New York

Washington

MEXICO, CENTRAL AMERICA and the WEST INDIES

ATLANTIC

OCEAN

Miami

BAHAMAS

Habana

CUBA

Camagüey   Guantánamo

Santiago   HAITÍ   San Juan

DOM
REPUBLIC

JAMAICA   Port-au-Prince   Santo   PUERTO
Kingston   Domingo   RICO   GUADELOUPE
                                                      DOMINICA
                                                      MARTINIQUE
                                                      ST. LUCIA
                                                      ST. VINCENT

CARIBBEAN SEA

GRENADA
TOBAGO
ARUBA   BONAIRE   MARGARITA   TRINIDAD
NDURAS   CURAÇAO

ARAGUA

Bluefields   Barranquilla   Valencia   Caracas
                              Maracaibo
an José Colón   Cartagena   ORINOCO R.
STA   San Fernando.   Ciudad Bolívar
ICA   Panamá   Cúcuta

PANAMA   VENEZUELA

Medellín

COLOMBIA

Bogotá

palacias

PANAMA CANAL

MAGDALENA R.

THE NEW LATINS

THE NEW LATINS

Fateful Change in
South and Central America

GEORGIE ANNE GEYER

DOUBLEDAY & COMPANY, INC.
Garden City, New York
1970

FIRST EDITION

Library of Congress Catalog Card Number 71–97662
Copyright © 1970 by Georgie Anne Geyer
All Rights Reserved
Printed in the United States of America

For my mother
and father

CONTENTS

INTRODUCTION

Like every national man in the world, the Latin American evokes a certain image in the minds of other peoples. But when you examine this image, it soon becomes clear that there is a peculiar one-dimensionality to it. There also is a superficiality about it, as though all Latin Americans were a mixture of Carmen Miranda and Emiliano Zapata. Compared to other national types, the image is disturbingly unreal—without depth, without understanding.

And there is something very curious about all this, too. For a long time—the last forty years, at least—Americans have been looking critically and analytically at other peoples. They have tried to dissect them ethnically, politically, culturally, socially. Cultural anthropology emerged as the most popular social science as the old isolationism of the earlier part of the century gave way to an international awareness based on the idiosyncratic behavior of other peoples.

But the enigma today is that the continent closest to us—and the one of most importance to us—is the one that has remained the least known to us. The largest amount of American investment in the world is in Latin America; it is here that nationalists of right, left and center most threaten the nationalization of American industry, as in the case of the International Petroleum Company in Peru and oil and minerals in general across the continent.

More interesting experiments in the development of under-developed countries are being waged in Latin America than anywhere in the third world. There is New Marxist Cuba, Christian Democrat Chile, New Military Peru, and a dozen other unruly combinations of revolutionary characteristics. Much, in effect, to learn there.

It should not be forgotten that the only serious threat to the continental United States in this century came, not from distant Vietnam, for whom we lost tens of thousands of men, but from Communist Cuba, only ninety miles off our shore. It should be remembered that John Kennedy, the most beloved American president of this century, was assassinated by one of the many tormented men of this century who were inspired by the revolutionary example of Cuba.

And Che Guevara—what about him? It was that romantic failure who, in death and martyrdom, was to become the hero of a new generation of young Americans devoted to changing and sometimes overthrowing a United States they deemed materialistic and unjust.

All of this raises the big questions—really vital questions for the United States. What kinds of societies are the Latin countries going to be? Basically democratic egalitarian societies like us? Societies we can, through a profound convergence of structures and beliefs, call our real friends in the world? Or obstreperously neutral or New Marxist societies who will come to remain distant and apart and hostile from the North America they originally patterned themselves after?

Most of all, what kind of policy should the United States, in whose natural sphere of influence Latin America falls, formulate toward the Latin countries? Should it be the permissive brother or the strict brother? How will Latins react to different roles? Should it be a Rooseveltian Good Neighbor Policy, an Eisenhower praise-for-the-strongmen approach, an idealistic Kennedyian Alliance for Progress policy, Johnsonian pragmaticon, a Rockefeller "let's-go-and-listen" visit? The fact that American policy *has* wavered so, the fact that it has shifted back and forth so constantly and so dramatically, is another example of the lack of firm, intuitive and empirical knowledge that we have about the area.

Despite all this—underneath it and above it and around it—the interest, little by little, grows. Latin American literature becomes constantly more and more popular in North America. John Kennedy and then the men of the Nixon administration remind us over and over that Latin America is the most important area of the world to us. Slowly it ceases to be only a romantic travel poster.

And yet there still are problems—and the fault is not wholly our own. The very difficulty of isolating the Latin American man— of understanding him and knowing him—is complicated by something strangely amorphous in his own makeup, something that is as bewildering and frustrating to him as it is to those looking at him.

When someone asks today, "Who is the Latin American man?" the question is met with superficialities and then a resigned silence. It is difficult to find his form, let alone to seize it and dissect it. Qualities flick in and out of the mind, but nothing palpable remains to establish an easily identifiable figure that can be set on the world stage—like the American, the Frenchman or the Russian—to point to and say, "There he is!"

Why this is true is a fascinating problem—almost as interesting as the question of who he is. And if you proceed a little further, you emerge with another frustrating problem. For not only does the world scarcely *know* who the Latin American man is, the world has barely *cared*.

Most of the world hardly knew he existed. To Americans and Europeans, the Latin American was a man marginal to the world's great currents and causes. He existed, but he did not count.

His countries, barely divisions of the land's surface, could hardly be called nations; often he did not know the name of the country in which he lived. Yet he squabbled endlessly over borderlines and fought bloody wars—the Chaco, the Triple Alliance, the War of the Pacific—in which nameless men suffered and died while the world barely knew of it.

There was never anything original about his world. He copied his culture from Europe and his political structures from the United States. And when he did copy other ideologies and concepts, they were so late in reaching him and he was so slow to respond to them that they took on bizarre forms.

There were nineteenth-century anarchists in Uruguay and Argentina in the mid-twentieth century, long after the ideology of nihilism and destruction had disappeared from the rest of the world. In the Andes in the 1960s, men ardently proclaimed themselves Trotskyites, while in the rest of the world Leon Trotsky, who had dared Joseph Stalin in the name of world revolution, was a dinosaur of the revolutionary past. Latin America was a political and social vacuum, an open receptacle for the worn-out, tossed-off ideologies of the world.

It was also a place where wanted men went to hide; to go there meant dropping off the surface of the earth. Nazis, Communists, confidence men, swindlers, politicians out of power in the Middle East—they all fled to Latin America, and they were gone. Colonies of Germans, Poles, Japanese and East Indians immigrated there, but they were not assimilated as they had been in North America. They remained intact and spoke their own languages. They neither formed a new culture nor contributed to the existing one, for there was no "Latin Americanism" to mold them into something new.

The Latin American's compulsive revolutions, which broke out with such distressing regularity, offered a small respite from the big wars. But like so many other things in Latin America, they were not quite real either. Latin America made famous the "palace revolution," a political innovation which introduced one cardinal principle—the more revolutions occur, the less things change. The men at the top revolved, while the social quagmire at the bottom remained the same.

And there was the comical quality of it all. Bolivia, by mid-twentieth century, had had 179 revolutions. Men still challenged each other to duel in Argentina and Uruguay. The Bolivian dictator of the last century, the evil Melgarejo, when asked how he would go to the aid of a European ally, said grandly, "We shall walk down the valley."

But if Americans and Europeans found little to take seriously about Latin America, they also found there something they deeply lusted after.

The South was different. There stretched the vast expanses of the Amazon jungle, half a continent living in the damp, moldering shadows beneath the rain forest. There were the last savage

Indian tribes on earth—dying, typically, not of anything indigenously Latin American but of outside diseases, the common cold,
syphilis, flu. And there were some of the most breath-taking land
formations on earth.

On the West Coast, the black pagan Andes fell like a sculptured
spine from Colombia to the bare remoteness of Tierra del Fuego.
There, black-necked swans flew and the almost extinct guanaco
raced in packs across the unrelieved loneliness of the last place on
earth. On the East Coast, the Amazon jungle stretched out across
2.7 million square miles—wave upon wave of trees breaking in an
evil green sea. In the center was the waterless Chaco, that
worthless green pothole that Paraguay and Bolivia had fought over
so insanely. And falling down from the Andes to the Atacama
Desert in northern Chile were the barren mineral valleys, some
with as many as two hundred geysers, others with pink bacterial
lakes and pink flamingos.

For those seeking relief from the obsessive order and the structured emotions of the Anglo-Saxon North, the tropics provided a
magic pull that began in the last century and continues today.
Orderly northern man looked south and he saw a cluster of basically untroubled countries with simple, passionate people; a fiesta
of the senses; people unencumbered by the moral chains of the
Puritan North; men living out their lives in sensual celebration.

If Latin man was not taken seriously, his world was at least rewarded with a jealous appreciation of its emotional qualities. The
Latin was simpler, easier to get along with than his serious, con-
science-ridden northern counterpart who lived in the real world
of business, war and ideology. The northerner often had a nagging
suspicion that the Latin American had the better of it.

The countries were fabulously rich—botanically, geologically,
humanly. They offered northern man, often hungry for experience,
a universe in which to exercise his manliness, to build railroads,
to explore for lost cities and to find new species. Northern man
saw an opportunity to prove how much the positivism and pragmatism of his culture could do for the waiting, basically dependent and feminine cultures of the South.

In the 1870s, when most of Latin America was still slumbering in its feudal past, the American adventurer Henry Meiggs was importing Chinese coolies to build his railroad over the Peruvian Andes. In 1878, Philadelphia engineers, led by the American investor and builder Percival Farquhar, were cheered from the wharf as they left the United States for Brazil to build the "train of the century" deep in the Amazon jungle. It would open the Amazon to the world and bring the rubber, the gold of the New World, to the sea. It was a clear example of North America acting on South America—male on female—northern positivism showing the southern fatalists how it could be done, with technology and reason.

With the adventurers and the builders came the great naturalists. With less predatory purpose, they too mulcted Latin America —but of its beautiful green secrets. Charles-Marie de la Condamine went to Ecuador in 1735 to measure the arc of the earth. An unknown, young Charles Darwin, sailed to South America in 1832, through the Strait of Magellan and up to the mysterious and bleak Galápagos Islands. Surrounded by the remnants of the world's animal past, he evolved the theory of evolution. Alexander von Humboldt, Richard Spruce, Alfred Wallace and many others —all penetrated the waiting, receptive, dependent, pliable South, and emerged with unimagined wealth. It was all there in South America, waiting, and it all had to be found by foreigners.

The fact that Latin America had developed so slowly and sluggishly, the clinging persistence of the dead and frozen structures of Latin society, the way that nothing ever seemed to move right or turn together—all this was explained away, to those who even bothered to think about it, in easy terms.

The Latin American was a different man, a man of the South; to him, progress was not important. He was a simpler man, a happier man, neither aggressive nor ambitious for himself or for his countries. Work, progress, activity as a value in itself—none of these mattered to him. Yet, despite the lack of recognition tendered him by the rest of the world, he *did* live in the world; he *did* have to be taken into account, particularly when he occasionally threatened the peace of the rest of the world just by existing.

The Cubans rebelled against Spain in 1898, and the United

States felt compelled to step in. In 1904 President Theodore Roosevelt proclaimed that "chronic wrongdoing, or an impotence which results in a general loosening of the ties of civilized society, may in America . . . force the United States . . . to the exercise of an inter-national police power."

In 1915 American Marines landed in the Dominican Republic to put the customs house in order. Nicaragua came next, and then the Dominican Republic again.

The paternalistic big neighbor "knew better" and felt he had to intercede for his Latin American brothers. And this reaction, which continues to this day, is the one that has most shaped certain present-day attitudes of the Latin American toward North America.

But, who *is* the present-day Latin American? Who is the man beneath the myths, the suppositions and observations supplied by outsiders? Why doesn't he speak for himself? Why doesn't he interpret his own reality and arrive at his own solutions? Is he Fulgencio Batista and Rafael Trujillo, those old-style *caudillos* with their regal bellies and sagging chests covered with medals, their compulsive sensuality, their Mongol cruelty? Or is he Eduardo Frei and Fernando Belaúnde, those new leaders with their deep thoughtfulness, their grave simplicity, their dogged determination to change Latin America, once and for all time? Or is he the new young military men, with their cold certainties? Is he the Latin American standing on the coast with his eyes and heart in Europe and the United States—proud, involved with his own prestige and place, obsessed with class and station? Or is he the ragged Latin American with his fanatic attachment to the land, clinging to it like a child to a breast, searching for a secure place in the world?

In the present search for identity going on in Latin America, and gaining impetus like a careening meteor, there is a strange repetition of old journeys. Now the foreigners who come are trying to impose their own social imprint on the continent, to project their ideologies into the vacuum they feel is Latin America. One after another the peripatetic pilgrims come, hoping to fill the void.

There is the United States, whose imprint upon Latin America already is so enormous, particularly psychologically, that it can be compared to no other influence.

Then there was the way Charles de Gaulle went to Latin America, like a priest seeking converts for his concept of "latinidad," trying to draw the people back to their "natural" Latin world. He regaled them with pleas—often directed to the descendants of the Incas jammed together in the old Spanish plazas—for union among the Latin people. For were they not at heart Latin?

Yugoslavia's Marshal Tito also visited, for is not Latin America part of the third world—is it not marginal to the world's great powers? The Soviet diplomats went to Cuba with their ideology, for is not Latin America destined to be Marxist? The Asian and African "third-worlders" set up office in Havana under the Tricontinental Conference, for is not Latin America one with the striving, underdeveloped sectors of the world?

Germany's president visited Peru and Chile, for does not Latin America belong to Europe, to Western and Catholic civilization? Portugal and its African states suggested a Portuguese-Brazilian-African community, for is not Brazil sister to Portugal?

The efforts and interpretations from outside sources never cease, as the world attempts to fill the empty chalice it sees as Latin America, with some other, foreign ideology. But these efforts are already too late; they are already being superseded and over-shadowed by what is happening inside the continent.

For there is, today, a new Latin America, still barely known outside its borders and little understood within them. And it is at the very heart of the matter that there is a new Latin man emerging —stepping out of the past and entering the future—who is something new in history.

To put it at its simplest, the new Latin is not ruled by the extreme egotism, the obsession with prestige, the acceptance of testimony over scientific proof that was the web of his grandfather's personality. Where the man of the past sought personal privilege, the new Latin seeks unity and community. Where his forefathers allowed their lives to be molded, influenced and interpreted by foreigners, he is beginning to have enough confidence to dissect himself.

Obviously he is in transition. Obviously in him are mixed tormenting and often conflicting characteristics. National character is difficult to dissect; discussing "changing personalities" anywhere in the world is fraught with dangers. Nonetheless, today you can begin to see the shadowy figures moving in the worlds he says he will create, and you can begin to hear the voices from Latin America itself.

Father Roger Vekemans, the brilliant Jesuit priest and the sociological genius behind Chile's Christian Democrat experiment, when asked about his conception of Latin America, answered, "I would say it is partly colonized. Here you have urban colonials who believe in Europe and the United States. They are really colonials with regard to the hinterland. I still doubt you can call them countries, not in the sense of the nation state. You have the backbone without the skeleton, without the tissue."

Victor Alba, the noted Spanish-born Mexican political scientist agrees: "Latin American countries are not nations; they are not integrated, and the great majority of their people form subsocieties quite separated from the official 'society.' To convert these countries into nations will require long and hard struggle against both the inertia of the masses and the oligarchic system."

But, as these men also see, Latin America is beginning to flesh out. The tissue of nationhood is beginning to grow—politically, socially and, most important, psychologically. It is evolving unconsciously, as in Peru, as well as consciously, as in Chile. It is coming about in revolutionary Christian ways, as in Chile, and in revolutionary Marxist ways, as in Cuba. It is coming, in many countries, through the missionary zeal of new military men.

In becoming itself, Latin America is, in historic form, related to Europe, but it will not be Europe. Although its political forms are influenced by the American experience, it will not be the United States. It will be something new, something totally new.

For the first time, you can begin to call them a people—the Latin Americans. And as this Latin American personality and position in the world begins to emerge, the historic myths about them, clung to with such romantic reverence for so long, must be replaced. The continent must be seen, not as a series of isolated, unrelated semistates, as they have been throughout history, but as an emerging unity—Latin America. For greatly outweighing its differences are its common social and psychological realities: national economies as extensions of family groups; a propensity for political authoritarianism; caudilloism in politics; social marginality as the divisive and deadening element in society; the overriding importance of the personal in opposition to the universal. There are many other such realities. To ignore these significant similarities and to stress the minor differences is to miss the most important point.

The Latin Americans themselves feel this. They are enjoying a new sense of identity. Students, when asked where they are from, have begun to answer, "I am a Latin American"—without naming their countries. Slowly, very slowly, the continent is stumbling toward unity. There is a demand to be recognized, to have its say in the world, whether it is brought about as Fidel Castro did it or as Eduardo Frei did it or as the young officers want to do it.

There are still those observers—they are in the majority—who, standing outside and thinking of the past and not the present, say Latin America will never have importance in the world community. They cite the absence of centers of power and claim there is no real hope for development, as the underdeveloped world falls daily further and further behind the developed world. They insist that Latin Americans are peculiarly suited to authoritarian governments, despite the numerous examples of spontaneous democratic development on a grass-roots level among the Latin American marginal people and the persistence throughout Latin American history of the democratic impulse.

But at the same time there is also an extravagant re-evaluation of Latin America loose in the world. Arnold Toynbee sees the seeds of a new Renaissance in Latin America. John F. Kennedy saw Latin America as the single most important area of the world for the United States, echoing the reminders of many that Latin America is not Africa or Asia, that it is the only part of the underdeveloped, uncommitted world that is Western.

Speaking for the Roman Catholic Church, Monsignor Luigi Ligutti, delegate of the Holy See to the Food and Agricultural Organization of the United Nations in Rome, predicts that in the next century Latin America will move to the position of leadership of Western civilization.

"I love Latin America," Monsignor Ligutti says. "I am an optimist about Latin America. We have seen nations in the bygone millenniums called to leadership in civilization after civilization, each successful to a greater or lesser degree. We may go back to Babylon, Egypt, Greece, Rome, Great Britain and now the United States.

"A century from now, and perhaps less, it will be Latin America. The human resources of Latin America—and they come first—contain in themselves the greatest possibilities. There is the greatest potential, from a biological viewpoint, from a material viewpoint, from the viewpoint of Christian culture, that no other part of the world has possessed in like fashion thus far. In these possibilities, there is no limit."

This assessment may seem quixotic to many. Yet it is clear that the yeast of change has begun working in Latin America. It is there for all to see. The changes in life style of two hundred million men and women cannot be dealt with lightly, particularly when it is the continent that inhabits the New World with the United States.

And particularly when it is a continent of such exorbitant beauty, such charm, and such enormous potential talent as Latin America.

PART I

THE OLD LATINS

CHAPTER 1

The Amazon Syndrome

"I came for gold, not to till the soil like a peasant."
Hernán Cortés.

When you fly over the Amazon basin, the precise center and in many ways the symbol of Latin America, the potential wealth of the continent seems endless and obvious. The forests break on the jungle plain like green waves on a sea that seems to roll on forever. The statistics on everything are so extravagant as to exhaust any ordinary imagination or measuring stick.

They will tell you that the Amazon river system constitutes the greatest one in the world, covering 2.7 million square miles, almost one-twentieth of the total land area of the earth. At high water, 32 million gallons of water pass through its mouth every second. Waters rush back and forth—from the ocean to the river, from the river to the ocean.

In the spring, when the water pours down from the Andes— where the river begins in a thousand tricklets dripping off 20,000-foot-high glaciers—the river can rise fifty feet within an hour or two. The huge island of Marajó at the Amazon's mouth, bigger than Switzerland and home to roaming bands of water buffalo, is inundated. Ships 120 miles out in the Atlantic pass water drearily discolored by the four billion tons of mud the river carries away every year.

Later the sea pays back the visit and sends ocean tides forty to

fifty feet high rushing up the river, flooding the Amazon as far
as four hundred miles upstream. The local Indian tribes describe
this phenomenon in the usual haunting evocativeness of their
primitive languages. One calls it *pororaca* or "crashing waters";
another calls it *amacunu* or "the noise of water clouds."

There is the *pirarucu* fish weighing two hundred pounds, its
tongue so rough the Indians use it as a grate. There are red, black
and gray porpoises and floating islands drifting along the river at
the Amazon's speed of 2.3 feet a second. The rhinoceros beetle,
the size of a teacup, vies in frightfulness with the vampire bats
that suck blood out of a man's big toe while he is sleeping.

But equally as fantastic as the "natural wonders" of the Amazon
are the predictions of unlimited wealth that will emerge from it.
Every year the prophecies are made over and over—by enthusiastic
visitors, by military leaders on their way up, by men new in power
who wish to grow old in power.

Don't worry about anything, they say. The Amazon's alluvial
valleys will feed the world. Its lumber will build houses. Its vast
spaces will provide living room to the world's overpopulation. The
Amazon natives go even further. Unable to conceive of any
life-balancing force other than the hot primeval river that is the
source of their existence, they ask visitors, "What is your river
named?"

But when you begin to look closely, it soon becomes apparent
that everything is not what it seems. It becomes obvious that there
is what might be called an "Amazon syndrome" that applies to all
Latin America. It is a syndrome of failure—of apparent wealth and
well-being and underlying hopelessness. There are the vast rivers—
but they are filled with piranha fish that can tear a body apart in
seconds with their needle-sharp teeth. There is the nice weather,
the days when the temperatures never exceed eighty degrees—
but the humidity makes it impossible to move at a pace faster
than a shuffle. There is the "rich land," the "endless forests . . ."

Oliver H. Knowles, a handsome wiry Briton who was a United
Nations forestry expert in the Amazon, sat on the wide porch of
his screened-in house one day in Santarém and injected a bitter

note of realism. He shook his head when the "wealth" of the Amazon was mentioned.

"Only ten percent of the standing timber is usable at the present time," he began. "There are forty-seven botanical families here. From the point of view of the use of timber, it's an absolute nightmare."

In 1953, he explained, the Food and Agricultural Organization of the United Nations surveyed the entire Amazon Valley. Three men started at the river's mouth and walked six hundred miles through the jungle to the Madeira River. And they found that only a negligible percentage of the timber was usable.

The Amazon trees grow so closely that small trees must struggle for space and light. "Their branches fall off," Knowles explained. "They twist to reach the light. When a tree reaches the canopy, it straightens out. Though many of the trees look straight, the grain is crooked and defective underneath."

The only hope of ever making the Amazon forest really productive, he speculated, would be to start immediately on one of several possible plans of massive culling and replanting. "It would take a hundred years, but we could change the nature of the forest into a timber-producing factory," he averred.

Nor was he more optimistic about the soil. "That is an old error," he said sadly. "The soils are not rich and never can be. To grow food you need to clear the land. Once you clear the land, there is no soil. In three years, the leaching is so great there is only sand left, and even fertilizer can never help. It is totally impossible that the Amazon can ever be an agricultural area."

To the cynical, what all this represents is something that transcends the Amazon region, as important as that area is as the very heart of the continent. To them, it symbolizes the superficial magnificence of the continent—and all its inner emptiness. The Amazon, in contrast to the extravagant hopes ascribed to it, comes out as nature's great joke—and so, in many eyes, does the rest of Latin America.

They see something inherent in Latin America itself that prevents it from achieving the kind of modern, scientifically oriented, technically competent, development-minded society the rest of the

world, in varying degrees, is struggling toward. Reforms and
changes in the continent, as in the Amazon, are like suspended
wheels that turn and turn around the same hub, returning to rest
in the very same place. And a predestination to melancholy and
failure seem to override hope.

If such observations are true, then there is little purpose to the
striving and struggling convulsion within the continent. But if
they are not true, then we must look more carefully at Latin
America and try to isolate some of its skitterish and elusive traits,
to discover out of what dark warm soils they grew.

It soon becomes obvious that you must deal with four major
strains: the Spanish, the Portuguese, the Indian and the Negro.
Even today you can find pure pockets of each throughout the
hemisphere, but in the vast majority of cases the Latin American
is a *mestizo*—loosely, a combination of some mixture of the four.

In the Caribbean Islands, the mixture is largely Spanish and
Negro, and this mixture continues along the north coasts of
Colombia and Venezuela. In the highlands of Colombia, however, as in Mexico, Guatemala and the Andean countries of Peru,
Ecuador and Bolivia, the mixture is Spanish and Indian, with
large sectors of pure-blooded Indians living much as they did at
the time of the Incas.

To the south is "European Latin America"—Chile, Argentina
and the south of Brazil, where the predominant Spanish and Portuguese blood is mixed generously with that of other white Central
Europeans from a score of countries. Abutting them is Paraguay,
an almost thoroughly *mestizo* country where the native Guaraní
Indians blended so totally with the Spanish that a new race was
born that even today uses the Guaraní language interchangeably
with Spanish. The vast green, pregnant center of the continent
belongs to Brazil, that huge, unruly, buoyant country where the
tolerant, adaptable Portuguese mated enthusiastically with the
Indians and the Negro slaves, creating a beautiful, dusky-skinned
race that even today considers blonds a little parched-looking.

But despite the differences that these four major strains have
brought to the New World, they have also blended together,
through a process of syncretism, into a combination of new and

special qualities that characterize all of Latin America and define its unity. One of the most dramatic of these is the inflated importance of personal relationships over impersonal and institutional or functional relationships—something that is responsible for much of the charm of the continent and for much of its infuriating hopelessness, too. Another is the overwhelming amount of social marginality—where the masses of poor Latin Americans have not been integrated into their own society.

In contrast to North America, Latin America has far fewer racial attitudes; but it does suffer from a closed and inviolate class system. Growing out of the feudal Spanish tradition, the cities wield enormous and overbloated power; they are the tails that wag the dogs, the countries.

The traditional structure of all Latin America is authoritarian —in government, in business, in the family. Yet, within it, there has always existed a strong, spontaneous and seemingly contradictory impulse toward self-government and self-reliance. In its society, the male is dominant—not simply to a normal extent but to an extraordinary extent.

Latin Americans tend to strive for glitter and show in place of the real and the substantive, but even their apparent confidence is a façade. Their writing is filled with a prevailing "suffering over blood," with the idea that the mixed blood of the New World is bad, impure, without hope. They are legalistic, but lawless; fatalistic, but rebellious. And yet they have attempted to build utopias with the same unabashed hope of their northern brothers in the New World.

You find the roots of all these characteristics—the special blend of which is what makes the Latin American character unique— in the four predominant pasts that converged and clashed in the dramatic continent to the south.

If you begin with the particular Spanish characteristics—social class over racial exclusivity, the bloated importance of the cities, the importance of the personal, the conflict between self-government and absolute authority—you have to go back to the Moors, those brilliant Moslems who struck at Spain in A.D. 711 and ruled it for eight centuries, right up to the eve of the Conquest.

The most striking qualities of the Moors—their tolerance, their devotion to learning, their practicality—were always in sharp contrast to the predominant qualities of the Spaniards. Practical, unzealous and not driven to conversions, these North Africans lived peacefully with their Christian subjects, content merely to impose upon them exorbitant taxes. They organized schools, produced scientists and mathematicians, introduced paper to Spain long before it reached the rest of Europe, and preserved and transmitted Greek and Roman culture.

To both Spain and Portugal, where they also settled down for a time, the Moors gave a very special gift—a relative freedom from racial hatred or exclusivity. For both these countries knew the dark-skinned Moors as a superior and ruling people instead of as an inferior, slave people.

Then as Moorish power ebbed toward the end of their eight centuries' reign, they helped create something else peculiar to Spain—the overwhelming power of the cities. This came about when the kings of Castille and Aragon, to consolidate their power, strengthened their cities, purposely enlarging the middle-class population and creating city militias.

The cities were granted extensive immunities and special privileges which are called *fueros* in Spanish. These later carried over into the New World, where various social entities, such as the church and the army, had *fueros* like the right to impose their own laws and try their own members. This led to the institutional atomization of Latin American society and to an excessive and egotistical power on the part of individual institutions, which kept national societies from developing.

At the same time, the powerful cities formed *hermandades,* or brotherhoods for patriotic service, and militias, which also carried over to the colonies and continue to exist in the religious brotherhoods of today. Here is one forerunner of the concept of loyalty to personalities and to personal groups, instead of to the larger, more impersonal society.

By the end of the twelfth century, the kingdoms had also launched a form of parliament (the *cortes*), the first movement toward self-government. The *cortes* represented the nobility, the clergy and the citizens and had limited rights to discuss taxes and to petition the throne.

Then, just when Spain had rid herself of the Moors, just when the wealth of the New World was beginning to pour in, and just when Spain could have relaxed and liberalized, Martin Luther nailed his theses on the church door in Wittenberg in 1517. The Protestant heresy approached the very gates of orthodoxy in fanatically Catholic Spain, and the door closed. The Renaissance spirit of the Latins protested violently against the Reformation, with all that it meant in terms of Germanic individualism.

The threat of the enlightenment forced the formation of the Jesuits, who set out in the sixteenth century to buttress the threatened faith and came to forge their own empire in the center of the new continent. At the same time, the Jews were expelled from Spain along with the Moors, and Spain's industrial development began to lag behind the rest of Europe's. The world was privy to the strange spectacle of a poor and fanatic Spain adopting an obstreperous child of enormous potential riches, America. But once the riches began to pour in from the New World, they were used to create only a superficial glitter. It was never part of the Spanish heritage to work toward long-range, patient investment.

The differences between the Latin Americans of Spanish background and those of Portuguese blood have always fascinated observers, and they are of particular importance in attempting to know present-day Latin America. Where the people of Spanish background are rigid and absolutist in their thought, the Brazilians are athletically flexible. Where the Spanish-Americans are always driving toward the ultimate confrontation, the Brazilians are working on finding a way out. Where the Spanish are true believers to whom the idea of an inquisitional "one faith" comes as a natural thing, the Brazilians are tolerant and have always tended to think egotistically and familiarly that since "God is a Brazilian," everything is bound to work out all right. Where the Spanish-Americans saw the world structured in a perfect social and sexual hierarchy in which men and women lived out their lives within their own social layer, the Brazilians took in all classes and races with open arms and a happy innocent spirit. Yet both peoples came from the same Iberian peninsula. Both were peopled and formed by the same Iberians, Celts, Phoenicians, Greeks, Carthaginians, Romans, Visigoths and Moslems.

One of the main reasons for the difference was Portugal's long friendship with practical, commercial England, upon whom it relied for protection from Spain. Indeed, the battle against Castille, the predominant Spanish state, was won when English recruits aided a Portuguese army.

Part of the particularly free and breezy Portuguese spirit, too, was the result of its remarkable love affair with the sea. There were men like Vasco da Gama, who put out with four ships and 168 men, sailed around the Cape of Good Hope to reach India and in the process turned the eyes of their compatriots to the outer world.

The Portuguese were always practical. Merchants themselves, they appreciated a merchant mind. When a man rose in the commercial world, the kings invited him into the aristocracy. When rigid, apocalyptic Spain, acting on the imperatives of the one true faith, expelled the Jews in 1492, the accommodating Portuguese thoughtfully invited thousands of them to Portugal and then collected exorbitant fees from them.

The Portuguese had moments of apocalyptic religious fervor, but they always got over it the next morning with usually nothing worse than a bad headache. For the Portuguese faith was never so bleakly absolutist as the Spanish, being mixed with Moslem, African Negro and all sorts of other influences that penetrated the long, exposed Portuguese coastline. The prominent Brazilian sociologist Gilberto Freyre wrote that the Portuguese religion was not "the hard and rigid system of the Reformed countries of the North or even the dramatic Catholicism of Castille itself; theirs was a liturgy social rather than religious, a softened, lyric Christianity with many phallic and animistic reminiscences of the pagan cults."

Portugal's long experience with dark-skinned peoples would stand it well in Brazil, which became the racial and social melting pot of Latin America. In *The Masters and the Slaves*, Freyre wrote of the new man, the Portuguese settler who would become the

Brazilian: "In certain respects, he resembles the Englishman, in others the Spaniard. As a Spaniard without the warlike flame or the dramatic orthodoxy of the conquistador of Mexico and Peru; an Englishman without the harsh lineament of the Puritan. The compromiser type. With no absolute ideals, with no unyielding prejudices . . . of greater social plasticity . . . as compared with any other European colonizer."

The hit-or-miss Portuguese explorers came to Brazil and landed in a typically informal Portuguese manner. Blown off its course, their fleet of thirteen ships with twelve hundred men on their way to India landed in Brazil on April 22, 1500. Later, they were simply given the huge center of the continent by the pope's Treaty of Tordesillas, which awarded to Portugal all the land that lay "within 370 leagues west of the Cape Verde Islands."

Even after that the Portuguese were typically leisurely in the settlement of their vast "continent." It was such a big place. So they began by settling the coast and mating, in their fervor for procreation, with the Indian women whom they relished for their dark bodies.

Because of this racial tolerance, the new race created in Brazil had few of the neuroses that the *mestizos* had in the Spanish countries, where they spent two centuries suffering over the mixed race and attributing all the evils of Latin America to this "bad blood."

But the Spanish Conquest was different from the Portuguese Conquest not only because the Spanish were so different from the Portuguese, but because the Spanish stumbled, dazed, upon the great Indian empires of the Aztecs, Mayas and Incas.

The Indians, who probably came across the Bering Strait from Mongolia some fifty thousand years ago, had worked out life patterns that were generally judicious and balanced; they knew why they existed; they had their legends which explained every detail of their presence on earth. To the Mayas of Central America, as told in their sacred book, the Popul Vuh, the Creator of the world carved puppets of wood and they came to life; "They looked like man, they spake as man, and they peopled the face of the earth . . ."

To the Incas of the Andes, their empire began thousands of years ago when, Inca history says, Mama Occlo and Manco Capac emerged from the depths of Lake Titicaca, that icily blue lake that lies half in Bolivia and half in Peru. They had instructions from their father, the Sun, to instruct the Indians, then divided into warring and primitive tribes, how to live at peace with themselves. The two young gods wandered northward through the exquisite valleys of the high Andes and when they found the site of Cuzco, they founded their capital and their empire.

The Incas created one of the most balanced empires of all time, an almost perfect communistic state. They divided land among the people with absolute equality and then redivided it every year, with the larger community working the land of the widows and the incapacitated. There was no want. Granaries kept food for drought periods along the extraordinary highways the Incas built from the borders of Colombia to northern Chile, and running messengers connected the kingdom.

The Incas extended their hegemony largely by way of reason and persuasion, gradually bringing all the tribes of Ecuador and Bolivia under their benevolent despotism. As with the Romans, all the duties and rights of the empire were extended to everyone who came under its sway.

But it was the perfect obedience of the Indians to the Inca (at that time the term "Inca" was given only to the emperor and his family) that in the end caused the empire's downfall. The bastard Spaniard, Francisco Pizarro, whose remains lie in state in the cathedral in Lima, climbed up the Andes with a handful of soldiers and horses and defeated the Incas with a single act. They kidnapped the Inca Atahualpa and once the Inca was captured the empire was defeated, for all its power was centered in him.

The magnificence of the Inca's court in Cuzco, where solid gold corn, flowers and trees "grew" in the garden, was ended. Those gold works of art were melted down, made into bars by Pizarro's men and shipped to a Spain that was only further corrupted by its possession. The Indians were snatched from their harmonious, obedient collectivism and put into reductions or reservations. The Spanish devised the *encomienda* system by which the Indians were assigned and tied to the great haciendas to be bought and sold with the land and the animals. Some Indians fled into the eastern recesses of the Andes, to the hot, damp high jungle on the eastern slopes, where they built their escape cities such as Machu Picchu, today invaded by tens of thousands of tourists every year seeking a new form of escape. Indian rebellions such as the one under Tupac Amaru in 1780 were put down cruelly. Future Indian leaders were bought off by the Spaniards with certificates of "whiteness" which allowed them to enter, if peripherally, creole society. In the last two hundred years the Quechua-speaking Inca empire has fallen into total, deathly quiet.

There were many reasons for these strange and tragic events. In the face of the Renaissance dynamism of the Spaniards, all the Indians of the Americas were peculiarly vulnerable to destruction, having the same obsession with destiny and unalterable catastrophe. But when one looks at the old Inca poetry and songs, it is obvious that the Incas, unlike the blood-worshiping Aztecs of Mexico, were preoccupied with peace and with an orderly collectivism.

There is also a distinct melancholy in their songs, a sadness and an obsession with unshed tears. The dew of the night is the "tears of the moon." Weeping is the "juice of grief." The pastoral happiness of their own empire rapidly became drowned in the nightmares of the long night of the Spanish Conquest. A modern Peruvian historian, José de la Riva Aguero, has written about the Quechuas:

"There is a tender, gentle, doleful poetry of naïve charm and pastoral softness, suddenly darkened by fits of the most tragic despair. More reserved and bound by tradition than any other people, this race possesses the gift of tears and the cult of memory. Guardians of mysterious tombs and forever mourning among these cyclopean ruins, their favorite diversion and bitter consolation is to sing about the woes of their history and the poignant grief that lies in their hearts."

Guardians of mysterious tombs—that they are. Peru is a precious graveyard of great Indian civilizations and the one that was the greatest in the world. Even today the landscape is littered with the ruins of great temples, fortresses and cities the way American cities are littered with junk heaps and billboards. In the sand dunes of the desert coasts, Inca treasure is still being discovered. Nor have the Indians forgotten what once was theirs. Today, as the upper-class Peruvians walk by, speaking the more fashionable French, Indians sit on the curbs in Lima playing their ancient pipes and singing of the land and glory lost to them.

But in the last analysis, it cannot be said that the Indians were only overcome and ruled by Spain. If only by their overwhelming presence and perseverance, they helped form the new Latin American who is emerging today. It was the Indian who provided the values of the nobility of hard work, the honor of the person, the idea of sexual equality, the pervasive melancholy and the ultimate recourse to magic.

For the Negroes, not enslaved in their own lands on the ruins of their own empires as the Indians were, the New World experience was quite different.

Though slavery came to the New World of the South at the same time it came to the New World of the North, and though it came in the same brutal manner of seizing men from their tribal societies, transporting them in slave ships and replanting them in a hostile new land, the forms of slavery were very different in Latin America and in many ways more congenial. For people like the Portuguese, historically accustomed to the idea that dark-skinned men could represent a superior race, it was the condition of slavery that made a man unequal and not his color. Being a Negro alone did not carry any social stigma with it. On the huge, paternalistic plantations of colonial Brazil, the slaves were often trained to special skills, and *mestizo* children were educated and often came under the tutelage of the "big house" and the white mother.

Moreover, the Spanish and the Portuguese had a long experience of slaveholding, and the slave had a special place and status as a human being; he had certain rights, and a slave could improve his status and even purchase his freedom. Once he did so, in contrast to circumstances in the United States where even the free

Negro remained a pariah, the Negro in Latin America had a far more fixed place in society. Once free, he was like anyone else.

Today, there are probably twenty-five million Negroes and mulattoes in Latin America, with every possible shade of mixture in between. They, along with all the other mixtures, make up what the Mexican educator José Vasconcelos has called the *raza cósmica* or "cosmic race"—the new race of Latin Americans still being forged. Or, as the prominent historian Hubert Herring has written of them: "The talents, the temperament, the beliefs, the physical traits of the Negro are ingredients in that new race of man—the American."

Though in the New World the Negroes, most of them from the area around the Ivory Coast, gradually took on the characteristics of their Spanish and Portuguese *patrones*, in Latin America more than in the United States they maintained many of their old customs and religious beliefs. Many of them were Mohammedans from Senegal and there were Moslem slave revolts in Bahia during colonial times, showing a unity and persistence of custom and belief that did not exist in the United States. African tribal religions persisted as well, and persist to this day.

Each group—Spanish, Portuguese, Indian, Negro—brought its own contribution to the New World. And beginning with the Conquest, there began that great merging that would create a new man—a Latin American, the second new man in the second New World.

The fantastic qualities that stretch across all of Latin American history are particularly present in the Conquest. In Mexico, Hernán Cortés, with a few hundred men, was able to vanquish the entire empire of the Aztec emperor Montezuma. In Peru, Francisco Pizarro, that unlettered swine-tending, bastard son of a Spanish gentleman, took over an Inca empire of five million persons, with sixty-two horsemen, one hundred and six foot soldiers and a few cannons. Pedro de Valdivia marched from Peru to Chile, won the country and then died, legend says, when the Araucanian Indian hero Lautaro poured melted gold down his throat, saying, "You came for gold, now we give you all the gold you can use."

"I came for gold," Cortés had said, "not to till the soil like a peasant." And in this, as in so many things, the spirit of the Conquest of South America was totally opposed to the spirit of the Conquest of North America. The Pilgrims came for political and religious freedom and gratefully tilled the soil like peasants. The North Americans came with women, with their wives, and settled sturdy, home-centered colonies. They came to stay, whereas the Spanish and Portuguese came to look around, to adventure, to whore, to get rich and to get titles.

Once the early euphoria of the Conquest was past, however, the Latin Americans were forced to accept reality. For most of them, dreams of getting rich and returning triumphantly to Spain remained just that, dreams. So they stayed and worked. From 1516 on, the Spanish began to explore the Río de la Plata. In 1535 Buenos Aires was founded for the first time and was immediately destroyed by the Indians. But gradually the South, which was to become "European Latin America," developed, and all of Latin America pushed forward into colonial times.

Even as Spain and Portugal dominated the colonial period, the new Latin American culture already was developing. Imperial Spain tried to fix upon the New World the same hierarchical system it had nurtured at home, and to a great extent it did. The Spanish constructed their towns in Latin America in the Spanish form, with the plaza as the center of the town and of its life.

Whereas in North America, men rushed westward, as far and as fast as they could go, in Latin America "the colony sat down," as the Colombian historian Germán Arciniegas has put it. "If the United States had built plazas like those in Spanish America, it might have produced more politicians, men more unstable, more anarchical, less bourgeois," he wrote. "Spain built plazas instead of providing schools for the people."

The Spanish also put their particular imprint of legalism onto the new colonies, with their minutely detailed laws that covered almost every possible action of man. In some cities, judges were expressly forbidden to receive gifts of chickens from Indians, so explicit and onerously detailed were the laws. By 1635 more than four hundred thousand edicts were in force. By 1681, in an attempt to deal with this runaway proliferation, the number of laws had been reduced to sixty-four hundred in the compilation of the laws of the Indies. It was the beginning of the phenomenon of the letter of the law over the spirit of the law that would plague Latin America into modern times.

Politically, the governmental organization of colonial America grew directly out of the spirit of the Habsburgs of the sixteenth century. As in the Roman tradition, the cities were glorified, and the *cabildo* or city council was the major organ of political expression. It was not the natural blooming of the city as the center of civic expression which occurred in the twentieth century in the United States; it was the unnatural glorification of the central bureaucracy at the expense of the countryside, where the real wealth originated.

In the English colonies the town grew up to meet the needs of the inhabitants, and in the Spanish colonies the population grew to meet the needs of the town. This gave a bloated importance to the cities and retarded the development of the interior. It is an example of a prime metaphysical problem as well: the importance, in Latin American life, of form over substance.

The authoritarianism inherent in Latin life developed during colonial times, too. There was little political development from the grass roots up, as in the New England town meeting. Instead, everything moved from the top down. The *regidores*, or members of the *cabildo* were *appointed* to their posts, and they in turn *appointed* constables, collectors of taxes, inspectors of weights and measures, and notaries.

The first *cabildos* were appointed by the founders of the cities and, after a number of abortive attempts to have them elected by landholders, the king began selling such positions to fill his treasury. The only avenue through which the *cabildos* encouraged local democracy and self-expression was the *cabildo abierto* or open town meeting. Leading citizens were summoned to discuss particularly important issues. It was these *cabildos abiertos* that later became the rallying ground for the secessionists in the independence wars. But above all this was the most important and the most powerful figure in the colonies: the viceroy, the king's representative from whom all power flowed.

Still, it is a mistake to see the colonies as a simple posed tintype of imperial Spain, for New World man soon developed his own spirit and his own rebelliousness. Royal decrees handed down in Madrid lost force and potence as they traveled the enormous distances across the sea. Transplanted nobles and clergy in the Americas disputed the king's authority, arguing that his dictums did not fit the forms of the New World. Like many husbands, they pretended to honor and obey, but in actuality they didn't. It was a New World emanation of the classic Hispanicism, *Se obedece, pero no se cumple.* He obeys, but he does not comply.

The Spaniards and Portuguese brought with them certain libertarian impulses of the kind that seemed to grow and thrive in all of the New World, South as well as North. In Paraguay in 1762 a curious little revolt, called the revolt of the *comuneros* (those who live communally), broke out when Fernando Mompax, its instigator, insisted that: "The rights of the common people of any republic, city, village or hamlet are greater than that of the king himself."

He decreed that the people had the power to accept or reject any law or governor they desired for "even though it be given by the Prince, if the common people do not wish it, they may properly resist and fail to obey." The *comuneros* put Governor Cabeza de Vaca on a ship and sent him back to Spain, and the people sang a song containing the telling phrase, "But the king is very far away . . ."

Despite the fact that a heavy form of authoritarianism seemed on the surface to be omnipresent, underneath there always existed seemingly contradictory manifestations of social experimentation and ingenuity. In 1780, for example, Rousseau's social contract was so well known in Latin America that when Indians rebelled in Peru, Bishop Martínez y Companón attempted to pacify them by explaining the social contract in an adaptation that gave the king of Spain the right to delegate to the people their due powers.

Socially, it is true, life in the colonies was carefully stratified.

None the less, the very ebullient blood mixture out of which the Latin American sprang encouraged a more democratic way of life than that of Spain. The Spanish born in Spain, called *peninsulares*, stood at the top, holding the best posts, receiving the top salaries and inspiring the wars of independence with their excesses. Beneath them were the creoles, those restless men of Spanish blood who had been born in America. Landowners, business and professional men and artisans—all creoles—led the final rebellion against Spain.

Beneath them on the pyramid were the *mestizos*, the fruit of the union of the Indian woman and the Spanish conquistador. With no sure roots in either tree, with no secure place in the colonial world, and with a sure sense of their own despised state, these *mestizos* became the "marginal men" in Latin America, the men who did not fully share in either culture. In contrast to North America, where men uprooted from communal societies in Europe were immediately integrated into "Americanism" by the sheer force of the new ideas of American egalitarianism and democracy, in Latin America the great masses of men remained on the outside looking in upon a society whose life forces they do not share.

In colonial times, as in the Conquest, Brazil always differed from the Spanish colonies. Partially because of the high percentage of African slaves upon whom the economy depended and partially because of the Brazilians' own Portuguese-oriented personality, Brazilian life tended to be soft and paternalistic.

Life centered around the "big houses" where the patriarchal father ruled supreme. These self-contained units early usurped the power that in Spanish America fell to the cities and central governments. Unlike the Spanish colonies, Brazil had no plazas which were the center of everything; instead, Brazil developed in a feudal manner, with all power on the huge estates. In contrast to the rather successful paternalism of Brazil, in Spanish America the patriarchs were so unyielding, so cruel and so unconcerned with the welfare of their subjects that the wars of independence broke out in the Spanish colonies. Brazil never did have to fight for independence from Portugal.

The fight for independence from Spain was actually a fight for independence from all the economic absurdities that Spain had imposed on its colonies. Products from Buenos Aires had to go over the Andes to Lima, and from there they could be shipped to Spain. The colonies could not trade with each other, only with the mother country. And so there arose a group of young revolutionaries, nourished by the success and under the sway of the American revolution, who demanded a total severing of all ties with the mother country.

The two men who came to lead the wars for independence, Simón Bolívar and José de San Martín, would also come to typify two predominant strains in Latin America. Bolívar was the dashing, emotional, theatrical leader of that part of Latin America that is really "Latin"—the Caribbean, tropical, northern Spanish countries. San Martín came from Buenos Aires, and his every move and action represented the more "European" countries of the South.

Bolívar gloried in adulation and was the master of the dramatic moment; San Martín was humble and self-effacing. Bolívar was aware every moment that he was striding through history. San Martín forsook glory and eventually sailed quietly away to Europe, where he died, after quarreling with Bolívar. San Martín was a devoted family man; Bolívar typified the "macho" Latin lover. But both are responsible for the eventual severance of Latin America from Spain. Both forged the future of the southern part of the New World.

Simón Rodríguez, the eccentric liberal-minded tutor who so enormously influenced Bolívar, once inspired his pupil to take a walk with him in Europe. It was a romantic journey recommended by Rousseau—through central Europe to Rome by foot. In Rome the two men went up the Aventine Hill, where Bolívar made a vow: "I swear that I will not die until I have driven the last Spaniard out of America." And he did not.

But every step of the way, Bolívar, the man of the future, was forced to fight the depressive Latin fatalism. During the beginning of the independence war, a violent earthquake shook Caracas and a priest declared from the pulpit that God had sent it as punishment for the rebellion against the king.

"If nature is aligned against us, we must fight against nature," Bolívar cried.

For fourteen years, from 1810 to 1824, the battles for independence raged across the entire continent. Bolívar moved down from Caracas, fighting battle after battle, liberating Peru and finally dying in disillusionment as the liberators of Latin America clawed and fought among themselves for the bitter fruits of the Conquest.

Before he died Bolívar anguished over what form the new America should take. Although he was idealistic and hopeful, he was also doubtful of what could be achieved immediately. "The role of the inhabitants of the American hemisphere has for centuries been purely passive," he wrote. "Politically, they were nonexistent. We are still in a position lower than slavery and therefore it is more difficult for us to rise to the enjoyment of freedom."

Later, he wrote, "I desire to see America fashioned into the greatest nation in the world, greatest not so much by virtue of her area and wealth as by her freedom and glory. Although I seek perfection for the government of my country, I cannot persuade myself that the New World can, at the moment, be organized as a great republic."

In the end Bolívar died an embittered man. The independence movement had been successful in separating the colonies from Spain, but totally unsuccessful in building something new. It all broke up into petty squabbling and jockeying for power. One faction made an attempt on his life.

Before he died of tuberculosis in 1830, in Santa Marta, Colombia, he wrote the bitter words: "America is ungovernable. Those who have served the revolution have plowed the sea." Many, since, have agreed with him.

Yet one of the most hopeful aspects of the independence movement was the attempt to arrive at new "solutions" for Latin America's unbalances. It was a period pregnant with experimentation and innovation—a time to challenge the old staticism. The earliest independence leader, Francisco de Miranda, even suggested—and it was seriously considered—an *incanate* form of government, which would have been a hybrid of the English parliamentary monarchy and the Inca traditions, with a nobility composed partly of Indian chiefs. The idea of a revival of the Inca empire has emerged again and again throughout Latin American history.

In Brazil, as noted, independence came in a typically compromising way. Like the Portuguese, the Brazilians always considered fights-to-the-death a little excessive. And when it was time for independence, independence was simply arranged.

The Portuguese throne moved to the New World in 1807 when Napoleon moved into Portugal. Prince Regent João packed up his mother, appropriately called "Mad Maria," and the entire royal court in forty merchant ships and eight men-of-war and sailed away to Brazil. As Negroes danced around her car in Rio de Janeiro, Mad Maria kept screaming, "I am going to hell."

But this early assessment proved premature. Mad Maria went no farther than Rio, and the throne devoted itself to making its new capital a fit and royal place. Palaces were built, streets constructed and the city was beautified.

When João returned to a newly freed Portugal in 1821, he knew that Brazil would not remain under the monarchy. His sage parting advice to his twenty-three-year-old son, Pedro, was, "If Brazil demands independence, grant it, but put the crown upon your own head."

It was typically Brazilian, and of course it worked. Pedro stayed and one day in São Paulo, standing alongside the Ipiranga River, he ripped the Portuguese colors from his uniform and shouted, "Independence or death." Naturally, it was independence.

Brazil peacefully moved from a monarchy to a republic, and it was typical that even the Brazilian "emperors" were popular and kindly "fathers of the country." The most noted and the most beloved was Dom Pedro II, who ruled the country for forty-nine years.

The manner in which he became emperor was also typically Brazilian. In 1841 the young Dom Pedro was only fourteen, but the Brazilians needed someone on the throne to prevent anarchy.

Arciniegas reports in his brilliant *Latin America, a Cultural History* that one of the deputies simply presented a legal statement declaring, "Senhor Dom Pedro II is declared of age from now on." He then suspended the chamber of deputies to avoid a vote on the matter and people in the streets sung:

> We want Dom Pedro the Second,
> For now he has come of age.
> He was born to dispense our laws,
> Long live his Majesty.

As Dom Pedro matured, with his six-foot-four-inch figure and his large white bushy beard, he looked the perfect patriarch. In most ways he was. Men were appointed on the basis of worth rather than social class, and men of high caliber appeared in public office. Abroad he traveled incognito as Dom Pedro de Alcantara, and his democratic attitudes endeared him to everyone. In Europe he became known as "the most popular royal person." He sought out Victor Hugo and when he visited the United States in 1876 he met John Greenleaf Whittier, a shy Quaker whom the emperor stunned by attempting to embrace him in the Brazilian style.

Henry Wadsworth Longfellow had him to dinner and described the royal guest as a "modern Haroun-al-Rashid wandering about to see the great world as a simple traveler, not as a king."

Dom Pedro opposed slavery and freed his own slaves, but it was not until 1887, when he left his daughter, Princess Isabel, as regent while he traveled in Europe, that she signed the emancipation proclamation.

In 1889, peacefully and upon demand of the army, the republic of Brazil was proclaimed. The emperor simply left, refusing the offer of a large sum of money. He lived for two more years in France, busying himself with studying Tupi, Hebrew, Arabic and Sanskrit.

In contrast, the post-independence in the Spanish countries was marked by anarchy, chaos and the changeover to home-grown *caudillo* rule. Politically, the continent was in chaos. Economically, it withered without the control and markets of Spain. Education declined. Not one man in ten could read or write; how *could* the new system work? What's more, the new constitutions that had been modeled after that of the United States were in no way applicable to the Latin American reality.

There were fights between liberals and conservatives, between centralists and federalists, between anticlericals and devout Catholics.

To referee these fights, the Latin American *caudillo* or strong man emerged. For the next century, and in some countries longer, the *caudillo* ruled supreme across most of the continent. He was the Latin American "boss" who played much the same role as the machine boss in big American cities during the period of large immigration. Almost all of the Spanish republics went down to dictatorship in the next fifty years.

Latin American history is, if anything, the history of a constant struggle for Latin man to find himself, to define himself, to find a Latin American way in the world that would somehow balance the often contradictory ideals of liberty, brotherhood and democracy with the need for stability and order. The North American established his identity early and knew what it was "to be an American"; the Latin American still does not know.

The nineteenth century again found Latin America turning over and over the two contradictory sides of the coin: authoritarianism versus experimentation with democratic approaches; military versus civilian rule. Even while the age of the *caudillo* was at its peak, Latin America was searching for better "solutions." And the nineteenth century was the time when the search was directed abroad, toward the fertile tree of European scholarship and influence.

Late in the century, Auguste Comte's philosophy of Positivism gained large numbers of adherents. In Brazil, its sway was so pervasive that the Comtian motto, "Order and Progress," is written to this day on the Brazilian flag. Ideally Positivism was to permit man to progress naturally to an orderly, scientifically oriented world. But it did not come to have precisely that effect in Latin America, and it lost much of its force when, in the end, life continued to go on pretty much as usual.

In the twentieth century the search continued. Much of the inquiry again was directed abroad—toward Marxism, toward the various movements of radical Christianity, toward revolutionary young military officers. For the first time, on a massive scale, however, the search was also directed inward, toward the roots of Latin Americanism itself.

The first dramatic instance of this was *aprismo*, the philosophy of returning to the tenets of "Indo-America," espoused by the brilliant Peruvian politician and intellectual Victor Raúl Haya de la Torre. But *aprismo*, having aroused the undying hatred of the Peruvian military for its attacks on it, was never allowed to take power.

Instead, the first real social revolutions—in contrast to the old palace coups—would occur elsewhere. First came Mexico, in 1910, with its total revolution, a revolution whose flaming stage alone lasted more than a decade. Between Mexico's totally transforming revolution and the next—the Bolivian—the area would have to wait two generations, until 1952.

After Bolivia's upheaval, dramatically transforming that backward country which is second in the hemisphere only to Haiti in poverty, there were only seven years to wait—until 1959—for Cuba's, the third great social revolution.

Meanwhile, all across the continent, even without the invigorating qualities of revolution, Latin Americans were searching for themselves and searching within themselves. They were defining a new man, a new Latin religiosity, a new place in the world for themselves. They were evolving new purely Latin American political and cultural "solutions." Latin America was feverishly embarked on a search for ways to modernize its feudal and sluggish societies and its feudal and sluggish mentalities. If the search was to be successful, it would have to end with Latin man finding himself.

CHAPTER 2

The People Who Never Win

"All the battles we celebrate are losses, but they are grand losses." A Latin American.

"I am a Peruvian, and I could not allow them to annul the goal of my people." Victor Matías "Bomba" Campos, who started the 1964 soccer riot in Peru in which 319 persons lost their lives.

If it were only outsiders who had always perceived Latin Americans as a people who never win, the judgment would not be so corrosive. But, it is they who perceive themselves as chronic failures. Their historic inferiority complex is a pervasive reality that poisons every aspect of Latin American life. As individuals, as nations, as a unified entity, they have never experienced the luxury of winning. And so generosity of spirit is budding but weak, and confidence shatters at the first slight threat.

One of the predominant strains in the conglomerate psyche of Latin Americans throughout history is that they are a people who cannot bear to lose. Yet they are at the same time a people which has always lost. There are very few Latin Americans who, nationally or personally, have known lives of victory or lives which they have controlled. And so they emerge a people with such deep historic feelings of inferiority that they cannot react with

grace to the slightest displeasure from without or exact from themselves the minimal discipline to advance technically in the bigger
world. Neither can they accept responsibility for what they are,
a fact that leads to the gnawing dependency of blaming everything
they are on forces outside themselves.

One of the most pathetic examples of all of this occurred in
Lima on May 24, 1964, an ordinary Sunday in an ordinary Lima
winter. The capital of Peru is a somber city in the winter, when
a low fog creeps over the city and nearly chokes it. The foothills
of the Andes are obliterated. Tangible life is reduced to the level
of the curbstones and tree trunks, for often you cannot see the
tops of buildings or the tops of trees. It becomes hard to breathe
and harder still to keep your wits about you. It is not surprising
that *limeños* grow cranky, nervous and depressed. Life is hard
enough anyway, sitting in the middle of a great desert, being
brushed by the cold Humboldt Current that originates in Antarctica, and coping with a life that was better four hundred years
ago than it is today. You do not need the added burden of the
Peruvian fog from April to October.

That Sunday, Peru was playing Argentina in a soccer match in
the Lima stadium, a huge cement ring which is one of many stolid
public buildings scattered around the city that were built by the
dictator Manuel Odría as proof of how dictators "get things done."
It was an important game. Not only were the two countries old
enemies—Argentina looks up upon itself as white and European
and looks down upon Peru as brown and *indio*—but the winner
would represent Latin America at the Olympic Games in Tokyo.
All the nameless, faceless *limeños* were there who do not belong
to the Club Union, an aristocratic haven where the affairs of the
country have historically been settled. They had come in from
the *barriadas* and the *callejones* and the other poor sections that
infect the old city like a growing poison, and they wanted to win.

Soccer is more than just a sport in Latin America, it is a religious fever. It is the place where the poor go for a cathartic
exoneration for their lives, and in many instances a passion for
soccer supplants patriotic fervor. Jokes about soccer and national
character abound. In a favorite Brazilian joke, a Spaniard, just

off the boat in Rio, comes across a crowd running down the street
and yelling, "*Botafogo . . . botafogo . . .*" In addition to being
the name of a favorite Rio soccer team, this also means "Set fire."
The Spaniard, with his politically oriented background, happily
joins the crowd, shouting, "*Al palacio del gobierno*"—"To the
palace of the government."

But to get back to the story, during this Sunday soccer game at
the last moment the Uruguayan umpire suddenly ruled against
Peru on a goal that would have made Peru the winner. A howl
of rage rose from the stands, but nonetheless it seemed to by-
standers that the angry crowd would accept the decision. Several
newspapermen left and went back to their offices to file the story:
Peru had lost something—again.

Just when the crowd seemed to be quieting down, however,
a hulking Peruvian Negro named Victor Matías Campos, known
in unsavory circles as "Bomba," could no longer bear the humiliation. Later he told the police, who had made his acquaintance
before, "I am a Peruvian, and I couldn't permit them to annul
the goal of my people." Eluding the guards, he ran onto the field
with a broken bottle to attack the Uruguayan umpire, thus setting
off a melee in the stands.

Something snapped. The young Peruvians, whose nerves are
always as tight as taut violin strings, poured out onto the field
and all the strings suddenly broke. Forming a flying wedge
around the umpire and the Argentine team, the police managed
to get them safely to their dressing rooms. The bewildered umpire
was hidden in a downtown hotel and flown to Argentina in the
middle of the night.

As police battled the rioters, the fight grew more and more
vicious. A common hatred of the authority of the police erupted.
The rioters flung one policeman to his death from the top of the
stadium. Another was strangled with his tie. When police were
forced to use tear gas, they inadvertently lobbed several bombs
into the stands. The masses of soccer fans had been watching
the melee with attentive interest, as Latin Americans always observe acts of the most wanton violence with an absorbed, almost
scientific curiosity. But now they stampeded to the gates. It was

already half an hour after the official closing of the game and the doors should have been opened. But it was typical, too, that the gatekeepers had not opened the gates. They had been watching the riots.

Later that night, in the hospitals across the city, as the infuriated cries of the day faded into the dull dirge of the night, you could see the corpses with the cross marks from the gates impressed on their bellies. In the outdoor patios and the dingy hallways, the bodies lay in long lines. As they stampeded from the stands, hundreds of persons had been caught at the closed gates. And as body pressed against body, the life was squeezed out of them. Later, when the gates were opened, the corpses tumbled onto the pavement: three hundred and nineteen of them. Before the bodies could be transported to the hospitals, the local toughs of Lima put a final touch on the Kafkaesque scene by robbing them of watches and money.

Early in the evening the fog turned into a fine, steady rain, unusual for Lima. There seemed to be air nowhere. Lines formed outside the hospitals—long patient lines. People spoke in low voices; inside, there was an eerie quiet. Methodically, people were allowed in in sixes and sevens. They crept from body to body —many were children—seeking to identify. Occasionally a woman would find a son or a husband. One middle-aged Peruvian woman, with a black mantilla over her head, suddenly came upon her sixteen-year-old son. "I knew it, I knew it," she screamed, "I knew he was here." She fell to her knees, clasping her hands. The man supporting her said to the empty room around him, in stupefied explanation, "It was her only son."

Lima is a city that had to be careful as to how all this was handled. Mass funerals were held the next day. President Fernando Belaúnde immediately proclaimed a state of siege, for he feared that leftist elements would attempt to exploit the ill-defined, amorphous violence.

And then the questioning began. Latin Americans are not, in general, notably self-analytical, but a certain amount of investigation had to be done. A reason had to be found and given for the carnage. And the explanations for the greatest sports tragedy

in history poured out in a welling up of righteousness and indignation.

With no exception—either among individuals, in newspapers
or in government communiqués—there was only one explanation
ever offered: the umpire—a foreigner—had ruled against Peru. No
one claimed that the umpire had ruled incorrectly. It was never
mentioned that, right or wrong, the umpire rules and his will
must be accepted, that such is the essence of good sportsman-
ship. What was central to everything at the time was simply the
fact that he had ruled against Peru.

Neither were such sentiments reserved exclusively to the poorer
classes. When a high-level investigating commission of judges,
public officials and lawyers was formed to investigate the reasons
for the tragedy, the commission's explanation was that the
Uruguayan umpire was the "intellectual author" of the stadium
massacre.

It was a curious statement, but it was typically Latin American.
And others had other explanations. Weeks later, far from the
stadium and the stadium people, Dr. Humberto Rotundo, one of
Peru's foremost psychiatrists and a man known for his work
throughout the world, sat in his book-lined office in the luxurious
Miraflores section of Lima. A few blocks away stood the cliffs
overlooking the gray ocean with the strange sea animals that the
cold Humboldt Current washes up from Antarctica.

Dr. Rotundo is a short, somewhat rotund man with a lively,
human face that compliments his intellectual vigor. He was interested in the soccer tragedy, in the real reasons why it could
happen. "But of course I must give you a psychological explanation," he began, almost eagerly, with the fine excitement over
ideas found in the best Latin Americans. He shrugged genteelly.
"There is no other explanation."

"The relation with the mother and the father in the lower
classes is very complex," he said. "The child has a terror of the
father; and because he is there to inflict his authority and not to
guide the child, the child sustains a devaluation of the father.
This leads to a lack of faith in figures of authority. They do not
respect the father figure. He hasn't been a model for his children.

The mother is stronger, but she also is in the condition of being a victim because of the absence of the man and the aggression toward women.

"There is the psychological element that people's aggressiveness does not show itself day after day. When they get into a mass situation, it releases itself." The doctor's reasoning about the stadium disaster was quite logical. The boys grow up with an ingrained distrust for authority. It does not make their world run fairly; it humiliates and downgrades them, as they see it. When they go to the stadium, expecting victory, they find new authorities and further humiliations.

They find a foreign umpire who rules against them, and the police use tear gas. They find a foreign team that takes pride in being "white" while they are "*indio*." Is it possible to lose again? Clearly not. Losing drives them to fury and they strike out. And they are crushed to death at the gates.

How to explain the terrible sense of inferiority and lostness exemplified by the soccer tragedy? How to explain the lack of progress and development in the America to the south—particularly in comparison to the extraordinary feats of the America to the north?

The Latins, when they are not being particularly introspective or self-critical (one of the things they have *not* picked up from the Marxists is their dour propensity for self-criticism), have easy answers. It is American imperialism, American and/or European colonialism. The Japanese take advantage of them commercially; the Vatican, spiritually. The soil is bad, the land inhospitable. All non-answers. All superficial. All magnificently self-pitying.

But those more secure Latin Americans who have searched more deeply and systematically for answers have found other reasons. These men—writers, poets, even politicians—have, throughout Latin American history, always suffered over "Latin Americanism." Crying and rhyming out their despair over the Latin American's not knowing who he was, these men have usually come eventually to the theory that it was his racial mixture itself that condemned him to inconsequence in the world. Was it not, they asked, the vile mestizoization—the rapacious mixture of the in-

nocent Indian woman with the arrogant, lusting conquistador—
that brought forth the bastard son of the New World? A man with
no place, a human soul with no form.

The sensitive Brazilian writer and historian Vianna Moog is
only one who has voiced the recurrent fear: "What, indeed, could
be expected of half-breeds conceived and reared outside of marriage, the issue of scandal and sin? Well-adjusted, integrated individuals, healthy in body and soul? Of course, that could happen
only exceptionally. For three centuries, the rule would have to be
as it was, emotional imbalance, inner discord, insecurity, instability, hearts hardened by resentment, marginalism, laziness, melancholy, vague desires of return to childhood in search of the father,
an ideal father, 'the father of the poor,' revolt against the real
father, maternal fixations, generalized social maladjustment . . ."

The Mexican philosopher Leopoldo Zea saw the Hispanic American as unable to accept his past—it seemed so black and evil to
him that he had to reject it outright. "He surrendered to the difficult task of no longer being that which he was," Zea wrote, "in
order to become, as if he had never existed, something entirely
different. Our heritage is the complete opposite of what we want
to be and what we should be. We carry our defects in our blood;
let us rid ourselves of this blood if necessary."

From wherever men looked, they seemed to find only hopelessness. Even Europeans, such as Hegel, looked at Latin America
and found it existing only as an echo and a reflection of the Old
World—as a shadow, and not a reality. How different from the
buoyant optimism of the American to the north, whose history
proclaimed the birth of a supremely confident New Man, a man
who built life block by block to his own master plan.

What the Latins did not themselves fully realize until recently
is that there are, in truth, two Latin Americas. There is the old,
aristocratic Latin America, with its heritage from Spain and its
men who were basically Europeans. And there is the new—some
say the real—Latin America of the "marginal" masses, which existed and exists on the peripheries and margins of this tradition.

It was not the "mixture of blood" that prevented Latin America
from progressing and developing, it was the cultural formation of

Latin Americans. The way they were, with the cultural attributes they had, they could not enter the modern world. Whether society's structure, the family's structure or the structure of the Latin personality—it was not such that it could serve as the basis for a modern, technically oriented society in which change was built-in and institutionalized.

One of the most primary problems was the lack of social integration—the massive percentage of "marginals" who were not taking part in Latin society. As Victor Alba, the Spanish-born political scientist who is a specialist on Latin America, has written: "The Latin American countries are not nations: they are not integrated, and the great majority of their people form sub-societies quite separated from the official 'society.' To convert these countries into nations will require long and hard struggle against both the inertia of the masses and the oligarchic system."

It was not only important to integrate these "marginals" in order to release their energies to society, it was important to integrate them to bring into play the new and more modern and more democratic values held by the men.

Even by the 1960s, these masses of Latin men—men who held the kernels of change for the future inside them—were taking relatively little part in the major currents of their societies. They were outsiders looking in. They were marginal men—marginal men politically, socially, economically and, most important, psychologically—and marginal men never win.

They existed on the peripheries of their societies but not in the center. They had a place in society—in their families and in small local groups—and in many ways it was a firmer and surer place than that of their individualistic North American brothers, who seemed always to be flailing their arms in their society of equals trying to find a place to sit down. But it was not a place where they had power or where their values came into play.

They did not belong to the inner circles of their societies, for they took no part in the decision-making process. Nor did society belong to them. Latin American life continued to be dominated by societies where the masses lived out detached lives, taking little real part in the decisions of society except to obey and, from time to time, to help put some *caudillo* in power.

The figures of marginality are impressive. In Brazil, it is estimated that 64 percent of the people live outside the money economy; in Chile, it is 30 percent; in the Indian countries, it includes most of the Indians. In Peru, with some twelve million people, only two million vote, when they vote, and almost all voting takes place in the urban centers. In the Dominican Republic and Brazil, 67 percent of the rural population are illiterate. In Guatemala, 51 percent of the farms cover 41 percent of the total arable land; in Ecuador 17 percent of the landowners possess 37 percent of the land. These figures of marginality exist because the masses of Latin Americans do not have the tools—literacy, the vote, land, influence, respect in their society—that would integrate them as citizens of a modern society. They have little real sense—in contrast to the artificial and exaggerated importance of the soccer game incident—of nationality or self.

The class system in Latin America, in most of the countries, has largely been frozen. At the top is the 10 to 15 percent of ruling creoles, descended from the early Spanish settlers and usually having some in-mixture of Indian or Negro blood. They are from the upper and middle classes who control government, send their children to Europe and the United States to be educated and generally look with disdain upon their compatriots. Since World War II, a middle class has been forming, particularly in Argentina, Chile, Peru, Colombia and Mexico, but it is not a middle class like that of the United States. It has no principles or ideology of its own and has no sense of itself as a class with any binding standards. Its aim is to imitate the aristocrats and to have what the aristocrats have. Consequently, having two maids in the house becomes more desirable than having milk for the children.

Below the ruling creoles are the real marginals. They differ from country to country but today they are alive and moving. Most of the marginal population is *mestizo* and the *mestizo* or mixed-blood is historically a confused, schizophrenic, traumatized man. Germán Arciniegas provides a clear explanation of the *mestizo*: "The *mestizo's* situation is not the same as the Indian's. The *mestizo* received no more than half of the things that came from Europe—everything about him is by halves. He is a native product, and an illegitimate one to boot, born of the contact between the white man and the Indian woman, an under-the-counter product, as it were. If he was a child of love, he enjoyed some consideration on that account. But the social background from which he was born, with a right to it that was never complete, made him a rebel, or a difficult man at best."

Beneath the *mestizo*, particularly in the Andean countries, the marginal people are often called *cholos*. A *cholo* is a Westernized or citified Indian. He can also be a mixed blood, for basically *cholo* is a cultural term and not a racial term. In Guatemala, *cholos* are called *ladinos*. In the eastern regions of Bolivia, they are the Camba people. In Brazil, they are similar to the Candangos or workmen from the Northeast who built Brasília and the Northeasterners from the Sertão who trucked down to São Paulo for work—both a mixture of white, Negro and some Indian.

Many of the marginal people are avid wanderers, for they are restless and searching. Latin American life is not static; it has changed enormously in the last hundred years from the traditional frozen society that it was and that many foreigners still think it is. Within the last twenty years, it has disgorged masses of people onto the public scene, tearing them out of their traditional community patterns. But in Latin America there was nothing like the American ethos, to absorb the European immigrants and to create a "new man." Neither would the upper classes allow them into the centers of society.

It is difficult to characterize these marginal people, for they represent diverse mixtures. Yet they represent some constant characteristics, too. They have never had power over themselves, but today they want it. They are, ironically, both cynical and hopeful. They are cynical about the central governments in the capital cities, because they see them draining off the wealth of the rural areas. Yet they are hopeful enough that the world can change that they keep working toward unrealized goals. They have done an amazingly good job of organizing themselves for community and political action. They are hypersensitive and touchy enough so that they do not easily expose themselves; they are probably more realistic in many ways about Latin America's failure than the even more hypersensitive middle classes. In contrast to the intellectuals and the middle class, they tend to be idealistic about the United States. They seldom criticize the United States and more often praise it with such comments as, "It is no wonder Americans run the world and not the Latin Americans, because the Latins don't work."

I remember a machinist in the fishing boom town of Chimbote in Peru, where all the money that rolled in was squandered on alcohol and women. He told me, "Peru doesn't live methodically. It always lives in a poor state of affairs. There are many who earn money, but what happens is that the people who have a lot aren't dedicated to a methodical way of life. Alcohol, a lack of discipline, vices—these are the heritage of the Peruvian."

This is a typical reaction among the marginal people in Latin America, who have a childlike admiration for the United States. It shocked the Mexican intellectuals, for instance, when a poor Mexican was quoted in Oscar Lewis' book *The Children of Sanchez* as saying he thought Mexico would be far better off under an American president. It rang perfectly true to anyone who has spent any time talking to the poor in Latin America. For they are the people who never win. The poor in every country of the world respect power, and to them the United States is the country that always wins.

But it was not only the basic aspect of marginality that has led to the Latin Americans' inferiority complex, particularly in face of their brother colossus of the North. It was a crucial element, but there was more. Partly the Latins were especially suspicious, cynical and ungenerous because they had lived through so many periods in which man was to have been reformed and society changed for all time.

The dreams of the Independence were to turn Latin America inside out, to create new societies of justice, equality and independence. Instead the Independence wars were followed by the era of the great *caudillos* and one of the most wanton periods of authoritarianism the world has known.

Then toward the end of the nineteenth century there was another period of euphoria, this time an essentially abortive industrial euphoria that lasted up to the second half of this century. After 1880 another new Hispanic America seemed to arise, based on a belief in the efficacy of education in changing man's lot. Railroads were built, industries grew, and "liberty," "progress," and "democracy," rooted in science and in Comtian Positivism, were to fashion a new world. The unscientific Hispanic past, with its superstition and fatalism, was gone. Or was it?

Strangely and tellingly, this era saw not only the defeat of Latins at the hands of their unwieldy continent, but also the defeat of the pollyannish and positivistic North Americans. It was as if the "Amazon syndrome" was a curse on everyone. It was in this epoch that Henry Ford attempted to develop rubber in the Amazon, only to be defeated by the recalcitrance of his *mestizo* laborers and his disregard for the laws of the jungle. It was in this era that Teddy Roosevelt, huffing and puffing with confidence, went to Brazil to explore unknown parts of the jungles. After weeks lost in the rain forest, his naïve exuberance turned to panic and desperation. Man after man died; and as they roved in hopeless circles, the president himself came down with a malady that eventually helped to kill him. Before he finally found his way out, he discovered one unknown river. And the man who was probably the most hopeless optimist of all time named it "The River of Doubt."

There is another story that carries the Amazon drama and the drama of the world's great losers a little further, that typifies the Amazon's—and thus all of Latin America's—apparent imperviousness to change and improvement. It is the story of the Madeira-Mamoré Railroad which runs deep into the western parts of the Amazon jungles, from Pôrto Velho to the Bolivian border. Like Ford's disastrous Fordlândia, the Madeira-Mamoré was a study in faith that the interior of Latin America—the "real" Latin America—could be developed, and developed rationally, if only man would use his technical knowhow to do it.

I visited Pôrto Velho and the Madeira-Mamoré in 1964, half a century after it was finished, and the skeletal structure of the great experiment was still there. Having flown to Pôrto Velho from Manaus, I found a little town deep in the jungle that still looked reasonably modern, with paved roads, little square houses, and a huge stone hotel with a veranda across its front, with complete tables and umbrellas. From the veranda, you could see the jungle steaming all around. Inside the dining room, there were incongruously romantic pictures of the forests, with heroic-looking tigers and happy rubber gatherers. On the night tables of the rooms were orchids standing in little vials of water.

Late every afternoon, the visiting businessmen from São Paulo who were doing trade in the cassiterite that had recently been found near there, would gather on the veranda and sit around and complain. "Every time I come here I feel good," one Paulista merchant said. "I feel I've worked out my sins being here." "This is the end of the world," another broached as if everybody didn't know it. But soon after I arrived and announced my intention to ride on the old Madeira-Mamoré line, the conversation changed. Then it was, "The heat has driven the girl mad" and "Don't do it, don't do it, my dear." One got angry with me for persisting in my plans and eventually he snapped, almost triumphantly, "You are going to suffer!"

The railroad has been called a number of things—in appreciation and in anger—but the most common nicknames for it are the "Mad Mary" and the "Devil's Railroad." Still, it didn't look as bad as one might have guessed from reading or hearing descriptions of it. The railroad yard was still neat and, though the machinery was old, it appeared to be in good condition. The creaking, listing wooden houses for the workers and officials still stood there, most of them with wide porches and sagging overhanging eaves.

When I presented myself at the railroad office to ask for the next train, the stationmaster announced glumly, "Ah, but there is not a train for three days." When I mentioned I could not possibly wait that long, he pointed out that a freight was leaving at 4 A.M. the next day and would carry me to Bolivia in only two full days of riding. He pointed to some sacks in the freight cars and suggested that if I just fluffed them up a bit they'd make quite a comfortable bed. When I demurred, he finally agreed to give me my own little railroad car and I left the next day to travel the steaming two hundred miles on the Mad Mary.

The driver of my little yellow railroad car, which was open on the sides and had two seats, was an extremely amiable young Negro named George Edson McCauley Davis who immediately told me, in almost understandable Caribbean island British, "My mommy and daddy came from Trinidad and British Guiana and I've never forgotten my English." And so we set off, at seventeen miles an hour, for two days of travel to the Bolivian border.

The territory of Rondônia is hot, flat, green and scrubby. It is home to the rubber gatherers, Indians, ocelots, mosquitoes, swarms of pretty yellow butterflies and four-foot-tall anthills that take on grotesque shapes and forms. Alongside of us, much of the way, languidly twisted and turned the Madeira River; when it turned a bend and ran into the Mamoré River, we would be in Bolivia.

I soon discovered that the men on the veranda were quite right about one thing: the rails did wave. And not only did the little yellow car throw you back and forth constantly, but there was an enormous roar from the original Ford motor. Still, George Edson McCauley Davis was ecstatically happy and filled with the realization of the importance of his job of escorting a foreigner on "the road." Whenever we stopped in a village, he introduced me as the personal guest of the president of Brazil.

At nightfall we made the first stop at the little settlement of Abunã—all the passenger trains stop overnight—and I checked into the hotel that looked as though it might be Charles Addams' summer home. All of wood, it was built in 1910, which was also the last time it was painted. It had broad overhanging eaves that protected its wide, rotting porches where the chickens pecked at the wood. For some reason the windows, which were large, were painted black, so inside you felt as though you were in a dark cage. The beds had straw mattresses and sheets and the food in the dining room was surprisingly good—rice, beef cooked in brown gravy, fruit, beans and coffee. Room and board was two dollars a night.

The town itself consisted of two rows of low stucco stores, some sturdy stucco houses and some thatched huts. All around, as a weird white moon came up, the strange shadows and sounds of the jungle moved, whistled, moaned and shifted. After dinner, four of us—one businessman, two malaria workers and I—went out and sat on the tracks in the moonlight. One of the malaria men kicked at the wavy tracks and voiced the old belief about the railroad, "A life lost for every crosstie . . ."

It was in 1878 that a group of Philadelphia contractors, with great fanfare, left the United States to make the first attempt to build the Madeira-Mamoré Railroad, a classic example of hope in Latin America. They would defeat the jungle and give Bolivia a way to the sea. But in a year they had abandoned the whole project: 904 men had collapsed from malaria, 221 were dead, and a few miles of rusted track were laid.

By 1903 Bolivia and Brazil were at each other's throat again. Brazilian rubber gatherers were poaching on Bolivian territory. The matter was settled when Bolivia ceded the area to Brazil. In exchange Brazil agreed to build a railroad which, though spanning only two hundred miles, would give landlocked Bolivia a way to carry its rubber to the Amazon and thus to the Atlantic, bypassing the rapids of the Madeira River.

In stepped a remarkable American Quaker and business titan, Percival Farquhar, who tackled the "impossible" railroad with zest. "I hoped the achievement would be my calling card," Farquhar is quoted as saying. He bought the concession for $750,-000, formed the Madeira-Mamoré Railroad Company with capital of $11 million and set out to vanquish the jungle. He laid out Pôrto Velho, built screened-in housing similar to that used in Panama during the construction of the canal, and fashioned a questionable asset—the first baseball diamond in Brazil. Hampered by Farquhar's sober Quaker beliefs and regulations against alcohol, the workers took to drinking a cheap brandy that had been brought in to rub down the mules. There were no women available until the very end, when prostitutes from Barbados were imported under the guise of "laundresses."

Despite the hardships, the builders were convinced they were building the "train of the century," that it would carry "fabulous riches" in rubber, oil and minerals out from an unknown world. But soon Americans were pushing their fingers into their skin to see if they had beriberi. Roused by fear of the change the railroad would bring, the Indians began to attack, and they were followed by malaria and yellow fever. In the end, thousands of men died building the railroad—Indians, Negroes from the islands, English, Americans and Brazilians. Farquhar said thirty-six hundred died. Probably it was more. It wasn't a life for every one of the 615,000 crossties, as the popular old story went, but it was a good number.

The best of the world's modern knowledge had been used in the task of taming and molding the jungle. Farquhar built an excellent hospital, the Candelaria, which set standards for the care of men in the tropics and treated over thirty thousand patients. Nevertheless, as the Madeira drops from flood stage, millions of mosquitoes breed at every cataract. It is one of the deadliest spots in the world for malaria and yellow fever. Though the men were paid exceptionally high wages (six dollars a day for skilled work and three dollars for unskilled), the turnover was 95 percent in every three months in 1908. Pôrto Velho ended up with not only a model hospital but also a model cemetery.

The rubber boom had brought development to Amazonas, but it was a temporary and superficial development. With the Latin liking for spectacle, the economic influx went into creating a little of civilization's frosting in the Amazon instead of being used in long-range investments. Manáos (later Manaus), right in the center of the Amazon, became a city of 180,000, and Sarah Bernhardt played in the pink opera house that still stands. At the height of the boom, a man had to wear a white shirt and tie to ride on the streetcars. It was the first town in Brazil to have electricity. The extent of the romantic qualities of the boom was personified in the planter who imported a Napier car from Europe in 1905 and let it stand for years on blocks. There were no roads on which to drive it.

And the Madeira-Mamoré? And the hope that anything could be done if you applied rationality and technical knowledge? The line was finished in 1912—the year the rubber boom collapsed. Farquhar's empire went into receivership and tongues wagged from London to New York about the railroad that went "from nowhere to nowhere." The railroad that had cost $33 million and that was to have been Farquhar's calling card in the world of financial empires never paid its way. The British ran it for a time, but in 1931 it went bankrupt and the Brazilian government ran it after that, always at a loss.

The Latin Americans never won and neither did anyone else who meddled in their ill-fated continent. The area seemed to be cursed. After each period of hope, new political tyrannies arose that were more refined than the old ones. When new industries were built, the oligarchies took them over. The Latins, frustrated and angry, blamed their problems on forces outside themselves —usually the United States and foreign "imperialism," but also anybody else they could find. And they looked at each other with a hostility and suspicion that destroyed their chances of working together—the one thing that could have helped them advance.

Colombians tell the story of the peasant who, when visited by the village priest who came to bless his fields, asked him to go instead and curse the fields of his neighbor. A Colombian writer wrote that his people "cannot stand, in the individual or the collectivity, the success of our neighbor." A maid in Peru who worked for an American family heard them talking about Americans working in the poor sections—Peace Corpsmen. "Yes, your people are out there too," she said knowingly. "They want some of the land that's being given away."

The Argentines cannot bear the thought of the historic accident that set them down in Latin America and they despise the very thought that they might be Latin Americans. They are "Europeans," they say constantly. Yet all of their problems are exactly the exaggerations of the Latin American problems. "And so," sighs the Argentine novelist Ernesto Sabato, "The Argentine is neither Latin American nor European. He is nothing." Their neighbors say the Argentines hate themselves, and it's likely—and not an improper emotion—that they do. There is a typically cynical tango that goes: "Today it is the same to be a traitor, ignorant, a wiseman, a man without shame or a contrabandist. All is the same, nothing is better. It's the same to be a burro as a great professor."

For the Indian mixtures, of course, it was even worse. In Peru, when psychologists gave Rorschach tests to the Indians, they continuously saw men with no hands and no feet. Pictures of a mother talking to her son constantly evoked the interpretation that it was a mother about to abandon her son. If you looked carefully, in a country like Peru, you soon came to the realization that all those heroic statues on podiums were of generals who had lost battles.

It is telling and typical that Latins have reacted with vigor to the American policy of sending Americans of Latin descent as ambassadors to Latin America. Washington innocently thought of it as a compliment, but the Latin Americans most insistently did not. They deeply resented the *pocho*—the name given to a presumptuous, Americanized Latin. As one usually calm Latin diplomat muttered, "These half-Latin diplomats seem to be constantly reminding us, 'We have made it in the important world, and you're still where you were.'"

Nor have the Latins been kinder to their heroes. Because they have not succeeded themselves, most Latin Americans cannot easily countenance the fact that some of their own men *have* succeeded. They have turned on almost every one of their great men, usually banishing them—and their success and nobility—from their sight. All the liberators died in exile, forgotten by their own people—the people they liberated from Spain. San Martín spent his old age in Europe. Bolívar died in exile from Venezuela, despairing and disillusioned. Sucre left Bolivia, which he created, after his troops rebelled against him, shot at him and wounded him in the arm, only to be ambushed and murdered. José Gervasio Artigas, the great gaucho who led Uruguay in the 1800s, spent the last thirty years of his life a simple farmer in Paraguay, his only companions a Negro and a dog.

Even when a Latin American succeeded—and succeeded beyond the wildest hopes of man—he could not bear his Latin Americanism and sought his identification elsewhere, in Europe or in America.

Perhaps the most dramatic monument to this phenomenon is in the Bolivian city of Cochabamba, that low, warm, flowery city that contrasts so warmly and so dramatically with the cold bleakness of the rest of Bolivia.

It is here that the story of Simón Patiño took place, and it is bizarre and wonderful enough for several fairy tales and a handful of Horatio Alger stories. That little Aymara Indian, whose wife once worked in the village market, was wandering across the Bolivian moonscape toward the end of the nineteenth century when he happened upon a mountain filled with tin. It was the mountain that was to become Catavi. Patiño became one of the five richest men in the world, but to the Bolivian *rosca* or screw, the term given to the aristocratic classes, Patiño never was anyone. He was simply an upstart *cholo* social climber who didn't know his place.

But Patiño thought he knew his place, and it wasn't Bolivia or hankering over the Inca empire. In Cochabamba today, if you get special permission, you can see quite clearly and dramatically where the tin king thought he belonged in the world. His city apartments, for the times he was living in Cochabamba, were, appropriately, above the bank building. They are huge aristocratically turned out rooms; they have Gobelin tapestries, Grecian figures, a Moorish room, carved billiard sticks, an elaborate old billiard score marker, and a huge grand piano that has never been played.

But it is at his big house, his "Portales" palace on the outskirts of Cochabamba that the picture is completed. When you enter the huge palatial yellow and white building, built in early French and Italian styles (it is impossible to isolate styles in Patiñoesque, except to say that they are all European), there are two large, full-sized formal pictures. On one side is Patiño, the little Indian who found a vein of tin, and he is standing in a very formal pose, dressed in black evening clothes. Across from him is his wife, her dark, fat Indian face emerging from a formal European gown of the period.

The palace itself is a weird fantasy. There are pillars of marble, a fireplace with a huge picture above it of the coronation of a European king, elaborate wood carvings, and a copy of the Sistine Chapel ceiling in the upstairs hallways. But there is a sadness, too, about so much wealth and ostentation. The marble is false—it is painted—and the "king" who should have been living there never did. No one ever did. The Patiños could not stand being close to their homeland, even though the shock of such primitiveness was dulled by the insulation of a full European palace. They moved to Europe shortly after the big house was built. Their children married lower-level royalty and Patiño died in 1938. His mines were nationalized by the revolutionary government that took over in the name of the Indians in 1952. The name Catavi became synonymous with violence and revolution. It was Catavi that became the center of leftist miner agitation all during the middle of the century, as the Indians began reclaiming their own.

But, today, almost before your eyes, you can see even these historic traits and problems changing, and changing dramatically. As the marginal men begin to take more and more part in their societies, as Latin man's character changes as generations pass, as the church and the military transform themselves as institutions, the search for identity is growing. It is a search that is beginning to find answers in the dreams and actions of the New Latins.

CHAPTER 3

The Importance of Form

"*Se obedece, pero no se cumple*"—"We obey the order, but we do not carry it out." Old and common Spanish saying.

You soon learn you don't have to pity the people of Chimbote, though it is hard to believe they might have built their city the way they like it. It's a mongrel city, impassively facing the Pacific with its thousand adobe and mat hovels. It lies on the coast of Peru, just north of Lima, and you can smell the city before you are able to see it. The miserable, gnawing stench of the fishmeal industry overpowers you as you approach Chimbote on the desert highway and carries you, a limp and subdued prize, into the center of town.

There is a strange, ethereal bay, light blue from a distance despite the floating filth, with white guano-covered mountains hanging like piles of white ash outside its perimeter. The "city" boasts dirt roads lined with little square houses of adobe brick, pieces of tin, board, cardboard and a good bit of spit. Chimbotans all spend an unusual amount of time spitting. At any one moment, too, approximately a quarter of the city's population appears to be engaged in urinating, almost any place the urge comes upon them.

But you soon learn that the people of Chimbote have built their town exactly the way it pleases them. There is plenty of money; the people are not poor. This is where the fishmeal industry boom originated in the 1960s, making Peru first in world production of the precious fishmeal used in high-protein animal foods. Fishing boat captains living in those miserable hovels earn up to six hundred dollars a month and spend it all on women and liquor. Chimbote is the way it is because it chooses to be that way. Any attempts at civic upgrading are met with an unregenerate attitude on the part of the citizenry.

Nevertheless, I liked Chimbote from the start. It has a certain animal energy about it; actually it is more of a human energy, for animals would probably adhere to some order. Chimbote, population grown to 180,000 in only five years, is the ultimate in human chaos.

One experience I had in Chimbote particularly demonstrates and dramatizes the way in which form takes the place of substance in Latin American society and the way in which the appearance of things seldom conforms to reality.

I had gone there to write a story on Chimbote, which was "sister city" to Pensacola, Florida. Under the "sister city" plan, United States cities "adopted" poor cities abroad in order to be "good neighbors," and cities were expected to "exchange" people and help each other in various ways. This particular "sister city" program had won first prize in the experiment. I expected to write a rather typical "good news" story, and that would be that.

But after two days in Chimbote I felt strangely uneasy. I had the basic story, yet I knew I couldn't leave, for everyone I had talked to had hinted at something more. I was convinced that everything was not what it appeared to be.

Pensacola, to help poor, whoring Chimbote, was sending fifty thousand dollars to build a sports stadium on the sand outside the city for the poor boys of Chimbote to grow into good sports. The money was being collected by Girl Scouts, among other exemplary types, and was being relayed in weekly installments of one thousand dollars. There was a supervising committee of six—three Chimbotans and three Americans—to watch over the program. A bishop, the Right Reverend James C. Burke, an American, was chairman.

The half-finished stadium looked splendid from the outside. It

was a large circular cement block affair out on the desert sand
dunes with the Andes rising directly behind it. But everyone kept
hinting to me—rather obviously, since Latins are hardly subtle
hinters—that it was not the perfect project.

One day I was interviewing one of the city officials when the
latter suddenly asked, "You know about the contract?" I shook my
head. He didn't say anything for a moment and then he added
slowly, "Well, there's supposed to be a contract—a secret contract
—somewhere. Something about the mayor getting the land by
making certain promises to the man who had donated the land."

The man who had donated the land turned out to be a land
speculator and nightclub proprietor named Pedro Farro García, a
robust *cholo* who had grown rich on Chimbote's growth. I discovered that on his property of 610,000 square yards adjoining the
Pan American Highway, about a hundred yards from the stadium,
stood "Mexico," Chimbote's most notorious (and legally licensed)
house of prostitution. The owner of several other clubs up and
down the coast, he was sometimes called the "Al Capone" of
Chimbote.

Farro had the land, or title to it, through a curious Peruvianism.
The land belonged to an Indian "community" that had been artifi-
cially created for political reasons. The people that had held title
were not even remotely Indians, but they, in turn, had issued
title to Farro for part of it in exchange for some commercial concessions. The local "Chimbote-Cuzco Indigenous Community"
was really a fiction.

I did a good deal of looking around and finally found Farro,
who turned out to be a big, garrulous man with a huge belly. A
local newspaperman invited Farro over to his house and the three
of us sat around drinking red wine and discussing the "sister city"
project. Finally I mentioned to Farro, who was growing more and
more talkative as he drank more and more wine, that he didn't
look to me like a man who would give land away for nothing.
I said it admiringly—and he immediately and enthusiastically
agreed.

"You should see what I got!" he exulted. Then he leaped up
from his chair and ran out the door. A few minutes later he was

back, holding a big rolled-up paper—*his* plans for the stadium. As we looked at them on the table, it seemed to me that something was very wrong, for all around the stadium he had sketched in little rooms, using the stadium wall for the back wall. Then he told me that he had got the right, in the "contract," to build "stores" all around the stadium, to have all concessions inside the stadium, and to get city permits for anything he wanted to build on his adjoining land. In leaving, Farro said that he had given the land because he "wanted the children of Chimbote to remember me."

So the Girl Scouts in Pensacola were collecting dimes to build a stadium in Chimbote and, in the process, to make the local land exploiter rich.

There was still another building in Chimbote that is symbolic of the same Latin divergence between appearance and reality. It is the neat, modern-appearing hospital that sits along the bay.

Built in the late 1940s with American aid, the hospital *looks* modern. It is a low stucco building with clean lines and modern doors and windows. But when you go through it, as in so many public buildings in Latin America, you discover some remarkable deficiencies. You find there are no sheets—the people have to bring their own. To the rear of the hospital, women were washing what linens and towels there were in huge black pots. They stood there, stirring them, looking like nothing so much as Shakespearean witches stirring a brew. Inside the building the nurses used huge barrels of rainwater for water. It was the only water they had because the water system had not worked for several years.

The head nurse explained that the building had been built, yes, but then no funds had been provided from Lima for its maintenance. It was another case of the form without the substance, of external development without the necessary and corresponding internal development. It represented one of the curses of Latin America, and one that has many manifestations.

It is there in the importance of the word spoken—but never acted upon. It is there in the voluminous social welfare legislation present in almost every Latin American country and in the Latins who point to "the book" and say, "See how developed we are!"

—but the laws are not carried out. It is there in the manner in which Latin Americans always ceremoniously take your address and then never write. It is there in the promise made which is never kept, because the important thing is to make the gesture. It is there in the importance of theory over practice and the emphasis on hierarchy over mobility. It is there in the strange ritualization of violence.

These paradoxes are not malicious, nor even a matter of being careless. They are rooted in that part of Latin society, whether Italian or Spanish or Portuguese, which confuses spectacle with reality, the word with the deed, the theoretical with the practical, the form with the act, the ritual with the accomplishment, the saint's day and the idol with the worship of God, the way a man looks with what he really is.

The tremendous importance of dress and appearance once affected even the great Simón Bolívar. During a campaign, he went on a trip to the Colombian village of Girón with two of his aides-de-camp, a Britisher and a Frenchman. The two foreigners were dressed in their uniforms, but Bolívar was wearing cotton trousers and a linen shirt. When they stopped at a little hut along the way, the peasant woman immediately gave the two uniformed officers the only two chairs in the house. To Bolívar, the Liberator, she offered a hide on the floor. Not wanting to embarrass her, Bolívar, a modest man, calmly sat on the floor. Just before he left, he was chatting to her about her personal problems and, touched by her poverty, pressed a gold Spanish doubloon into her palm. In astonishment, she realized it was the Liberator.

It is particularly easy to find many aspects of "form and place" in student life in Latin America, for it is filled with so many rituals. One evening in Guatemala City, a group of us sat at a meeting of leftist students at the turbulent university area outside the city. It was at the height of one of the many periods of trouble in Guatemala and there had been a large amount of guerrilla activity in the hills. A presidential election had just been held in which the military, which had been in power and had controlled the electoral machinery, unexpectedly had lost to the democratic civilian candidate. From moment to moment, it was a tossup as to which colonel would take over the city. Or whether, on the other hand, it might not be the guerrillas. Or whether the electoral results would be respected or annulled. Or God knew what. In short, it was a not untypical Guatemalan evening.

The student meeting had been called as an "action" meeting, to decide precisely what they would do to deal with the crisis. But, as with so many Latin "action" meetings, it slipped, instead, into the old, old rituals of Latin America. In every speech the word became substitute for the deed. It became obvious that what each speaker wanted to do at that moment was not to plan for action at all: he wanted to express himself—eloquently and unforgettably. As each speaker got up, he would show some sign of forcing himself to speak, some small nervousness like licking his lips or grasping the back of the chair in front of him and rattling it. Then he would begin to emote, his eyes looking nervously about the room, and the words would ring out with that peculiarly fulsome Latin resonance. "We are victims of the most ferocious oppression . . . great quantities of students and *campesinos* are suffering this despotic state . . . it is clear that the recent elections will not solve the problems of Guatemala . . . Guatemala is being converted into a concentration camp . . ."

It is part of the ritual of being a Latin American student, as much a part as the ritual dance of the demonstration, where the students present themselves to the police, all the while crying against the society they find themselves in and daring the police to shoot. The police know the ritual and, eventually, they do shoot. The dance twists and turns and some poor young man—the sacrifice—falls in the sunlit street and dies, green and unblossomed. The dance becomes a dirge. The police fall back, the students form a line and carry the tender body away. The sacrifice has been made, the martyr fulfilled. It is done.

It was typical that night that at the very end when a real *campesino*—a voluble and well-spoken peasant leader whose land had been taken away by the government—talked to the students, they barely listened. What he was saying was important. It was the only relevant thing that had been said all evening, for he offered facts. But they squirmed and twitched impolitely and clearly showed their boredom. What they had come for they had done: they had expressed themselves before their fellows in their most forceful and *macho* manner. "The word" had been spoken, the testimony had been made. They voted to do nothing for the moment, and dispersed.

To what can you attribute this obsession with form in Latin American society? What accounts for the lack of convergence between the outer shapes of society and its inner practices and realities?

When the Spanish came to the New World, they brought with them, first of all, themselves, and this meant a mentality that reveled in theory and absolutism. They saw the world in monistic terms of black and white, right and wrong, holiness and heretics. They were people who lived in the mind and treasured ornamental culture: Don Quixote was their prince charming, their John Kennedy, their Che Guevara.

In contrast to the openness and mobility of North American society, Latin American society reveled in hierarchy and place. The Latin Catholic Church was burdened with hierarchy, and obedience to the forms of the religion came to take the place of the practice of it. Idols, saints dripping blood, fetishism—these were Latin religion. In society, man tended to stay within his own rigid social class; he had a secure, ordained place there and he did not find it seemly to aspire to leave it. In politics, the forms were preserved; the Organization of American States, for instance, still sometimes goes through dress rehearsals of important meetings, so when it is all enacted publicly the form will be perfect.

Generally the Latin American states adopted Roman law, in contrast to North America's common law. In Roman law, man must prove himself innocent, and so in countries like Peru if a man hits another man with his car, the driver is immediately taken to jail to await trial, often at some distant date. Roman law also stresses the letter of the law over the spirit of the law. Under Roman law, laws are written out in meticulous detail—and this is especially true in Latin America—while laws are seldom enforced. The lower-level "marginal" Latin Americans are coming to understand this very well and they resent it. As a lieutenant in the mountains of

Peru said while discussing social problems, "There is a law, but here in Peru they pass a law and don't carry it out."

Great struggles—with vast amounts of eloquent verbiage—are waged in order to pass laws. All the rituals of self-expression are endured. Eventually the law is passed, with great ceremony, never to be heard from again because there is no will or disposition to comply with the law that has been created. He obeys, but he does not comply.

The great chasm between the atomized individual and the law, and the man at the top, is then dealt with in two ways: resorting to *personalismo* and favors, and by a fatalistic acceptance of the "fact" that the average man can do relatively little in life without a patron. Traditionally there have been no intermediate groups, no lines of control from the citizen to the leadership group. The average Latin man is fatalistic about this and he cultivates friends at the top—friends with personal obligations to him, if possible. If not, he slips back into fatalistic resignation.

Latin American fatalism often throws weird shadows across the landscape. Much has been written about the peasant leagues that blossomed in northeastern Brazil in the 1950s and 1960s. Invariably the picture is of violent, angry peasants, burning cane-fields and united against brutal, reactionary landlords. Yet the peasant leagues actually started in 1955 when João Firmino founded the first league to gain for the peasants the right to be buried in wooden coffins. The right to a proper death was the cause—not the right to a proper life.

In contrast to the United States where, outside of the big city immigrant communities and immigrant politics, a man is judged on how he functions and not on his personal relations, in Latin America *personalismo* is everything. It constantly interferes with attempts to build functional relations and to build institutions that depend not upon a person's *macho* or charisma but on how well an individual functions in an interpersonal position. There is no idea whatsoever of any "interchangeable man."

Henk Van Roosmalen, a young Dutch sociologist who was working in northeastern Brazil with the Roman Catholic organizational group in Natal, found this lack of functionalism to be his most important problem. "It is the lack of relationship between personal relations and functional relations," he told me one night in Natal. "You make a nice structure and you find it disturbed the next day by personal relations. After elections, people have no control of politics—this is the contrast between the formal organization and real organization. It is a lack of cultural experience. When you have a cultural tradition, norms are internalized. When there is a lack of culture, as here, people do things only when others control them."

So traditionally there has been little self-generated political activity in Latin society. People generally have acted under force or for the rewards of ego. I once was discussing this with the attractive and perceptive wife of a Peace Corps director in a Latin American city. Both she and her husband had been born of poor Mexican-American parents in the Southwest United States and raised in a poor *barrio*. "When I was a child living in the *barrio*," she said, "the teachers used to come—they were all *gringos*—and they could have come from another planet. They stressed all the *gringo* values—cleanliness, for instance. Well, my mother stressed this too, but for another reason: for prestige. And punctuality— you've got to be there on time! Why? We didn't see why this was so important." She smiled. "Now *we're* the *gringos* trying to change *these* people."

Another brake to action of the compulsive North American type, and a brake that is closely allied with the importance of form, is the theoretical and absolutist tendency of Latin American intellectuals. They tend to interpret the world within a strict theoretical framework—something that afflicts both the right and the left and makes the stride to Marxism a particular easy step for Latins. The political officer of an American embassy in Latin America once explained this to me: "What motivates a Latin is his great conceit in his intellectual achievement. They rather think you can move mountains with concentration, if you just have the right approach. When the intellectuals talk about the Cuban people being better off under Communism, they mean that their ideological basis is more sound. Since we Americans are basically pragmatic, it's very difficult to understand these people who prefer not to do something than to do it for the wrong reasons."

During the Dominican Revolution, Jaime Benítez, rector of the University of Puerto Rico, was discussing how his viewpoint differed from that of Juan Bosch, the attractive but emotional and theoretical ex-president of the Dominican Republic. "Bosch has a different mentality from mine," Benítez said. "He sees the world in forms and theoretical structures. It's always amazing to me how sure he can be of everything. I was educated in the case study of law at Georgetown and the University of Chicago. I was educated to judge each case on its own merits, to see that the world is not a series of formulas and frameworks."

He grinned suddenly. "It always amazes me when he does come out right. Bosch said to me when four hundred Marines had landed in Santo Domingo, 'You watch, there'll be twenty thousand.' I said, 'Twenty thousand, that's absurd.' And within days there were twenty thousand." What these two men represent is the basic difference between North American and Latin American society—the one deriving its mode of action from empirical knowledge, the other living off the "truths" of evangelical testimony in which right and wrong are unchangeable throughout time.

It also symbolizes a difference in two types of intellectuals. In Latin society the intellectual is the man closest to society's core. He often rules. He is always admired. His studies and concerns may be remote from the marginal groups in Latin society—they *are* remote—but still they are awarded prestige. In North American society, on the other hand, the intellectual stands on society's periphery, jealously looking in at the centers of power. Until very recently, his insights were ornaments to real society, rather than rules every man intends to live by. And he is more than slightly distrusted, for in American society it has been the practical man of action—the technician—the man who "gets things done"—who is most admired.

Along with the theoretical, absolutist turn of mind of the Latin intellectual goes the idea of the abstractness of knowledge, of art for art's sake and knowledge for knowledge's sake. This strain runs throughout both Spanish and Portuguese history and infects Latin American education on all levels. The Brazilian author Vianna Moog wrote of his country's past: "This taste for the show of erudition, for fake humanism and false universalism, this preoccupation with *purely ornamental culture,* was to affect all the centers of education in the country . . ." The terrible thing was not the not knowing how and the not learning how to extract gold from the depths of the earth, or how to organize the sugar trade on a permanent basis; the awful thing, the inexcusable thing, was to be ignorant of the latest European events, of the most obscure passages from Vergil, of the subtleties of the grammarians, of the minutest rules of rhetoric.

Another Brazilian writer, Alberto Torres, author of *The National Problem of Brazil,* published in the 1920s, declared that, "On the general level of society and as regards the higher forms of culture, dilettantism, superficiality, dialectic, empty flights of language, a taste for ornamental phrases and for conceits consecrated by notoriety or by the sole prestige of authority, replaced the ambition to educate the mind for the purpose of guiding conduct. Applause and approbation, the satisfactions of vanity and self-conceit, compose the whole ambition of men's minds. To attain to the truth, to be capable of a solution, to train the mind or character to resolve and to act, are things alien to us."

Latin Americans have always been harder on themselves than any foreigner ever could be.

The Brazilian educational system, which led to this type of mentality, was typical of the problems of all the Latin systems: schools were created to train small elites, specialized in rarefied subjects like philosophy and law. When an American educational team did a study of the Brazilian system for the U. S. Agency for International Development in 1966 and 1967, it found that only about 2 percent of Brazil's college-aged students were involved in higher education; only twenty-two thousand students were graduated annually in a country of eighty million persons. At the same time, admission requirements were so stiff that half the applying students could not meet them. There were more students enrolled in law than any other field "though Brazil already has a surplus of lawyers."

Though a reform of the Brazilian system was desperately needed, the response to the report of the American team was typically Latin American and typically self-defeating. The students vigorously protested the Americans' "imposing" a foreign system on Brazil. It was the old story: they could not modernize without changing and they could not change, they felt, without losing themselves. Their self-definition was simply too fragile.

Always the Latin Americans have become lawyers where there was no respect for the law; poets when 90 percent of the people could not read; economists when 75 percent of the populace lived outside the economy. Until recently, no one was moved to become what Latin America needed—agronomists and sociologists and construction engineers—because such examples of knowledge —and working with one's hands—were simply not esteemed. What the traditional Latin American man has wanted was not the opportunity to serve his country or people, but to gain prestige and a place in society. He got this through a title ("In Latin America, a man becomes a doctor to be a doctor, not to work as a doctor," one Latin commented), and titles are always used with the "Mr." It is "Señor Arquitecto" and "Señor Ingeniero." Often the accouterments of position are pathetically absurd, as in northeastern Brazil, where plumbers carry their tools in briefcases so as to appear to be white collar workers.

In such a society, truth seldom stands alone and objectivity does not exist. Everything serves a point of view. Every newspaper is the organ—the vehicle—for a political movement; every writer is an advocate. Clemente Marroquín Rojas, the salty Guatemalan journalist and, for a time, vice president, commented: "The difference in our ideas of freedom of the press is that you think of it as freedom of information. We think of it as freedom of conscience—you cannot say things that would hurt the country."

Until recently there has been little revolt against the importance of place and form and, indeed, Latin American literature is filled with baying against the formlessness, the classlessness, the chaotic

political and cultural egalitarianism of North American life. Even
the common people, whom it serves so poorly, defend it.

An Ecuadorean waiter, complete with black tuxedo, blushed a
delicate purple one day when an American woman called him the
"waiter." He appraised her with an icy-cold look and voice. *"They
are the waiters, I am the maître d'."* An Ecuadorean maid provides
another case in point. An American woman whose husband worked
for the American embassy in Quito went back to the United
States, leaving her Spanish housekeeper to stay with a friend of
hers, another woman at the embassy, for a few days. The Ecuadorean maid of the friend asked her employer where the housekeeper would stay. When she was told it would be in the upstairs
bedroom, the maid resigned. It was in bad form for any servant to
be so well treated; it was an improper household.

Cynical Latin Americans constantly deal with this respect for
position and prestige. An American woman, trying to get a ticket
for a certain plane at the Caracas airport, was told by the reservations clerk who was trying to help her, "Come later and bring a
letter to the manager, on your office stationery, saying that you
have to get on that plane. You see, he's not really the manager.
But he'll see the official letter and it'll make him feel important. I
know him. I know how to do it."

Latins are not angered by what North Americans would consider infuriating unfairnesses of the system. There are numerous
cases of a bastard son of a wealthy man who is finally accepted by
the family, only after he rises to a high position in politics. The
sons do not seem to resent this cavalier treatment, as Americans
would. In Ecuador, in the military junta that came to power from
1963 to 1966, one member of the junta was the bastard son of a
well-to-do family. When he rose to power, they welcomed him to
the family and he apparently was pleased. "They took him back,"
a friend of his commented. "He's up, they're down. He's delighted."

There is beginning in Latin America today, however, a deep
concern about and revolt against the division between the form of
society and the reality that has been existing apart from it. It is
taking place on various levels. Young, modern-minded politicians

are launching programs designed to "make the people conscious" of their plight, of their inconsequence to society as it is constituted, and of their ability to change things. In all the countries with democratic governments, there are deliberate programs to organize the marginal people in order to integrate them into society.

Many Latins are deeply conscious of the division between shadow and substance—in the family, in the Church, in political life, in mentality. The major thrust of sociology, a thriving discipline in Latin America, is to identify the areas of alienation and to discover tactics to deal with them. More and more Latins are realizing that, like a badly focused photograph, Latin American society has had its images juxtaposed unevenly.

To look at just one example—the Catholic Church—it immediately becomes clear that the young priests are particularly conscious of the great division in Latin life, of the vast schism between the form and the substance. A major report on the Church states: "Traditional pastoral structures, especially those of the parish, are more and more becoming mere formalities. They no longer meet the needs of daily life, and they grow in what might be called a cancerous fashion. Today the very channels of transmission are being changed. In the future there will be less and less 'automatic' Catholicism; less and less will one be Catholic merely because one is Argentine, Brazilian, Colombian or Mexican. Besides, a new society, and even a new culture, is arising, since we are witnessing the establishment of numerous new institutions and social roles. The Church faces the task of jacking up this new culture and this new society and of putting under it a foundation of structured Christian values."

All across Latin America, priest-sociologists are studying the "real" Latin America, underneath the forms. The Colombian sociologist Father Germán Guzmán says that "in the family there is a formal structure and there is a real world that the formal structure does not reach." The Catholic Church is finding that its dicta have no reality in the "real" society of poor Latin America. On birth control, Father Vekemans of Chile has said, "Our studies

show that about three percent of the people are all that know that
the Church even has a policy on birth control."

Nowhere is this vast division between appearance and reality
clearer than in the Colombian Church, where it has come to be
reflected in a dramatic generational conflict between the old
priests and the young priests. I sat one day with Cardinal Luis
Concha Córdoba, seventy-six, in Bogotá. Aging, retired, and feeling set aside, the cardinal sat in the quiet and lonely splendor of
his red brick mansion and mused over the Church that had been
torn apart by the division.

I asked him whether he had seen many changes in his fifty-two
years as a priest—years that had encompassed the Vatican Councils, Pope John and the entire trauma of the revolution in the
social doctrine of the Church. "No great changes," he answered
slowly, his aged hands resting in his lap on the black cassock that
had changed little in centuries. "But there has been an improvement in spiritual life. To me it seems that the religious life here is
very good. In all the churches of Bogotá, there are masses from
morning to night. The churches are filled with people. Every day
things are better and better."

This is the kind of statement that infuriates the young priests,
just as, on other levels, it infuriates the young politicians, indus-
trialists and sociologists. But it was understandable. The cardinal
and his generation looked with satisfaction upon the surface of
Colombian society, seeing only the solace of the traditional
religious forms; the younger priests looked at its ulcerated en-
trails, seeing only its internal anarchy and contradiction.

The younger clerics saw a country, famed for being the "most
Catholic" country in Latin America because of the personal piety
of the people, that was tormented underneath. A religion that was
form and idolatry, nothing else. Criminality running rampant.
Family life so deformed that many lower-class women, out of desperation, seek illegitimate children, knowing that men will abandon them and that only children are a security for old age. A
backwoods riven with fanaticism, the most horrible emanation of
it being the schizophrenic *violencia*, the mammoth pathological

killing that took some three hundred thousand lives between 1948 and 1957.

And so it is that all over Latin America the battle has been joined—often in the most dramatic ways—to bring the archaic formalisms of Latin American society into line with the real Latin America and, more, to bring the Latin American's mentality into conformity with the kind of world he wants to build.

CHAPTER 4

Three Keys to Traditional Latin America: Authoritarianism, Individualism, Personalism

Primero soy yo—First come I. Common Argentine saying.

No se meta—Don't get involved. Common Argentine saying.

In the pretty little central plaza of Asunción, Paraguay, stands a curious monument to the traditional authoritarianism of Latin America. It is a small chapel dedicated to the Virgin but serving actually as a shrine to the brutal dictators of Paraguay, who lie there in the dubious splendor of a copy of Napoleon's tomb. Two soldiers guard the "Pantheon of the Heroes" and inside the building stand heroic statues. On the stained-glass windows are etched the names of Solano López, Carlos López, Dr. José Francia . . .

After the pantheon was built in the 1920s there was disagreement over whether the dictators should be allowed into the Virgin's shrine, but the Catholic hierarchy gave in. A second dispute arose some years later over whether the ashes of Eliza Lynch, the famous Irish mistress of Solano López, should also be permitted to rest there. This curious ascension was pushed by ultra-nationalists who favored Eliza. But here the hierarchy held fast and Eliza's ashes remained in the Ministry of War in a kind of Paraguayan purgatory.

The walls of the pantheon are lined with plaques that recall the extraordinarily martial history of Paraguay. There is a Club de Leones' (Lions' Club) "Homage to Heroes" plaque; an homage to the Argentine army; a plaque from the Chilean army; one from the Paraguayan League of the Rights of Women; one from the Heroines of the Chaco, which was the association of nurses of the Chaco. The tombs of the bloody Francia and Carlos López are there, along with a statue to Francisco Solano López who, it says, died on the first of March 1870, "with his sword in his hand and his country's name on his lips, at the front of his soldiers and upon his last campaign of battle."

There is no purer worship of authoritarianism in Latin America —or perhaps the world today—than in little Paraguay, that "Garden of Eden" in the precise center of the continent. Pastorally exquisite, with vast green waves of farmland and a bright blue tropical sky, Paraguay, it was once said, was paradise. When you look out today from the heights of the new Guaraní Hotel in Asunción, the land is so green and spreads itself out so flat for so many scores of miles around the lovely little capital that it seems you are surrounded by an emerald sea.

Nor was Paraguay always an unhappy place, though it was always a peculiar monument to authority and paternalism in all their forms. Founded in 1537 by the Spaniards, it early became an orderly country, particularly under the Jesuit missionaries who arrived in 1538 and gathered the Guaraní Indians, perhaps up to a hundred thousand of them, in *reduciones* or mission villages. This was the Jesuits' perfect little theocracy in the heart of Latin America and they protected the Indians against predatory civil landholders, Spanish landowners who wanted slave labor, and the slave-hunting *bandeirantes* of Brazil. The craft skills which the Jesuits taught the Guaraní and the churches they built in this outpost of the world are still there in the deep forests of Paraguay and Argentina. The half-disintegrated, moldering faces of the saints they carved are remnants of the strange little state that once was.

The Jesuits were efficient administrators of their missions and developed agriculture and industry. They treated the Indians well, but they controlled them like the autocratic masters they were. From inside a large wooden image of some terrible-looking saint a hidden Jesuit would give the Indians instructions. Writers like the Brazilian sociologist Gilberto Freyre have found among the descendants of Brazilian Indians who came under this regime only hatred for the memories of the past.

When the Jesuits were expelled from all Spanish territory by Charles III in 1767, Paraguay turned from theocratic paternalism to authoritarian dictatorship. The Paraguayans were singular in several ways. They became the first totally *mestizo* nation when the Spanish mixed their blood with the Indians. Even today Guaraní is used interchangeably with Spanish. Its people fought with an almost insane passion, time after time, against outside invaders. But in order to protect themselves from being swallowed alive by their big and hungry neighbors, the Paraguayans delivered themselves to as cruel and bizarre a series of native dictators as any land has ever experienced.

Dr. José Gaspar Rodríguez de Francia, austere, frugal and cruel, was the archetype of the worst aspects of the Latin American's characteristics that revolve around authoritarianism, individualism and personalism. Originally trained in theology, he did not let that subject's humanitarian aspects stand in his way once he became absolute master of the nation. He broke off relations with the Vatican and appointed his own bishops and clergy.

In an orgy of exclusivity and antiforeign passion, he closed off the country to the outside world. Spaniards who owned the best lands and businesses were jailed, murdered or exiled. Paraguay became a hermit nation, with *el supremo*, as Francia came to be called, the unchallenged authority. He imposed order, hard work and progress—in a nation totally sealed off from the rest of the world. The next dictator, Carlos Antonio López, vain, fat and ugly, opened the country and welcomed immigrants. He was only a little less cruel. Then he turned the unfortunate little land over to his son, Francisco Solano López, who ruled from 1862 to 1870. A bloated little man, he ordered uniforms like Napoleon's and a replica of the Corsican's crown. Perhaps he is best known for bringing back with him from Europe the celebrated Eliza Lynch, who soon became the leader of Asunción society and whose theater is today the dining room of the old Gran Hotel del Paraguay.

To the second López's credit goes the most terrible and sanguinary war in Latin American history, the War of the Triple Alliance in which Argentina, Brazil and Uruguay fought against little Paraguay, outnumbered ten to one. López provoked the war by attempting to march his troops across Argentina in order to attack Uruguay. Everybody—little boys of twelve, old men of sixty —was drafted to fight in López's mad war, and resistance brought torture and slow death.

By the end of the war, Paraguay's population had been reduced from 525,000 in 1865 to 221,000 in 1871. There were 28,746 men left in the entire country. Quiet existed then in Paraguay, but it was the quiet of the graveyard. Brazilian soldiers who occupied the land until 1876 became the fathers of modern Paraguay.

There were other wars, like the 1932 war over the Gran Chaco, a wilderness of scrub and swamps between Bolivia and Paraguay, in which both contenders suspected there was oil. Proud but humiliated, Paraguay looked upon it as a chance to vindicate itself. At the height of the brutal three-year conflict, there were fifty thousand men on each front, fronts that were either flooded swamps in the rainy season or waterless savannah in the dry season. The Gran Chaco was the most deserving of the "green hell" description that has been used indiscriminately in describing so many areas in Latin America.

This time Paraguay won, and the treaty of 1938 vindicated Paraguay's "honor." It had won, said one historian, "twenty thousand square miles . . . at the cost of about three Bolivians and two Paraguayans for each square mile."

After a number of democratic presidents, Paraguay reverted to its traditional dictatorships, ending in the total authoritarianism of General Alfredo Stroessner. Stroessner was born in a little anti-Semitic German colony in Paraguay whose members had been handpicked, some by Nietzsche's sister. But even this son of selective breeding mellowed eventually among the orange blossoms of Asunción. By the mid-1960s, Stroessner allowed the opposition to operate again, some said to expose graft and irregularities among his own people that he did not want to expose himself but wanted brought to light. Still, the military budget was estimated at anywhere between 26 and 65 percent of the national budget, and some four hundred thousand Paraguayans still lived in exile. Stroessner's sense of humor was a little stiff. I once asked him, in a set of written questions, "Is Communism a threat to Paraguay?" This violent anti-Communist answered, "No, *señorita,* Paraguay is a threat to Communism."

But Paraguay is only one example, if the most extreme, of the presence and persistence of authoritarianism—and even the virtual worship of it—in Latin American life. It has traditionally been found in every area, and it is embodied not only in the political structure but also in the social and mental structure of the man as well. That this is changing—that new and conscious efforts are being made to undermine authoritarianism by forming a self-conscious, scientifically oriented and independent man—is one of the most salient aspects of life in Latin America today. Yet the old authoritarianism still persists, like a nagging hangover from Spanish colonial times. As the great Spanish philosopher Miguel Unamuno, speaking for all Spaniards, said, "I feel within myself a medieval soul."

It is present too in the marginal people who, even while they had organized democratically on a base level, have, until mid-century, voted time and time again for traditional strongmen. It is there in adults addressing their social "superiors" as *su merced* (Your Grace) or *patroncito* (Little Boss), and in all the inescapable signs in tone of voice and manner that denote grades of superiority and inferiority in stratified societies. It is present in the words of aristocrats who still believe that the poor are poor because that is the social hierarchy of heaven and that the wealthy *manda* (order) and the poor obey in harmony with some eternal celestial plan.

Just before the historic 1964 election in Chile, which is one of the least authoritarian of the Latin American countries, when it was obvious to anyone that the only two possibilities to win the presidency were the Christian Democrat candidate or the Marxist candidate, I visited the heart of the *fundo* or hacienda area around the southern town of Talca. The election was extremely important because both men represented a desire on the part of the masses for a new kind of man—a president who would represent their interests, give them importance and integrate the "outs." In different ways, both represented a trend away from the traditional aristocratic authoritarianism of the past.

At that time I went to see what might well be Chile's most beautiful *fundo*, the one belonging to a handsome aristocrat of an old, old family. Eugenio Correa Montt, descendant of the Montt family after whom Puerto Montt was named, is a strikingly handsome, dark-haired man. His house is a low structure surrounded by trees and decorated in impeccable taste. When we drove into the courtyard, the sheer beauty of the scene made me catch my breath. The courtyard is paved with bricks, around it is a low fence and, in the center, Don Eugenio and his young manager were sitting on perfectly formed horses with their long, brightly colored Chilean ponchos flowing down over the horses' shiny sides. On the men's heads were the broad-rimmed Chilean *guaso* hats, tilted at a rakish angle. It was a stunning scene.

"The present situation in Chile does not correspond to the Chilean reality," Don Eugenio was insisting later in his charming manner. "The people are not divided between Allende and Frei." Then, as we sat in his comfortable parlor drinking cocktails, he went on to insist that it was inherent for the Latins to want to be ruled. "What they want is a strongman, someone who can order, a *caudillo*." He felt that his candidate, an equally elegant, ultra-conservative named Jorge Pratt, really represented the desires of the people.

In answer to my request to talk to some peons, he rounded up a number of his workers, set me in a little room, and presented them to me, one by one, before he left to stand outside. Shy to the point of embarrassing me, the peons stood with their heads down and their hats held in front of their private parts. To a man they answered my questions by agreeing that Don Eugenio was a *"buen patrón"* or a good boss. But *patrón* is more than a boss in Latin America. The *patrón* is the father of his workers. He orders their lives as well as supplies them with work. (The peons worked twelve hours a day, six days a week, for 1.25 *escudos* a day or about $.39 at that time.)

But when election time came, the peons of Chile, all of whom are white and of Spanish descent, voted into office the Christian Democrat, Eduardo Frei, the man who most represented the antithesis of the strongman. Second was Salvador Allende, the Marxist. Poor Jorge Pratt was nowhere to be seen, but when I saw Don Eugenio a year later, he was still insisting that the people wanted someone who would *manda.*

The penchant for authoritarian systems and the presence of authoritarian mental structures in the Hispanic-American countries came straight from Spain and has been examined a thousand times in analyses of the Spanish character. It was partly due to the fact that Spain was cut off from Europe ("Europe ends at the Pyrenees"), partly due to the fact it early came into contact with the Moors and, in defending itself, somewhat like Paraguay developed its own exclusive authoritarianism. It was also imbedded somewhere deep in the Spanish man himself, in the absolutism of his faith. Perhaps it was something about the barren, sun-soaked, harsh emptiness of the Spanish plains or the starkness of the colors that made him so rigid a man, so *todo o nada,* all or nothing. So *primero soy yo,* first come I.

The Spanish brought their systems to the New World and imposed them as best they could. But the evangelical inspiration of the Spanish throne, which tried to regulate and ameliorate the treatment of the Indians, was wiped out with the Wars of Independence. After that, Latin American life, instead of aspiring to the idealistic ideas of independence and liberty espoused by the liberators, fell under the even more predatory controls of the creoles. Now there was no crown to control their excesses. Now there was no appeal to anyone and God seemed far away, perhaps back in Castille. As Bolívar had seen clearly, Latin America still needed a strong government; he had felt strongly it was not ready for the Anglo-Saxon forms.

Without exception the structures of the Latin American countries laid down in these days were totally centralized. Generally only the president and the congress were elected, if there *were* a president and congress. Even today in most of the countries the president appoints prefects to rule the departments or states. In most countries there have not been municipal elections. Power flows from the central government and the wealth of the country flows to the capital city, where it stays or goes abroad. Illiterates still do not vote in most countries and respond to leadership in the most basic and emotional terms, to the strongman in the plaza, who can be a very compelling figure.

Today in the less-developed countries, everything—including personal requests and petitions—is taken directly to the president or the dictator. As in earlier times, when people brought requests directly to the bishops and would see no one else, today, particularly around the Caribbean, the poor and not-so-poor, the women needing some supreme power to make some young scoundrel marry their pregnant daughters, the down-and-out men needing bank loans to avoid bankruptcy, and the spiritually needy desiring a kind word blessed with the sanction of coming from a high place—all come directly to *el jefe,* to the man in charge. It is partly this that is responsible for the insufferable inefficiency of many Latin American governments: everybody is waiting to see *el jefe.* Nobody else can make decisions. And to stay in power, *el jefe* must put his healing touch on each of them.

General Miguel Ydígoras Fuentes, president of Guatemala between 1958 and 1963, once explained to me the plight of the *jefe* caught in this system. "You have to help everyone," he said, with a wry smile. "One day a woman came. Her son needed a brain operation. I gave her a note to the Roosevelt Hospital in Guatemala City. She said, 'No, he has to go to Washington.' I had to give her money to go. Otherwise she would go to the newspapers and say, 'The president has no heart.' Then men come for money to bail out their *fincas.* I would often just give them a note to the bank saying, 'Please help this man in accordance with your regulations.'" He threw up his hands.

Another Central American country, a very poor one, gives its president $250,000 a year in a special fund which he uses just to spend on personal favors. In the Dominican Republic, before the important election of June 1965, Dr. Joaquín Balaguer, who had been the dictator Trujillo's mentor and was representative of the old style of Dominican politics, stood hour after hour, day after day, on the upstairs porch of his formal Spanish mansion in Santo Domingo, receiving the peasants who had been waiting on the streets for hours to see him. They would see only him, for no one else possessed power. And when they finally got to him, the little timid-looking Balaguer would hold their hands and nod in that frightened way he has and maybe write a note about the problem and give it to one of his aides. (It was indicative that his opponent, Juan Bosch, a far more modern type of politician, did not do this. Bosch greeted his followers with *abrazos*—embraces— and treated them as self-sufficient individuals. He did not hold court.)

The people know where authority is and, as in Ydígoras' case, they know how to manipulate it. It is the way of the weak man— the man who, like traditional woman, must capitalize on his weakness and lives by threat and wile instead of right.

The admiration for authority and the tendencies toward authoritarianism are still so strong in much of Latin America that, as in Cuba, what starts out as a revolt against authority ends at least in part as a new and often more extreme celebration of it. Despite the real and avid attempts of the democratic reformers, there is still the chance that Latin America will "progress" only to a new and more refined and more total authoritarianism.

The famous APRA party in Peru is a particularly depressing and dramatic case in point, for the Apristas were the first party of the Democratic Left and the first party to have a Latin American ideology which then spread to other countries. The Apristas started under their leader, Victor Raúl Haya de la Torre, in the 1920s when there was no representation of the masses in political life in Peru. Haya, a handsome aristocrat, walked down from his birthplace in the mountains to the university and began to realize some of the truths of Peru, which had always rejected its Indian heritage.

Haya's face showed his own Inca blood: he had the customary hooked nose and dark skin. Yet, he realized, his family pride dictated he must be pure Spanish. As a dapper young student in

Lima, the eloquent Haya set not only Peru but the entire continent on its ear. His ideology was the first indigenous ideology for all of Latin America, which he preferred to call "Indo-America." For he believed, as he told me years later, when he was an old but very alert man, that "Latin America was different. It would not be Europe. It would find its own way."

Aprismo—the philosophy of the party—quickly caught on with the growing urban working class and the peasants and soon it was raising hell. The conservative Peruvian military reacted to it with the cold horror of men who feel their time might just have come, and persecutions of Apristas rang down twentieth-century Peruvian history with the sounds of blood cries. One December 24 in Trujillo, the northern Peruvian city where Aprismo was born, the army surrounded a meeting of party members and killed nearly five thousand of them. In Latin America they call Christmas Eve *"la nochebuena"* or "the good night." It was a characteristically bizarre use of the night.

Under the dictatorship of Manuel Odría, Haya was hunted and eventually took asylum in the Colombian embassy in Lima, where he lived for seven years. The angry Odría, forced to respect the right of asylum, had his troops tear up the streets around the embassy. Eventually Haya, who had become the greatest *cause célèbre* of Latin American history, was allowed to leave. But he was never allowed to become president, though he was elected at least twice, in 1931 and 1962. The military annulled the elections to keep him from taking office.

In the years of being under fire, however, the great APRA, which had served as the model in the formation of innumerable other parties of the Democratic Left in other countries, itself hardened into an authoritarian party. Taught how to fight in the brutal battles with the Peruvian military, the Apristas learned too well. They developed their own thugs, called *bufalos*, and by 1962 they were beating up not the military but rival democrats. It had become so totalitarian in its methods that many democratically minded people saw APRA itself as a threat to the future. It startled everyone after the 1963 election, which Fernando Belaúnde won, by making a pact with the formerly hated Odría.

Its political *machismo* kept it from allying itself with Belaúnde, even though both shared the same reformist philosophy. Had they merged, they would have represented the overwhelming majority of the Peruvian people. But Latins do not work together; they do not compromise. Instead APRA went into the opposition in an alliance with Odría and proceeded to serve the interests of the oligarchy and the military by keeping Belaúnde from realizing many of the reforms Peru so badly needed.

APRA also developed into a strange religion, with Haya as its high priest. In the headquarters of the party, a little Aprista guarded Haya's room and he would take you around it telling you about it in whispered tones. I remember clearly one night in Lima when it was Haya's birthday. We all stood in the square waiting for Haya to appear at midnight. Tens of thousands of Apristas stood in the square, in the darkness, while candles burned and a loudspeaker announced every few minutes, as if the Apocalypse were imminent: "Ten minutes to midnight" . . . "Five minutes" . . . "Two minutes."

Then "Great teacher of our heart . . . brother and teacher . . . our beloved leader . . ." Precisely at midnight, Haya arrived. He was standing in an open car with his right arm raised, as if in salute or blessing. The ocean of faces was whitecapped with a hundred thousand waving handkerchiefs and the voices shouted themselves hoarse: "Happy birthday, Victor Raúl. Happy birthday, Victor Raúl."

This is heady stuff. In the darkness, in the old plazas, sometimes in the rain, it makes the blood run faster. It takes the place of the months of no recognition, of nothingness in the society. It makes man one with his leader; it makes him something.

Many of the same principles—in particular the way that the recurrent impulse toward democracy and self-government rotates to authoritarianism—are also present with the military in Latin America.

On the one hand, Latin Americans have consistently given their support and their passions to progressive, democratic, liberal, idealistic civilian statesmen. The bright side of the moon. On the other hand, they have just as consistently regressed to authoritarian, puritanical, unrepresentative military dictatorships. The dark side. This strange political and psychological seesaw motion is one of the most bewildering—and one of the most telling— aspects of Latin American life.

In a speech delivered at Colombia University, Eduardo Santos of the famous Colombian newspaper family, asked: "Against whom are we Latin Americans arming ourselves? . . . We have no reason to fight one another; we have reasons only for drawing closer together and living in brotherhood. Have we any military roles to play in the great international conflict, perchance? Never. That would be an act of foolish braggadocio that could not be sustained for five minutes." He concluded with ominous words: "We are building armies that are meaningless in international terms but devastating to the internal lives of our countries. Every country is being occupied by its own army."

It was as if he were saying that every human body is occupied by its own destructive impulses; as if every man is being "occupied" by his own failures; as if Latin America is being overcome by its own ego.

Yet though most Latin American countries share the same outwardly centralized political structure (often under the *form* of democracy) and the same authoritarian military standing watchful guard against the exercise of excessive democracy, there are great differences in spirit.

In most of the countries of Spanish descent you find this same admiration for the *macho*, authoritarian leader, father *caudillo*, although in a country like Chile it is tempered by a more central European legalism. In Colombia and Chile, the militaries are almost entirely nonpolitical. In Brazil, too, with its flexible Portuguese background, the spirit is different.

Brazil emerged out of an intensely paternalistic past. In the *fazendas* or big houses on the farms, the patriarchal father had the power of life or death over everyone under his sway. Often he actually did kill, or order killed, his own sons or slaves for certain offenses. But toward the eighteenth century the absolutism of the father was tempered. The doctor, the priest, the director of the school, the judge, the police chief—all gained power at his expense.

But this paternalism never had the qualities of *machismo*—an obsessive concern with masculinity—that so contorts life in the Spanish countries. The Brazilians tell a story, for instance, in which a Brazilian man is walking down the street in Rio with his wife and a companion when a third man says something very insulting to his wife. The companion is livid and demands, "Aren't you going to do anything? Aren't you a man?" The man looks at his friend calmly and answers, "Well, yes, I'm a man, but not fanatically . . ."

But even in Brazil, where the impulses may be more successfully paternalistic, they *are* paternalistic, and they are at heart authoritarian. There is the same phenomenon, which tortures all Latin America, of expecting everything from above, a phenomenon about which the Chilean President Eduardo Frei says: "A very bad habit, a result of the present order, is to expect change from a benefactor rather than from a true promotion of the people. Yesterday it was the *patrón*. Today it is the government and outside aid. This is the same phenomenon experienced by people under dictatorships. Everything will come when the tyrant is overthrown. When freedom does not come, the onus of too great hopes and the ignorance of the ways of freedom usher in anarchy and again the hope is reborn that another dictator will step in and put things back in order."

The greatest inherent problem in the rule by authority, by *the* man who holds all knowledge, all power and all means of intercession, is that it dims questioning and seeking. In education, in religion, in political life, man accepts the testimony of an all-knowing leader and defends that testimony as truth, which is seen as unitary. But as the Chilean priest Father Roger Vekemans has pointed out, it is exactly this acceptance of such testimony which makes it impossible for Latin American man to enter the modern world—that is, the scientific world that is necessary to development and modernization and in which testimony holds not the slightest importance.

"It is a fact," he has written, "that in the empirical sciences the weakest logical argument is the argument of authority, the argument through testimony, for testimony necessarily implies a human mediation between the object to be known and the receptive conscience . . . For the Latin American, the realm of knowledge is essentially a world of revelation, of testimony, of vertical and receptive dialogue, of tradition. Consequently, through his mental structure he tends to have the conviction that he possesses truth, said fully and once and for all, and he is not inclined to curiosity, at least not in the systematic and methodical manner characteristic of science. Being in possession of truth, he has no need to enter into the darkness of scientific questioning; he has no need for the rigorous approach of research. This explains his vulnerability to the 'prophet' or *caudillo*, who is taken as a Messiah and practically invested with all divine attributes."

Father Vekemans, who today has vast intellectual influence in Latin America, has injected an extremely provocative idea into the Latin American debate. He has said flatly that under typical Latin American authoritarianism, Latin America simply cannot develop into a modern society. It must, he insists, suffer a "cultural mutation": man must change.

Commodore Francisco Rivera Caaminero of the Dominican navy, a very typical Latin American military man of the old school, sat in his makeshift office in the Dominican Congress during one of the constantly shifting interim governments at the time of the Dominican revolution. Hefty of build and darkly handsome, he could have been one of any number of old-style Latin military men sitting in their lairs and looking suspiciously at the world about them.

When I asked him why he thought some of the Dominican military had taken part in the revolution that erupted that fateful spring of 1965 to try to force a return to constitutional government, he smiled and beckoned over to us a young captain. "He took part," Rivera Caaminero said. Then he instructed him, "Tell her why."

"For the ideals of youth," the captain said first. Then he looked at the floor. "I really don't want to talk about it," he added. "I realized I was wrong and I came back."

"What ideals?" Rivera Caaminero demanded.

Then he rubbed his hands together and spit out the word "*Dinero!*" Money.

What the man answered next I felt was spoken largely to assuage Rivera's cynicism about the revolution. "I did it to get a better post and money," he responded. "To sit where he's sitting." Everyone laughed. Whatever his real motives, form had been preserved; man acted only in his own self-interest, and not for any external ideals.

It is called Spanish individualism, and it has roots deep in the individualism of the traditional Spanish man. But in Latin America, where characteristics were transformed in transplantation, it comes out as pure, unalloyed self-interest. Individuals are taught, from childhood on, to look out for their own interests. "*No se meta,*" says the Argentine. Don't get involved. Suspicion, not trust, is the constant byword of Latin American society, and cool exclusivity, not community, has traditionally been the rule. It could historically have been said of the Latin American what the Spanish author Angel Ganivet said of the Spaniard: that he was a man who carried on his passport the imaginary words, "This Spaniard is authorized to do whatever he wants."

The stories about Spanish individualism are often bizarre to the point of disbelief. The Spanish author Fernando Díaz-Plaja, a critic of his countrymen, recalls a rallying cry from the 1930s: "Workers, do not vote! The vote is the denial of personality." In all his examples of Spanish arrogance ("Arrogance," he says, "offensive in its equivalents in other languages, is a word of praise in Spanish"), the finest one concerns Miguel de Unamuno, the famous Spanish philosopher.

Unamuno had gone to the court of Alfonso XIII to receive a decoration. In accepting the honor, Unamuno noted that he deserved it. The king smiled and exclaimed, "The others who are decorated always say they do not deserve it!" "And they are right," answered Unamuno.

This kind of individualism, carried to extremes, leads to a total and destructive atomization of society. An American doctor assigned to the hospital ship *The Hope*, commenting on the Latin American doctors who came aboard to work, said, with a note of sadness: "They won't teach others what they know. It is a kind of secret medicine. Everybody keeps to himself what he knows. There is no patient-doctor relationship. It is very rough, because people love it when they get some consideration. But the older doctors keep telling the younger doctors just to do it themselves."

Another, outrageous example of individualism occurred in the Dominican Republic, which is a kind of exaggerated example of all the rest of Latin America, a place where even the virtues are slightly gangrenous. Several months after the revolution of 1965, there was a little rebellion in the northern city of Santiago.

An unregenerate rightist plotter, Tomás Alcibiades Espinoza, rose against the provisional government which had been installed as an interim measure to carry the country through to elections. The man who supplied arms to Espinoza was then police chief of Santiago, and he acted in conjunction with a Dominican politician named Augusto Lora. When the comic opera revolt was put down, Espinoza fled to the house of Joaquín Balaguer, who was to become the next elected president and was also in on the plot.

When Balaguer did become president some months later, the group was able to blackmail him to the extent that the Santiago police chief was made police chief of the capital, Espinoza became minister of the interior, in charge of all internal security, and Lora became vice president. It was an *opéra bouffe*, but of such cynical cadence that it could hardly be outdone in Al Capone's era.

Some would probably insist that this kind of political and moral corruption stems from other things in Latin life, but it seems actually to stem from the Spanish sense of individualism, the all-important *yo* or "I"—the person who most enchants each Spanish man. It is there in the atomization of terrorist groups in Latin America, so that, even in a relatively "civilized" country like Uruguay, the terrorist groups neutralize each other; there are so many of them and they are so opposed to each other. It is there in the historic figure of Don Juan, the ultimate nonromantic, who seeks only to use women to assuage his own ego, not even to enjoy them. In Mexico, it is there in that part of constitutional law known as the *recurso de amparo*, which is a suit that can be brought before a federal court against any authority or law that infringes on the rights of the individual.

But most likely it stems from the idea of man's direct relationship with God. Despite the hierarchical way of the Spanish Catholic Church, there remains the distinct idea that man can go straight to God. Spanish individualism is not the kind of Anglo-Saxon individualism in the sense of every soul being equal before God, the law or his wife. Spanish individualism stresses the uniqueness and innate dignity of each individual.

V. S. Pritchett, the writer who is one of the best interpreters of the Spanish personality, writes: "The egalitarianism of the Spaniards is not like the citizenship of the French, nor the anonymity of the English or American democracy, where we seek the lowest common denominator and try to hide our distinctions. The Spanish live in castes but not in classes and their equality— the only real equality I have met anywhere in the world—is in their sense of nobility or, rather, in the sense of the absolute quality of the person. One will hear this sentence spoken of people living in the lowest wretchedness: 'They are noble people.'"

The fact of any man's having equal status has absolutely nothing to do with it. Nor does Hispanic individualism mean a man will "stand up for what he believes." Latin Americans almost never, as individuals, "stand up" for something that is contrary to the crowd consensus, as Americans do. As a very perceptive Peace Corpsman said of his Latin friends in a key Latin university: "They will not talk against the decisions of the leaders. They seem to need to follow a strong leader and once they have elected him, they feel they have no more responsibility for his actions. Let him do the thing. They will not protest a popular action. In my university, they only voted for a Communist slate in an election where there was a closed ballot. There is no idea of a man standing alone with his conscience."

This individualism, in which every man does what he wants or can get away with, contains no loyalty to the larger community, as in North America. Jaime Benítez has noted that one of the great problems of Latin America is the absence of social solidarity. There is no "loyal opposition," he says, "because Latin America has not effected the great transition from feudal ordination of guilds and corps and established the superiority of state and political power." He points out that every organized group keeps its own power inviolate and that "any time two groups get together—say, the church and the army—down goes the government. Each structure is, like the Middle Ages, a law unto itself. Each has its own private laws." It is another assertion of what Father Vekemans says—the absence of nationhood, or the condition of pre-nationhood.

In the Spanish tradition, such institutions as the church, the army and certain other corporate groups had the aforementioned *fuero*—the right to try their members and to apply their own laws, to the exclusion of other laws. Originally, in countries like Colombia, both the church and the army had this privilege, but in recent years only the church retained it to any extent. One sociological study reports, however, that "although in the formal sense the institution of the *fuero* has nearly completely disappeared, the attitude that justified it has survived; that is, no one general law applies to all individuals, but every individual is regulated by such law as is accepted by the group to which he belongs."

Where this is particularly prominent is shown clearly in the case of the universities, which under the "university reform" that started in Córdoba, Argentina, in 1920, made the universities separate and autonomous institutions. The "university reform" was, to Americans, a peculiar business—until the university riots of the late 1960s. On the one hand, the avant-garde students who promulgated it insisted they were doing so to bring the universities closer to the societies in which they existed. On the other hand, they celebrated Latin individualism to the point of profligacy—to the point where the students had all control over the universities and to the point where the centers of learning were totally removed from any control by the larger society.

The manifesto of Córdoba proclaimed in one part: "The only recompense to which the students of Córdoba aspire is the spiritual redemption of American youth, *for they know that our truths are true* over the entire continent." The Córdoba manifesto, in short, was another outgrowth of the Latin idea of the unity of all knowledge, of the existence of one body of truth. They proclaimed the separate existence of the universities and bitterly fought the constitution of private universities because "*true* academic freedom can only exist in a national university, where another right is also recognized: the right to education for all the inhabitants of a country, without regard to their social, economic, religious or political background, where there is academic freedom and autonomy from central government authority over pedagogic, scientific and financial matters." Truth was easily come by, if only the circumstances were right, if only the state of mind and the objective conditions were right. They did not see that this would only open the universities to an even greater lack of freedom.

Since then, the universities have been used as shelters for students attempting to overthrow their respective governments. One, the Central University of Caracas, particularly became a haven for guerrillas and even assassins. In one case the police caught two Marxist psychology teachers giving tests to gauge criminal tendencies in students: those who came out best were given assassination and bomb-throwing assignments. In another case, the Marxist students kidnapped a police official, took him onto the "autonomous" campus, and then assassinated him by shooting him through the head and pouring acid over his body.

By midcentury a bitter debate and even a small war were going on in Latin America over university autonomy. It had not served the cause of modernizing Latin society. In the absence of sufficient textbooks, students were learning almost entirely from lecture notes, and since teachers were almost always part-time, this was a hit-or-miss business; testimony again played an inordinate part. And there was a great revolt against the traditional apartness of the university.

In La Paz, a technical university was established which demanded that abstract standards of learning be upheld. Another such school was started in Mexico. Catholic universities made a great point of the importance of universities for learning and not for political agitation. Venezuela, a democracy, invaded the university and stopped its autonomous existence; Argentina, a military dictatorship, did the same. The University of Puerto Rico fought a long fight over university autonomy, and its rector, Jaime Benítez, published a brilliant paper saying: "The theory of the university as a house of studies is incompatible in my judgment with the theory of the university campus as a proper place for political agitation, indoctrination and proselytism . . . As is well known, our 'house of studies' approach harbors and welcomes all types of political ideologies and heresies in the faculty, the administration, or the student body. But as part of this all-inclusiveness it is necessary to insist upon certain minimum restraints indispensable to a fruitful relationship of this heterogeneity we endorse."

It will doubtless be a long time before the "question" of university autonomy is solved. Meanwhile, it is the utmost in Latin individualistic behavior, symbolizing, too, the removal of sectors of Latin American life from the mainstream of society. It is another example of the abstractness of learning, of learning for learning's sake, art for art's sake, and the still unresolved division of personalism versus functionalism.

All over Latin America, there is one way to get something done: know somebody. It is the new immigrant mentality in the United States carried to its ultimate absurdity; it is the Boston Irish tribal reflex, magnified a hundred times. It is as deeply imbedded in the Latin American psyche as respect for authority and feeling for a man's innate worth and individualism. It makes much of Latin life exceedingly charming—and it makes much of it perfect hell.

In Mexico, it is common for anyone who is *anyone* to carry a card or a letter indicating he is no ordinary citizen but someone with—a descriptive Chicago word—"clout." They indicate that the "man holding this letter" is the cousin or a colonel or the secretary of the presidency or an official of the ruling party. In the United States, while this is done particularly in such new immigrant-dominated and tribally oriented cities as Boston and Chicago, it is not in the more universal-oriented sector considered good form; it is an exception to the traditional rules and most

Americans resent and ridicule such behavior. This is not the case in Latin America.

There it is common and accepted; it is even institutionalized. No one goes to the customs house or to a government office or anywhere, to get anything, without knowing someone or getting an uncle to call or—the way out for those without instant connections—without money for a bribe. There is one other way, but it is uncertain: if the person in charge takes a liking to you.

Personalismo is everywhere in Latin American life; it bitterly fights giving way to twentieth-century functional and institutional society. It is there in the form of address which must be employed. An American businessman in Argentina said one day, after talking to a local businessman, "You know, he was angry with me. I know why! I didn't ask about his wife and family before talking business."

It is often very charming, as for instance in the Latins' personalizing of inanimate objects. In most Latin cities, buildings are given names instead of addresses. The entire address, for example, will be Edificio Tacubaya, and the street address, if there is one, will be given only on insistence. Trucks too are personalized, particularly in the Andean Indian areas where the Quechuas name all their trucks; they give them such names as "True Love" and "If you see, you suffer" and "Always with the child Jesus" and "Death rides the Andes." When I asked one Indian why he named his truck, he said without blinking: "I thought it should have a name."

Taking the place of the relatively impersonal bonds of individuals in North American society are types of ritual "personal" bonds. Most countries have a form of *compadrazco*, roughly a form of godfathership which is an overwhelmingly important item in the Latin scheme of things. It is the one link—and an intimately personal one—outside of actual blood relationship that makes brothers of men and binds them in a form of community in the otherwise suspicious world in which Latins live.

Compadrazco is a kind of ritual kinship in which friends vow, at the birth of children, to take over the care of them if the parents die or are otherwise unable to care for them. It comes out of tribal society, it comes out of the Middle Ages and it comes out of godfathership in Europe. But in Europe, because functional considerations in society have taken over the care of the children, it is barely a serious thing. In Latin America, it still is. It is a realistic escape from the insecurity of daily life; it links man to man on a personal level in a society in which man fears man on a larger, more universal level. It exists because there is no public assurance of justice or security for the average, atomized man. Poor Latin Americans often seek to have Peace Corpsmen as their *compadres*; they trust the power and effectiveness of the United States.

Compadrazco is prevalent everywhere, and often it is used sagaciously in politics, as many politicians are *compadre* to voters in their area. At the Peruvian Andean town of Vicos where Cornell-based anthropologists organized the villagers to buy a hacienda and run it themselves, the resident Peruvian anthropologist, Mario Vásquez, was *compadre* to half the Indians, something that helped him enormously in his work.

A society based on personal considerations means many things. To the Latin Americans, it is a society that is more humanly honest than is the indiscriminate smiling hypocrisy of the American corporate structure—even if the American style is more "functional." The emphasis on personal considerations can also be very charming. It strengthens and succors the individual and often nurtures a stronger personality than the more viable North American system. But it also means a lack of any impersonal or universal morality that makes any one man treat all other men as equal or having value.

In traditional Latin America, this kind of morality is not considered necessary and there has been no hypocritical behavior demanded to expound it as desirable. As in southern Italy, morality has been extended only to one's family and to those whom, through such artificial but workable means as *compradrazco* or Freemasonry or the religious brotherhoods, one is beholden to as "near-family."

This is why every foreign woman in Latin America is looked upon as "fair game" to every Latin man and why he so obsessively guards his own family's women. He knows from his own impulses exactly how the other men would treat them if they could. It is why morality is so strained, so limited, and why generosity is tied up in such careful constraints.

Once in Santo Domingo—Santo Domingo again, for that really is a kind of archetypal example of all the ills of Latin America—I was talking to the "liberal" churchman Archbishop Hugo Polanco.

He was supposed to be the most forward-looking of all the Catholic clergy in a country where the Church was extremely conservative. A big amiable man in a white cassock, he sat in his small old office, around the corner from the old cathedral where Columbus is supposed to be buried, and he talked about sin (which was personal too).

"Other countries have lost the sense of sin," he said. "The Church here knows what principles are. They know what is wrong. The problem is when you lose that sense and never return again. We, for instance, never know a murder in the English sense, where murder can be a cold, impersonal thing. Here they murder for a girl, for politics, for the violence of the moment. But then they come crying, 'Pardon me,' and they mean it."

It was all very interesting. Here was a country wretchedly, insanely, grotesquely ill. In thirty-two years of Trujillo atrocities and savage sexuality, the Catholic Church had not spoken a word until the very end, when its privileges were threatened. The Trujillo clan's unimaginable bestiality had led to the sickness of this time. That morning we had watched a group of the restless, suicidal young people take the brains of a rebel who had been killed by the police and who lay in his blood for hours on the street. They ran down the sidewalk with them on sticks.

But when the archbishop talked about the Trujillo era, he talked about other countries having "lost a sense of sin." He talked about "responsibility"—the "responsibility" not of the Church, which was after all supposed to be the body to proclaim historic truths, but of the individual faced with Trujillo's killers.

"It was a case of a people demoralized," he said. "There was a man who came to me one night during Trujillo's time and he said, 'Father, a man was killed on the street again last night by

Trujillo's men. Please do something—talk to the police, do something.' I asked him if he would go with me and tell the police he saw the murder, and he said with horror, 'But no, they would kill me.'" He shook his head slowly. There was a very moralistic expression on his lips and in his eyes. "You see, if he would not go and testify, how could the Church?"

Morality, like everything else in Latin America, has been placed under personal considerations; it has been a formalism. Morality has been not missing a saint's day or not sleeping with a girl. There has never, until recently, been any exercise of public morality in Latin America or of abstract universal morality—not in government, not in the Church, not in the human being. And that is one more reason why they are a people who never win.

CHAPTER 5

Machismo *or* *The Unromantic Latin*

"A Latin man is a man who expects not only his wife to be faithful, but his mistress too." A Latin man.

The Latin man enjoys the world's most extravagant reputation for romance. His image on the world stage is an infinitely enviable one and when many American men go to Latin America they feel obliged to imitate him almost to the point of exhaustion. The Latin's elegant posturing, his tireless and single-minded pursuit of women, his sure manliness—all these are the apparent hand-maidens of the man who is *the* romantic male of the world.

Underneath this reputation for romance, there lies a curious concept, barely known in the rest of the world yet affecting and permeating every fiber of Latin American life. It is the concept of *machismo* and it is perhaps the prime reason why Latin America has not progressed more rapidly.

Machismo is present in all the Latin American countries to one extent or another, but it is more prevalent, for instance, in Mexico than in Chile and far more predominant in the Spanish countries than among Latins of Portuguese descent. In Brazil, it is over-shadowed by the irresistible urge to compromise, something the *macho* man looks on with about the enthusiasm he would have for being castrated.

Macho is used to refer to anything very, very male in certain obvious and often vulgar ways. When its values are imposed on the rest of society, the concept of *machismo* comes into play.

In the Hispanic view of the ideal man, which is greatly influenced by the Moorish sense of exclusivity and dominance of the male and the extreme dependency and public scarcity of the female, male virtues revolve around intense activity, competition, domination of other men and sexual prowess with women. It is not the truth of what the *macho* says that is important but the brilliance with which he says it (the form over the substance again). It is not the quality of the love he feels for a woman that is important but the number of conquests he can claim. It is not the substance of his political program but the power of his presence.

There must be a zest for physical action, which means a corresponding down-playing of the day-to-day, time-consuming, self-effacing work of experiment, scientific inquiry and intellectual investigation. This should be accompanied by daring speculation, which means a public disregard for the plodding businessman who seeks the kind of long-term investment that causes countries to progress rationally and steadily. In intellectual life, it is the brilliant speaker rather than the substantive man of knowledge who gains attention. In every sphere it is forcefulness and conquest which are most admired. They become ends rather than means.

It is part of the reason why Latin Americans have over and over again been able to harness their obstreperous energies to build great and dramatic projects (Brasília, for instance), only to let them fall apart once they have been built. It is one of the reasons why they have at crucial times been able to rise to the solutions of great problems (the Uruguayan welfare state, the Mexican one-party "solution," Costa Rica's democratic paternalism), only to lack the flexibility to change them again when these answers grew stale. It is partly why there is no institutionalization of change. As Jaime Benítez, the wise rector of the University of Puerto Rico, said of his Latin brothers, "How grand to die for a principle, how tiresome to live for it."

If you look for the typical assertive and theatrical *macho* in Latin American history, he is not hard to find. The brother of the Mexican president Manuel Avila Camacho was noted for keeping fifty-one mistresses at one time. When a nude statue was found missing one day in Mexico City, his brother remarked wryly, "Ask brother Max, he might have built a house around her."

The brutal Bolivian dictator Mariano Melgarejo, a presumptuous *cholo* looked down upon by the upper classes who ruled in the 1860s, flew into murderous drunken rages, lost vast expanses of land to Bolivia's neighbors and left his country in bankruptcy. Nonetheless he is still held up as a kind of *macho* hero. Though Melgarejoism is used as a generic term for completely wanton, selfish and brutish behavior, he is also begrudgingly admired. To vow allegiance to him, his followers were required to kiss the bare bottom of Melgarejo's mistress.

That is the ultimate in vulgar *machismo*, but Melgarejo's life exemplified the term. At one point, the Queen of England X-ed Bolivia off her map, symbolically banishing it from the sight of the world. The Bolivian dictator had seized her representative in La Paz, tied him to a donkey and beat him.

But it is not only among the ruling classes, whether upstart *cholos* like Melgarejo or aristocrats, that *machismo* is indulged. In Mexico City I once was driving with a lower-class cabdriver— unshaven, husky, in good spirits—who wanted to talk. "I have eleven children by my wife and two others," he began. And then he added sadly, "But I've never been in love." I sympathized with him as best I could, and he went on, "I never really could say I know what it is—to 'love' a woman."

Then he reminisced. A voluble sort. "When I was young, I was nuts about dancing," he said. "My whole life was dancing. Every night I was in the café. If I didn't go dancing one night, I couldn't sleep. Even now, I listen to Pedro Infante—you know Pedro Infante?" I said, yes, I knew the famous singer. "Well, every song he sings reminds me of another girl. And you know how many songs Pedro Infante sings?" I nodded.

"Now I go every eight to fifteen days to see the mother of my other two children . . ." Why, I asked him, did he need so many women? "It is natural," he answered, shrugging.

Mexico produces its share of *machos*—perhaps it ranks first in the continent. And they are indestructible. One Mexican businessman of Lebanese descent has a very elegant bedroom atop one of the office buildings he owns. All the floors in the bedroom slope—toward the bed. The imaginative *macho*.

An accessory of *machismo*, almost as indispensable as his lusting after women, is his weapon. *Machos* fight not with fists but with knives or pistols. It is common, particularly in Mexico but also elsewhere, to carry pistols to answer insults, giving rise to the Mexican saying that pistols are "pointed with hands but the triggers are pulled with the testicles." *Machismo* has a grim humor about it. Another Mexicanism is the joke about the *macho* curing his friend's headache by emptying his pistol into his head.

All of the elements of *machismo*—and honor is one, despite "vulgar *machos*" like Melgarejo—are intertwined and interrelated. *Machismo* is not simply power; the *macho* is not the American he-man. *Machismo* is very subtle. Sometimes men who are perceived by their societies as *muy macho* are physically unimpressive, even puny. Occasionally they are even homosexuals. *Machismo* is an elusive thing, having to do with a kind of life force inside the man or with a courage that makes him stand out among his fellows. Usually, too, there must be an element of *caballerismo* or gentlemanly behavior, or else the *macho* is simply an unseemly boor.

Of all the attributes of *machismo*, the most spoken of—and probably the most important for his public image—is the *macho's* sexual prowess. It can mean political success or failure. Yet it is complex and tied up with other factors. The ideal *macho* is characterized by ceaseless sexual activity, intense attention to women, and the idea that any woman outside his own family group is fair prey. He is characterized, on the one hand, by a puritanical and obsessively vigilant attitude toward his wife, mother and daughters, and, on the other, by a totally predatory attitude toward all other women. The wife and mother is perceived in the role of the Virgin Mary and even most "modern" young Latin men today say they insist their wives be virgins at marriage. The wife is also supposed to be sexually undemonstrative. Studies have indicated that Latin couples own to less sexual intercourse than their Anglo-Saxon counterparts, and Latin doctors have accused Latin men of being basically disinterested in sex—only interested in the appearance of it. It is from his mistress that the Latin man expects professional sexual behavior.

Latin Americans tend to be honest about sex, however, (they can afford to be honest about it since it is so carefully regulated) and Latin American history is filled with stories of famous mistresses and lovers that are considered part of the national heritage.

Dom Pedro I, the emperor of Brazil in the beginning of the nineteenth century, took as his mistress a high-spirited woman of determined temper, the Marquesa de Santos from São Paulo, and built for her a beautiful little white house down the street from his palace at São Cristovão outside Rio de Janeiro. On the walls he had painted the marquesa in the role of various women, including a bare-breasted Brazilian Indian woman. The marquesa became so involved politically that she eventually was obliged to retire from politics. In true Latin style, Dom Pedro decided to marry—not the marquesa, of course—and, the perfect Latin romantic, swooned when he saw the delicate young virgin princess Amelia whom he would take as his bride. Recently the Brazilian government decided to restore the marquesa's house, which tradition insists had a tunnel running to it from the palace, and workers from the National Trust on Historic Monuments started eagerly peeling off the layers of paper trying to find the bare-breasted Indian girl-marquesa. And they did.

There has always been a great deal of flair in relations between the sexes in Latin America, and the sheer size and openness of the continent sometimes added to it. President José Manuel Balmaceda began the greatest sheep-raising industry in remote and lonely Tierra del Fuego, the southern tip of Chile, on February 19, 1893, when he gave a million acres of land to the husband of a Sarah Brown. It seems that the president had taken a fancy to Sarah, daughter of a Russian Jew who made good in Chile. The land was a payment to Sarah's husband for her ample favors.

Although it differs from country to country, and also from class to class, and although this is changing radically with the younger generation, it is permissible—and in many countries considered far more natural than monogamy—for the traditional Latin man who can afford it to keep a mistress or even two or three. Often he is in love with her and often they have children—his "second family." She lives in a *casa chica* (literally little house) which he provides for her. To know a man's mistress and to spend time with them is to know the man intimately and to be considered his dearest, most special friend.

One Central American president, Anastasio "Tachito" Somoza of Nicaragua, is said to be madly in love with his mistress, though he has several children by his wife. His enemies applaud this, saying, "It is the only proof we have he is human."

In Bolivia the late President René Barrientos in the beginning lived openly with two wives—one in the capital, one in the second city. For a long time it was common knowledge. Both had the same number of children of the same ages, and when the second wife (second in influence) needed money she phoned the first wife. Eventually, however, it all became too open (*machismo* is a very delicate thing) and the public gossip became noticeably unfriendly toward the "arrangement." He divorced the second wife, and all was well. But every time he traveled around the country, he managed to spend a day—or a night—with her.

That the traditional patterns are breaking down is one of the most important things occurring in Latin American life today, as Latin men begin to observe more conventional sexual patterns. Today men have begun divorcing their original wives, as divorce becomes legalized in the countries which are undergoing intense revolutionary experiences. In Bolivia, for instance, divorce came into being with the 1952 revolution, which also disgorged from the lowest depths of society and flung to its apex an entire new class of Indian and *mestizo* leaders. Almost without exception, these leaders divorced their original wives and married women of a higher social class—a class whose status coincided with their newly acquired importance.

In the winter of 1967 there occurred another case symptomatic of the new thought. Puerto Rican governor Roberto Sánchez Vilella announced his intention to divorce his wife of thirty years. He wanted to marry his judicial assistant, a young woman many years his junior. Under old *macho* rules, this would have been as unnecessary as it was impossible. Even if the *macho* man got involved emotionally, he would never consider upsetting his marital arrangement or, moreover, feel any need to legitimize any other romantic entanglement.

Nor did the old-style Latin American woman, no matter how much she suffered from society's "arrangements"—and psychiatrists tell us that contrary to popular myth, she suffered a great deal—demand that anything change. She was wisely counseled by her mother and aunts to accept "the way men are," with such advice always having a strong tinge of woman's-superior-and-spiritual-nature-versus-man's-weakness-and-carnal-nature about it. It was only an insult to the wife if her husband chose a mistress less attractive than she. It is probably true that many women preferred and today prefer the ordered, stable life of Latin society, in which the family is sacrosanct and indissolvable and where they know they will always be the respected, virginal wives and mothers, no matter what other women their husbands enjoy.

As in all Latin society, in the world of love and privilege that the *macho* has set up there are precise and rigid forms, and love is generally spontaneous only within these forms. Almost always, he observes the exigencies of social class, for it tells a man—and a woman—where he or she belongs, how to act and how, when and whom to love. Latin Americans don't *need* to be loved in the often desperate way that Americans need to be loved. Security is gained rather by obedience to traditional forms, to class and to the historic prerogatives or non-prerogatives of sex. Latins don't depend upon the approval of persons outside their family groups to the extent that the atomized American does.

Love comes usually within the already-established forms. A certain kind of love—with marriage, say—can almost never come if you are not of the proper class. So people gain security through performing well the accepted actions of their group, adhering to their class and their sex, and through celebration of the unchangeable "place."

Just as "place" is important in the forms of love, there are places for love—physical places—which comply with the kind of society the *macho* has created. They serve him and his desires and his image of his world. These are places that tell a great deal about Latin American society; they show how specialized love is; they show how unromantically structured Latin society is. In North America, the places for love are fluid—any kind of love can take place anywhere—and motels, apartment houses, hotels, cars are interchangeable. The kinds of love are egalitarian, like the society. It is not like that in Latin America.

In addition to his home and his *casa chica*, the Latin American will often patronize the black nightclubs—those lightless, curtained places which proliferate from Mexico to Tierra del Fuego, but particularly in the "*macho* belt" that stretches from Mexico to the borders of Chile and Brazil. These "black nightclubs" are disconcerting at first to the North American who may innocently wander into them for a typical evening out and who considers that courting and lovemaking are more wisely done in a car or a bed.

These nightclubs are pitch black. Generally the headwaiter has a tiny flashlight which he uses to lead people to a table—that way they cannot see the others and the others cannot see them. In one of them, in Bolivia, the bottoms of the glasses glow so you can find your drink in the darkness. There is a certain surrealistic feeling in seeing the darkness pitted by floating, glowing glass bottoms. In Lima there is a club used largely by military officers and their mistresses where, when one opens the door to the bathroom, the light inside momentarily goes out.

One of the rules of *machismo* is that a man never takes his mistress to places where he might expose his wife to meeting her or even hearing about her. The dark nightclubs serve this specialized purpose. But there is a club in Mexico City which carries the ritual of the *macho* a step further. When you enter you first see a large, rather typical nightclub, with couples sitting at tables and a dance band playing. But there are seven rooms. In the second the lights are dimmer and there are open booths with low stools. In each subsequent room the lights grow lower, the darkness becomes more pervasive, the stools merge into couches and the couches into beds, the booths become curtained and finally closed. It is the specialization of love—the stations of love—carried to its ultimate degree.

Latin strongmen have always made their lovelife public and prominent, and none more so than the Venezuelan dictator Marcos Pérez Jiménez. He built a huge, stolid "hotel" in the mountains surrounding Caracas, each floor with a great circular suite, for the sole purpose of entertaining the Cuban prostitutes whom he and his men particularly liked. But in addition to these peculiarly specialized places, the exploration would not be complete without a look at the *posadas*, as they are called in some countries (although it should be noted that *posadas* is the common name for perfectly reputable hostelries in many places). In Cuba these are actually motels, sometimes low and sometimes in apartment complexes, which rent by the hour. They are the common place for a man to take a woman, they cost a few dollars for a couple of hours and drinks are served through a rotating shelf that provides for complete privacy.

After the 1959 revolution in Cuba, the government planned to close down the *posadas*. But there was such a display of civic indignation that the Communist government retained them, spruced them up and now runs them. How does socialist morality jibe with lovemaking motels, with mirrors on the walls? No one says.

Implicit in the world of the traditional *macho* is a double view of women that divides them with admirable simplicity into good and bad. A man marries the good women and the bad women he enjoys. This, of course, imposes upon the woman a definition that originates in man's desires and psyche and which Latin women no longer accept with docility. Latin men also often consider that it is all woman's fault—a projection of the primordial idea that original sexual sin is lodged in some dark corner within the woman's being.

As Juan Lechín Oquendo, the former Bolivian vice president, leader of the volatile tin miners and a *macho* par excellence, said one day in his laconic way: "I was seduced for the first time by a servant girl when I was five, again when eight by a girl fifteen, a virgin. I am a man who was corrupted by women." Though Lechín is known for his success with women (he once refused to join an insurrection because he was with a woman he liked—something that gained him admiration from all sectors), he is typically *macho*: he is not above insisting that the women maintain "standards." "If the West falls, it will be because of the degeneration of the standards of women," the tall, handsome, sloe-eyed Lechín told me once. "Women can't have the sexual freedom of a man. Russia started, and went back to strict morality." As to his own responsibility, he answered simply, "I only do what any man would do who has my chances."

The *macho's* relations with women, however, are not so simple as they may at first seem to the outsider. For although in society's terms, the man dominates his woman, he himself is most often dominated by his mother. The brutal Dominican dictator Generalissimo Rafael Leonidas Trujillo, who ruled bestially from 1931 to 1961 in the Dominican Republic, used women as cynically as any man in Latin American history. He had mistress after mistress and was pathologically incapable of keeping up any real relationship with any one woman. It was considered an honor for Dominican families to take their daughters to *el jefe* to be deflowered; and his sexuality seemed to know no bounds. "Nice girls"—*semi-señoritas*, they called them—who had fallen some hot Dominican night were kept in government jobs and given on a nightly basis to visiting American congressmen, a good number of whom were on Trujillo's payroll.

But like all real *machos*, the little, squat, squint-eyed dictator who tortured men casually in his dungeons across the Ozama River, had one woman in his life he adored: his mother. She was a wizened little woman who had been abysmally mistreated by his father, an errant sexual roamer. As is typical with traditional Latin men, the first thing Trujillo would do after work was visit his mother. When he was assassinated in 1961, he was busily erecting a statue to her on the spot where he was born in the town of San Cristóbal. The thirty-foot-high pedestal on which she was to be enthroned still stands, now defaced with vulgar scrawlings.

I recall once in Lima watching a young newspaper editor who

was the soul of *machismo*. In his office he ordered people here and there with that special peremptoriness of the Latin man. Then one day he told me why he had not gone to Bolivia to cover what would have been that active country's 180th revolution.

"I was dying to go," he said. Then he added, with both disgust and admiration blended in his voice, "My mother!" I must have looked puzzled. "I was all packed," he continued, "and she carried on something terrible. She cried and cried. She said, 'Do you want to kill me? Do you want to kill me? Then go!'" I must have looked a little bemused, for he said then, irately, "Well, did you want me to kill her?"

But if the key element to understanding the *macho* is his sexual behavior and his attitude toward women—mother, wife, mistress—another, and closely related, is his attitude toward power. For if we seek what the *macho's* attitudes do to politics in Latin America, we find the innermost core of the entire problem of political instability in that wildly mercurial continent.

There is a saying in Spanish, *Hay gobierno? Yo soy contra.* It means literally, "Is there a government? (Or: Is there authority?) I am against it." In Mexico, one of Benito Juárez's closest associates, a loyal general who had fought beside him, suddenly vanished when Juárez became president. When Juárez asked about him, his secretary informed him, "I'm sorry to have to tell you this, Citizen President; the general has just come out against you because you're in the government now."

In Latin American politics, it has been not the man who seeks to unite and to compromise and to heal wounds who was admired but rather the man who wielded total power—that classic Spanish type, the *caudillo* or strongman. Power could not be shared; it could not be dissolved in that curious Anglo-Saxonism, compromise. "It is not considered *macho* to heed the council of others," Dr. Alfonso Millan, probably Mexico's most respected psychiatrist, has explained. "In politics, as in the family, the father is not criticized openly." He sees *machismo* as "an almost neurotic compensation" for feelings of inferiority, personal and national. He further classifies it as "the admiration of power" and says that as a result "men often receive admiration not in proportion to what they deserve as individuals but in proportion to the power they wield. When they lose power, they lose admiration."

With political *machismo*, to oppose is to fight to the death, and to lose is to begin, at that very moment, plans to annihilate the winner. Latin Americans do not lose gracefully. Neither in sports nor in politics do they accept defeat, saying, "The best man won . . ." Latin men, indeed, are incapable of losing, for loss means diminution as a man; every contest is an attempt to justify one's existence and one's power in the world.

In the United States, at various crucial times in its existence, men of both political parties have linked together to put through the legislation and reforms needed to enable the country to survive. Because of political *machismo*, this is not possible in Latin America. It is typical that today with the masses of people in every Latin country having expressed over and over, with the vote, their desire for representative government and social reform, change is stymied because of *Hay gobierno? Yo soy contra.*

If this were the only principle at play, of course, the continent would be forever locked in a clash of absolute wills. There have to be ways to get around it, and there are. Part of the ritual of *machismo* is for a man's friends to plead with him in moments of intense confrontation and to beg him "for our sakes, for your children's sake, for your mother's sake, for your country's sake not to go the whole way." It is common to see two men about to fight, and each one finally led away by his friends. His *macho* comes out intact, for he has done something greater than rise to a confrontation: he has responded to the cries of friendship.

I recall a dinner table conversation in the Hotel Sucre Palace in La Paz, Bolivia, after Victor Paz Estenssoro had been deposed from the presidency in 1964. Three men were drinking heavily, and one, a former Paz politician, was saying drunkenly, "And I still say Victor Paz was the best president this country ever had . . ." He was becoming unruly when the other man started appealing to him: "If you weren't such a good friend, I would feel obliged to do something, but you are such a good friend . . . the ties of friendship are the only thing that keep me from taking action . . . but you are a friend, a real friend." Everyone was

saved, and the three walked out with their arms around one another's shoulders.

Politically, too, "ways out" have been found for the absolute
confrontations of *machismo*. Attempt after attempt has been
made to curb this destructive, runaway horn-locking through de-
vising "solutions" that will control it, by imposing, usually after
times of bloodshed and tribulation, rules that will control the excesses of individualism and male ego.

The most successful "solution" of this sort was Mexican, arrived
at after the bloody revolution which began in 1910 in which more
than a million people lost their lives. It was the one-party solution
that other countries have tried to copy and in which one party
expresses the will of the revolution and, therefore, the will of the
people. A president rules for only one term and he is chosen from
the bowels of the party, by horse trading and negotiation; the
power plays are not in public, so destruction need not be the ego's
revenge for losing.

Before the election, *the* candidate is coughed up from the in-
sides of the party and presented full-blown to the people, which
gives its approval ceremonially to the new interpreter of the revolution and of the people. He is the father of the people and he is
never criticized, for that would bring the destructive needs back
into play. But he cannot keep himself in power; his power is relative. He is not permitted, under any circumstances, to see himself
as the indispensable man, for he has accepted the solution of the
revolution which says that only the revolution is indispensable.
After one term, another man is suddenly coughed up; they have
molded *machismo* to a new idea—*machismo* serving the ideals and
the solution of the revolution.

Uruguay is another country which, at a crucial time in its history,
rose above and out of itself to find a "solution" to Latin underdevelopment, backwardness and *machismo*. Uruguay, which came
to be considered a model of order and progress, was traditionally a
country of frontier gaucho brawling and political instability. Then
in 1903 there came to the presidency a highly unusual man, José
Batlle y Ordóñez. Batlle, a staunch democrat and constitution-
alist, traveled to Europe and looked at Switzerland, where he got

the idea that subordinating the president in the political structure would be the panacea for Uruguay's ills—*caudillismo*, which is simply another word for *machismo*. He urged that Uruguay do away with the office of president and substitute a "collegiate executive," in effect, that Uruguay be ruled by committee instead of strongman.

The full transition from the one-man presidency to a nine-man ruling council did not come until 1951, but Batlle did succeed in diminishing the president's powers, and he created the famed Uruguayan welfare state, where workers retired at full pay at age fifty and there was no illiteracy or real poverty. Women could get pensions after a few years' work, if they had children. Unemployment was taken up by massive public employment.

By the 1960s, however, the "solution" began to sour, drained by its inflexibility and by the burdensome mass of unproductive social welfare laws. Of 380,000 on the public payroll, many simply did not show up for work, and the Uruguayans joked that a government worker had to get to work early to get a seat. "Uruguay is the largest office in the world that qualifies as a republic," the wags said. Once I met a charming young middle-class couple, both high-school educated, who were living in a rude board house with a dirt floor on the outskirts of Montevideo. They had built it themselves and had moved out from their city apartment house. With half of the husband's salary taken for welfare benefits, they had no money left to pay rent.

There was no flexibility built into the Uruguayan "solution." It signified again the Latins' enormous ability to rise to great occasions and find answers to complex problems; and it signified the inability to build the kinds of institutions, with intrinsic flexibility, that allow them to evolve. In the '60s the Uruguayans voted for the return of the presidential system, in a desperate effort to put the economy—riddled by a "benefits only" socialism, with little state planning to continue a sound economy—back on its feet.

Both the Uruguayan and the Mexican solutions were and are only temporary solutions, yet they creak on. The solution that turned out to be the most tragic was Bolivia's, for that was a country that had a total social and political revolution in 1952 and then allowed itself to fall back into the abyss.

There were four men who made the revolution of 1952, the second (next to Mexico) great social revolution in Latin America —Victor Paz Estenssoro, Juan Lechín Oquendo, Hernán Silas Suazo and Walter Guevara Arze. They were brilliant men, as attractive as you will find in recent Latin American history and idealistic to the extent one can be idealistic in a country as brutal as Bolivia. Under them the world changed. The Indians, descendants of the Incas, who had lived the most slavish lives in Latin America (they mined the great silver mountain at Potosí), took over the lands from the big landowners and began to get fat on their own crops. The tin mines were nationalized, the government became openly a people's government, and massive settlement of the eastern regions was begun. And there was an understanding, a "solution." "We were going to go the Mexican way," Walter Guevara told me fifteen years later, when it had all collapsed from the sheer imperatives of Latin ego. "Each of us was to rotate the presidency."

Under the party, the Nationalist Revolutionary Movement or MNR, they began taking their turns. First Paz, a bespectacled, deceptively scholarly looking man who had been the intellectual leader of the revolution. Things were going well. Then Silas, an emotional, dedicated man, for he was second-in-line.

Things were still going well when in 1960 political *machismo* began reasserting itself. It was Guevara's turn, but Paz said, "No." He himself must be president again. He was the only one to lead the country, the indispensable man. Paz's men trailed Guevara's men and left them hanging from light fixtures; Guevara himself was hounded from attic to attic. The "solution" was broken at that moment, but it took four more years for the men of the revolution to devour each other. For Paz was not satisfied with just one more term, he wanted still more. He changed the constitution so he could be elected once more, and he got himself in again in 1964, which was to have been Lechín's period to serve.

One of the things Latin Americans will not stand for—and another example of the basically democratic reaction of Latin Americans—is *prorroguismo* or *continuismo*, a man's continuing himself in power after his time. And this time it was all over. In the fall of 1964, the three he had double-crossed united to throw Paz out. And the country sank back into the bottomless abyss of political savagery, with each leader vying for absolute power for himself.

This is *macho* politics and Latin America is rife with monuments to it. One of the most dramatic is in the cemetery of Guatemala City, where barefoot little boys suffer the cost of the political savagery with no schools, no future: all they can do is sell water to mourners at five *centavos* a can. If you walk through the cemetery, you see the monument to Colonel F. Javier Arana, hero of the right, assassinated in the 1940s (assassin never apprehended), another to Mario Méndez Montenegro, hope of the democratic left in the 1960s, found mysteriously killed in 1965 (case never solved) . . . Others were luckier—they escaped into exile. One of them, General Miguel Ydígoras Fuentes (president of Guatemala from 1958–63), sat in his exile house in neighboring San Salvador one day going down the list of Guatemalan presidents in this century. "Not one was not either exiled or shot," he said, smiling a bitter-sweet smile. "Being president of Guatemala, being president in these countries—it is not a very good job."

The *macho* man who looks so romantic to much of the outside world is not looked upon as romantic by his most intelligent fellow Latins, who more brilliantly than anyone—and more devastatingly —have analyzed him. The Mexican poet-philosopher Octavio Paz, wrote: "One word sums up the aggressiveness, insensitivity, invulnerability and other attributes of the *macho*: power. It is force without the discipline of any notion of order; arbitrary power, the will without reins and without a set course."

To Paz, as to most of the others who have studied the *macho*-style man and written about him, the *macho* engenders hostility and hatred in his sons, who then turn to the mother and, embarrassed and confused by her humiliation, become *machos*—authoritarians—themselves and complete the cycle. "The essential attribute of the *macho*—power—almost always reveals itself as a capacity for wounding, humiliating, annihilating," Paz says. "Nothing is more natural, therefore, than his indifference toward the offspring he spawns . . . He is power isolated in its own potency, without relationship or compromise with the outside world. He is pure incommunication, a solitude that devours itself and everything it touches."

To Paz, the woman is to the *macho* the humiliated one, the creature the *macho* splits open—and anyone who opens himself to others, sexually, emotionally, politically, is despised. Life and the human being must be closed and safe. The verb *chingar* in Spanish is used to denote the woman's despised state. *Chingar,* he says, "is to do violence to another. The verb is masculine, active, cruel; it stings, wounds, gashes, stains. And it provokes a bitter, resentful satisfaction . . . To the Mexican there are only two possibilities in life; either he inflicts the actions implied by *chingar* on others or else he suffers them himself at the hands of others. This conception of social life as combat fatally divides society into the strong and the weak."

The background of *machismo* is not only in the Hispanic tradition but also in the New World experience, for it was here that the conquistadores came, in effect, to rape the land in their predatory lust. They literally did rape the Indian women, thus producing the new race of Latin American men who so often feel themselves the consequence of such raping. They lust after the figure of the father, the rapacious conquistador, yet they also hate and abhor him. For the figure of the mother there is sympathy and love, yet also the image of the victim, the figure of powerlessness. The man desires her largely as a mother to his children, and the more children he can have, the more a man he considers himself.

Dr. Humberto Rotundo of Peru, one of the most distinguished psychiatrists in Latin America, insists that Latin women do not like their role and that it causes them deep problems. "What the double standard does is it creates in women the devaluation of men," he says. A Latin American university woman insists that the "typical *macho* likes politics and sports better than sex, which probably he fears though he talks women all day. *Machismo* is the attitude of an incomplete man. It is the pampered boy who has never grown up. It is a form of immaturity, of underdevelopment. Our whole culture suffers from it. Perhaps that is why it is so hard for us to develop stable political and social institutions."

Where, then, is the "romance" of the Latin American man? Where the romantic Latin of pictures, songs and poems? Where the man who appears so sure of himself, so elegant, so proud?

If we take "romantic" to mean the extravagantly ideal, the *macho* is the most unromantic man in the world. He has ordered his life in the most cynical way possible, in the way least responsive to man and man's possibilities. He is driven not to love but to conquest; oriented not to the drive for unity and community among men, but to predatory apartness. Totally uncontrolled in physical passion, when it comes to spiritual love he is as coldly calculating as the most parsimonious Prussian burgher balancing his accounts. When it comes to marriage he weighs class, status and gain on a careful scale.

There is the wife for child-bearing and raising, and there are the women outside the family for carnal pleasures, for the symbolic ripping open. He is the ultimate man of appetite—but ironically he probably is a man who rarely enjoys that appetite because it always must serve his own ego.

In the past the *macho* has been the Latin American ideal, and he is one of the major reasons why Latin America has never amounted to anything. *Machos* do not work together. *Machos* are not real patriots because they use instead of help. *Machos* are incapable of selfless dedication, of sharing power, of political gallantry. When they lose, their instinct is to kill. When they conquer, their instinct is to gloat. When they love, their instinct is to use. They are incapable of long-term work, of scientific experiment, of the patient investigation that builds civilizations. They cannot acknowledge defeat, and they spend their days crying "fraud" about the winner and plotting the downfall of those who do succeed. They are incapable of anything not immediately rewarded by sexual pleasure, unfettered power or social adulation.

They can be charming, but they are men who inflict and hurt and humiliate. Perhaps worst of all, they are men who are incapable of creating modern societies.

CHAPTER 6

The United States and Latin America:
A Love Story

"You really do love us, don't you?" A Latin American
in conversation with an American friend.

The first time I met Cuban Prime Minister Fidel Castro in Havana,
we sat talking from midnight until six in the morning in the lobby
of the Hotel Havana Libre. He had talked about a number of serious
things—developing the economy, the sugar problem, subversion
toward Latin America, his sinuous relations with the United States.
Then, about 2 A.M., something came up that has symbolized to me
the peculiarly tormented, and at the same time often amusing,
relationship between the United States and Latin America.

Castro was sitting at the end of the couch and he appeared to
be tired. He kept his field cap on the whole time and his nose,
which is straight and prominent, seemed to lunge straight out from
under the hat, which was jammed down on his forehead. His manners were extremely correct—almost gallant, almost Victorian.
Only his free-floating beard, which grew out in all directions from
his chin, seemed to symbolize the historically flamboyant Fidel.

Suddenly he brightened noticeably and said to the minister of
education, José Llanusa, "Let's get some ice cream." Llanusa, a
tall, lanky man, shook his head. "It's closed," was all he said.

I knew immediately what they were talking about. When I had
come into Havana from the airport the previous night I had noticed
the enormous Coppelia ice cream parlor across the street from the

hotel. Indeed, you could barely miss it. It took in an entire city block of the choicest downtown real estate and it had carefully manicured parks around it, with flying buttresses tying the round, space-age structure down to earth. It was obviously a shocking extravagance for a country suffering the economic problems of Cuba. Obviously, too, it represented more than a random taste for ice cream.

"That's a pity," Castro said. Then he added quickly and with serious mien, "We now have twenty-eight flavors."

I was perplexed, and I asked, "Twenty-eight flavors?"

"Yes, more than Howard Johnson's," he rejoined. I must have looked even more bewildered, for in another minute he was explaining: "Cubans used to love Howard Johnson's ice cream. This is our way of showing we can do everything better than the Americans."

The Cuban incident was amusing, and one could let it go at that if it were not so symbolic of so many other things. For it speaks of one of the most active catalysts and irritants in every Latin American's life and one of the major components of the collective psyche of the Latin Americans—the overwhelming presence and influence of the "colossus of the North," the United States of America.

The strange role that the United States has always played in Latin America is little understood, and very often the opposite of reality is perceived. North Americans most often perceive that Latin Americans hate them, for instance. They see the violent anti-American demonstrations, the marching students, the "Yanqui Go Home" ("—and take us with you," they used to add in the Dominican Republic) signs, and they see no more.

But it is much more complicated than that. Underneath is the complex duality of Latin America's relationship with the United States—the deep love-hate, dependence-independence, admiration-despising part of it. In that other America, "Anti-Americanism" is born basically of a desire to emulate North America and to be awarded prestige therefrom; it expresses itself in violent actions which arise out of the fury and frustrations of failure. As one knowing, non-American anthropologist, who had worked many years in Latin America, commented, "They hate you because they want to be like you." In a curious way, it is a kind of thwarted love.

Latin American literature is filled with the story of it, and Latin American social scientists in particular have written of it; yet it seems to be a well-kept secret north of the Rio Grande. Gilberto Freyre, the Brazilian sociologist, has compared the relations "on a national scale, to those of a sociologically male in regard to a sociologically female, that is dependent, Latin America. The American south of the Rio Grande sees in the United States a masculine power that some of the most feminine Latin American nations are inclined to consider unstable, exuberant and irregular in its masculine, that is protective, behavior toward them."

Jaime Castillo, the Chilean Christian Democrat philosopher, also interprets the Latin American reaction as one hinging upon the amount of appreciation and care Latin America receives from the North. "Chile has to be against the U.S. because of the American intervention in Chilean life," he explains. "But the attitude is more collective than personal. Franklin Roosevelt easily awoke sympathy; John Kennedy even more. A negative attitude on the part of Latin Americans seems to go along with any lack of appreciation on the part of North America. When it appears a friend or good neighbor, there are no problems."

But any sensitive person who has lived much time in Latin America does not have to consult sociologists or philosophers for a confirmation of the Latin complex about the United States. It is with you every minute—sometimes engaging, sometimes pathetic, often outrageous, many times only tiresome. It is there with their constant resentment of the United States for pre-empting the word "American." With a perverse precision, they call citizens of the United States "North Americans" and persist in insisting that "We are Americans too." They constantly remind Americans, often with the appearance of hurt feelings, that "you helped Europe with the Marshall Plan far more than you ever helped us"—in effect, you loved them more.

Young Latin Americans in the democratic camp who are not caught up in the violently anti-American and dependent Marxist attitudes often speak, even unconsciously, of their mixed feelings about the United States. One American, leaving Peru, was saying good-bye to his Spanish teacher, a young Peruvian of unusual sensitivity.

Toward the end of the evening the teacher burst forth suddenly: "We look at the United States. We are both the same age, and the United States is a thousand times ahead of us." Then he added with emotion: "There's a strange bond between our continents. It's strange, but it's true." In extremely emotional terms, he then said, "You really do love us, don't you?"

I personally recall a party in Santo Domingo one night several months after the Dominican revolution had erupted with all its primordial ugliness. It was a party that told a great deal, a party attended by about fourteen Dominicans—mostly young writers and artists who had fought in the revolution—and several Americans.

Several persons were singing and at one point one of the young American women got up to sing. She leaned against a doorway and sang in a good voice but with a somewhat peremptory manner, "Fly me to the moon." The Dominicans all applauded, for she was in fact quite good. Then one of them said in Spanish, which she did not understand, "You see, they *all* give orders," and the others dissolved in laughter.

A few minutes later another of the Dominicans was saying to me, speaking to all of us Americans there, "We do this because we like you." He was very serious. "We are so close to you, we are all so much the same. If only your government understood what we want, we could be one great continent, America. You could be at the head—that is all right—but you must appreciate us."

At the end of the hot, sticky evening, everyone was sitting around; the mood was tired and mellow. The *merengue* on the phonograph was about the death of the dictator Rafael Trujillo: "And they killed the old goat on the highway on the thirtieth of May." Trujillo was something that was typical: kept in power with American support for thirty-one years, then assassinated with CIA help.

The months before this party had, after all, been a grisly time. A sick nation had gone mad. The streets had become insane asylums and everyone with a gun had gone out and shot, leaving the corpses to rot on the streets with the garbage that collected and collected and collected in those days. Several thousand Dominicans died, largely needlessly. But it had been a great cathartic event in the long history of the Dominican Republic, that tortured land in the Caribbean sun.

Toward the end of the evening, one of the better Dominican playwrights, a sweet, gentle young man, came over and asked if he might show me his play. Thinking it would be about Dominicans and the revolution, I evinced considerable interest. But when I saw the list of characters, I realized, with shock, that it was about the American soldiers—the invasion and occupation force. "We had Americans all around the house," he explained, "and we got to be very friendly. I really felt for them. This is about them. But there is nobody here to play the American Negro soldier. We have nobody that big."

An even more dramatic example of the strange psychological and social forces at work came at a meeting of the Catholic Inter-American Cooperation Program in Chicago during the early 1960s. This is the organization which the American and Latin American Catholics started, to carry through the pope's calls to the American church to aid the Latin Church.

It was one of those moments, almost of confession, when all the frustrations and all the pains of several lifetimes suddenly disgorge themselves from the dark consciousnesses where they are guarded. José Villegas, an official of the Pan American Union in Washington, got up and said to the assembled Americans, sometimes in an almost-breaking voice: "We think of you so much as supermen that we sometimes don't even think you are human. The Latin American sees only the superman propaganda. We think you are so perfect you don't even have emotions. This is one of my first experiences in which I see you in a human way."

A little like a fundamentalist religious meeting where the witnessing of one to the "truth" sets off a chain reaction that rouses the confessions of others, his confession spread. Marina Bandeira, a handsome and talented Brazilian laywoman who is a specialist in literacy programs, got up and said, again with emotion: "Several years ago, when we held the first meeting, we knew you felt disdain for us. There was hurt and resentment on our part. This meeting has been one of the first times I have not felt talked down to by Americans."

Then, with a note of joy in her voice over the words of the American priest, Father Leo Mahon of Panama, who had just praised what North Americans can learn from Latin Americans, she ended in a crescendo with the words, "Now you have helped us in finding solutions and you have ended up discussing your problems with us."

The key to the Latin American relationship with the United States is in an idea, or a reality, that as many analysts fervently defend as others vehemently deny: the existence of a New World personality, comprehension and way of life, something that unites the two disparate and, in many ways, different continents. The late Hispanic scholar Federico de Onis always said that he could recognize an American in Paris but he never could tell whether he came from North America or South America, for there was the same openness of manner, the same innocence and optimism about both of them.

Although others insist there is nothing at all similar about the two continents, Don Federico's position holds the most truth. His insight will become even more apparent as the "marginal people" in Latin America, whose desires have never come into play in Latin society, are integrated into society, for they are real "Americans." It is this too that is at the roots of the Latin American "complex," and we must call it that, about the United States.

The simple fact that we share the New World, and that here and only here were men in modern times given vast new continents to settle and a past to shed, is the crucial issue. But the United States, with its secular egalitarianism, soared into history, while Latin America, with its aristocratic exclusiveness, inched through it. Nevertheless, the fact of twin birth and geographical position in the world has meant that the only part of the world which Latin America can pit itself against in its striving is the United States. Because we share the same historic sequence and because we both inhabit the New World and because we are relatively the maturer

continent, it is a psychological necessity that Latin America, now
in its adolescence, find its own character and its own nationality,
in pitting itself, toe to toe, eye to eye, against us.

To understand the paradoxes at play, one must look at history.
Our two continents were opened for settlement at relatively the
same time and benefited from many of the same raw materials and
vast expanses. But the contrast in the extent of our respective developments is what gnaws at Latins and sends them into rages.

They look north and see a continent webbed with great universities and laboratories and roads and launching pads, with
skyscrapers, artists, writers, scientists and the best-paid workers
in the world. They see the most powerful nation on earth. They
see the womb of a secular democratic philosophy and a scientific
technology that changed the world for all time: a country that
knows its own name and shouts it for the whole world to hear.

When they look around them—the same age, remember—they
see barefoot Indians with dark, fearful minds dreaming of an
empire lost four hundred years ago, and arrogant, effete aristocrats,
mimicking European culture (poorly) and despising the lands
they live in. They see a land so untouched by a pragmatic hand,
that it seems man has only recently passed that way.

The history of relations between the two New World continents
does a great deal to illuminate this psychological swampland, for
the two New Worlds were always intertwined. The men who built
the revolutionary structure of the United States of America found
themselves drawn to the independence movement in Latin America, wanting to help its leaders. Thomas Jefferson, in particular,
sympathized with Simón Bolívar and was his friend and fellow
voyager in the New World's sea of enthusiasm over change.

One of the most dramatic incidents of early American sympathy for the Latin American revolutionary impulse came in 1787,
just before the famous Inconfidencia Mineira or Minas Conspiracy,
which was the forerunner of independence for Brazil. Inflamed
and inspired by the American Revolution, a group of six young
men who wrote poetry and thought of themselves as "Arcadians"
—taking the names of Greek shepherds and writing long, pastoral
poems—hatched a plot to overthrow the Brazilian monarchy.

They came out of the barren highlands, which in those days were glittering with ores. It was from this state, Minas Gerais, that much of the gold of the world came at that time. Moreover, the devoutly Catholic miners used the money to build cities of medieval splendor in the highlands. It was here that the famous Brazilian sculptor, the crippled Aleijadinho, created his famous prophet statues with their tormented faces.

Resentful of Portuguese rule and passionately interested in history and politics, the poets were joined by other intellectuals and army officers. Their leader was a lieutenant named Joaquim José da Silva Zavier, who practiced dentistry and thus earned the nickname *Tiradentes* or Toothpuller, a name that was to go down in Brazilian history as hallowed.

Inspired by the American Revolution, as was all of Latin America at this time, the group corresponded with Thomas Jefferson and in 1787 one of them traveled to France to meet Jefferson, then minister plenipotentiary of the newly formed United States. The romantic meeting took place in the Roman amphitheater at Nîmes —a meeting that more than anything else endeared the United States to Brazil in the ensuing independence era.

In the darkened amphitheater, where the empires of the past listened mutely to the dreams of future ones, Jefferson gave his moral support to and expressed his personal sympathy for the conspirators. He could do no more. But the young envoy who had gone halfway around the world to talk to the man from the country that represented man's most profound revolutionary ideals died on the way back to Brazil. The conspiracy of Minas went ahead. It was discovered; Tiradentes was hanged and quartered, his house destroyed and the ground where it had stood was strewn with salt in the Biblical symbolism of making a house barren forever.

Today Tiradentes and his men are buried in the main church in Ouro Prêto, that beautiful little town in the mountains of Minas. "Toothpuller Day" is a national holiday and every town in Brazil has its Tiradentes Square or Street. His house was not so barren after all.

But the ways of Jefferson, who sympathized so warmly with the

Latin revolutionaries, came upon hard and practical days in Washington. There developed the other reaction—the second head of the two-headed creature that is the American attitude to Latin America—that the Latins were not capable of handling themselves or their own affairs.

This was expressed in the Monroe Doctrine of 1823, which proclaimed the New World off-limits to European adventurism or expansionist lusts. It abetted the Latin independence movements, to be sure, but it also expressed North America's paternalistic concern over the instability of Latin America. In the 1800s, the United States fought Mexico, annexed Texas, and laid the basis for an American-controlled Panama canal; by 1895 the circle was complete. In that year Secretary of State Richard Olney exulted that "today the United States is practically sovereign on this continent, and its fiat is law upon the subjects to which it confines its interposition." The Latins understood very well.

American interventions in the Caribbean also spawned an odd, hybrid, half-American type of leadership: the pathological and evil Trujillo in the Dominican Republic, who always thought of himself proudly as a Marine, because he had been trained by the U. S. Marines; and the Somoza dynasty of Nicaragua.

One night in 1967 I sat with the third of the Somoza rulers, young "Tacho" Somoza, during his electoral campaign. All over that small, low, hot country, Tacho's boys had torn down all the electoral posters but his. There had been shootings. Other campaigning was allowed only under the most stringent restrictions, and the big blustering Tachito, known for his vicious temper, kept everything under control through the National Guard—another souvenir from Marine times.

To look at Tachito that night, one would have imagined him a slightly paunchy, slightly fortyish American business executive. The suit, the hand outstretched, most of all the almost perfect American southern accent—all came directly out of his American education. I asked him about the torn-up posters of his opponents. "Ah think that's they-ah tough luck," he drawled. I asked him what he thought about his opponent's saying that no one could win in

Nicaragua but a Somoza. "Ah think that's they-ah tough luck," he answered. And so it went with almost every question.

Before I left that country I also discovered that his wife and his children held American nationality. If they ever had to leave Nicaragua, they could all escape easily and quickly. They-ah luck wouldn't be tough at all.

For all these reasons, the Latin Americans, over the last century, began that suffering over their neighbors to the north that would preoccupy them for so long—what to do about them, how to react to them, how to deal with that extraordinary, aggressive, active spirit that was and is the United States of America. The North Americans were positivists; the South Americans, fatalists. The North Americans believed the world could be changed, for had they not changed it? The South Americans, as Octavio Paz so brilliantly put it, believed it could be redeemed. The South Americans hankered and yearned and suffered to have what the North Americans possessed. Yet to have what they had, the Latins had to give up what they were. And this is the core of the entire literature of frustration from Latin America, toward its American neighbors.

On the one hand, Latin America has undergone a tremendous negation of Hispanic America and of Spain in general. The renowned Argentine thinker Domingo Faustino Sarmiento (1811–88) led the pack of defamers with his "Do not laugh, oh, people of Hispanic America, at seeing so much degradation! Remember that you are Spanish and the Inquisition educated Spain in that manner. We carry this disease in our blood."

An even stronger condemnation of the Spanish past was heaped upon the Latin American psyche by Francisco Bilbao, (1823–65) the Chilean intellectual and critic. His book *The Civics of Chilean Society* aroused an enormous scandal, with its "Slavery, degradation: that is the past . . . Our past is Spain. Spain is the Middle Ages. The Middle Ages are composed, body and soul, of Catholicism and feudalism."

When the *Catholic Review* protested, Bilbao was tried for abuse of the press. Arciniegas describes his looking the prosecutor in the eye and demanding: "Who are you? Philosophy assigns you the name of reactionary. An innovator, that is what I am; reaction-

aries, that is what you are." Within a few minutes after the end of
his trial, the public had taken up a collection and paid his fine and
Bilbao was carried through the streets on the shoulders of his followers.

And if Spain was the black legend, unredeemable, unregenerate, the United States was goodness, positivism, a haven for free
man. Simón Rodríguez (1771–1854), Bolívar's tutor, cried that
"the soil of the United States is sown with liberal ideas—cultivated
by skillful hands in every spot—protected by an atmosphere of
freedom that all its citizens breathe."

The Argentine writer Juan Bautista Alberdi (1814?–86) wrote:
"My conviction is that without England and the United States,
freedom would vanish in this century." Sarmiento added: "Let us
emulate the United States. Let us be America, as the sea is the
ocean. Let us *be* the United States."

The romantic Bilbao, who opposed the continuance of colonial
institutions after independence, could perhaps be looked upon
as most symbolic of the great chasm, the intellectual conflict,
love-hate, admiration-fear, that the Latins felt toward the United
States. On the one hand, he was writing, "Those Puritans, or their
descendants, have given the world the most beautiful of constitutions, directing the destinies of the greatest, the richest, the
wisest and the freest of nations . . . they put into effect what
they think, and they create whatever is necessary for the moral
and material perfection of the human species. Their free individual
and political life and all of its marvels depend upon sovereignty of
the individual and upon the rational basis for this sovereignty:
freedom of thought. What a contrast with South America, with
what was Spanish America!"

On the one hand, outrageous admiration, uncontained. On the
other hand, dire warnings and fears. For in his darker moments
Bilbao wrote that the United States is extending its claws more
and more every day "in that hunt which it has undertaken against
the South. Yesterday it was Texas, then it was the North of Mexico
. . . and then Panama." And he added, as night fell they were
"looking at themselves and finding themselves so great; they have

fallen into the temptation of Titan, convinced that they were the arbiters of the earth and even the possessors of Olympus."

Already the duality was eating into the Latin American consciousness—childlike admiration and adolescent rebellion—devouring hope and stilling early love. But it was only beginning. The two natures of North American—Jefferson and Franklin Roosevelt and Kennedy and brotherhood versus Monroe and Teddy Roosevelt and knowing better. In 1898 the United States entered the Spanish-American War and then told Cuba, via the Platt Amendment, which gave the United States the right to intervene in Cuban affairs at any time, that it knew better, much better. This was followed by incursions into Santo Domingo and Nicaragua. Now it was the Marines, rather than Jeffersonian ideas about the rights of free man, which were penetrating the South.

Theodore Roosevelt seized Panama from Colombia to build the Panama Canal, and the Nicaraguan poet Rubén Darío (1867–1916) wrote his "Ode to Roosevelt," in the last verse of which he cries, "And though you count on everything, you lack one thing: God!"

Always the Latins fell into the same dichotomy—Latin spirituality versus American materialism and technocracy. So what if North Americans were the men of might? Latin Americans were the men of God and the spirit. North Americans were simply pagan technicians. The Latins were afraid they would lose themselves in North American positivism and secularism; they were afraid the North Americans would snatch them away from themselves.

It was a fear born both in a lack of faith in their Hispanic background and in an excessive admiration for the United States; a fear born not only of the threat of American power extending itself southward, but also of all those aggressive, proselytizing Americans with their ideas about social equality and their gadgetry—two things that perhaps have changed Latin America more than any invasion could.

To defend themselves, in their underdevelopment, from becoming culturally overwhelmed, they had to defend themselves as spiritually and culturally superior men. They had to defend their style of business, with its control by extended family groups, against the impersonal, efficient, egalitarian North American corporations. And so Juan José Arévalo, the "spiritual socialist" who became president of Guatemala in 1945, could write in his symbolic book *The Shark and the Sardines* (the United States is the shark, Latin America the sardines):

"In our resistance to the businessman mentality, we are still Spanish, stubbornly Spanish. Also, we have not left off being Catholic, nor have we left off being romantic and we cannot conceive of private life without love, nor of public life without chivalry, nor of our children's education without enlightening ideals. If you want to be our friends, you will have to accept us as we are. Do not attempt to remodel us after your image. Mechanical civilization, material progress, industrial techniques, fiduciary wealth, comfort, hobbies—all these figure in your programs of work and enjoyment of life. But for us, the essence of human life does not lie in such things."

But perhaps the very essence of the spiritual Hispanophile–materialistic Anglo-Saxon fight lies in the book *Ariel*, written by the Uruguayan José Enrique Rodó (1872–1917), and often considered the "Bible of Latin American Youth." Nothing could be clearer. Ariel is the Latin, the hero, the representative of the "spirituality that loves intelligence *for itself*, the beauty, the grace and the pure mysteries of the infinite." Intelligence without aim, beauty for beauty's sake, substance without object.

Pitted against him, throughout the book, is the North, represented by Caliban, a savage and deformed slave who enters the narrative exclaiming the inspiring words *"Necesito comer"*—"I must eat . . ." Caliban is utilitarianism, sensuality without ideals which leads to the "negation of charity, the dogma of the triumph of the strongest, the fight for existence."

The concern over the equality of the North, unthinkable in terms of the hierarchy of Latin life and which plays such an emotional role in "anti-Americanism" in Latin America, is here provided its rationale. "The leveling democracy, aspiring to the monotonous empire of the lowest medium, democracy poorly understood, Rodó combated with strong reasons and eloquence," proclaims the introduction to *Ariel*. It is a point of honor among the traditional Latin Americans that man is not equal.

Even today this fear of American egalitarianism is not dead in Latin America. I recall speaking to a liberal Peruvian priest from an aristocratic family, Father Carlos Alvarez Calderón, in the scabrous old building in downtown Lima where he had his office for trade union organizing. When I mentioned the American priests who were wielding such influence in Peru, he lost his regal composure. "They do more harm than good," he snapped, and accused them of everything from having nervous breakdowns on the job to imposing an unnatural "Americanism" (American parishes, $100-a-plate charity dinners) on the Latin Americans. "They put down their theology books and become pagan technicians," he concluded. At this time there were slightly more foreign priests than native priests in Peru, adding to the local paranoia.

But the Peruvians and the Latin Americans of the shantytowns of Lima and the other big cities and the miserable villages of the interiors do not feel that way. Over and over, the "marginal people" of the Lima *barriadas* tell visitors that they prefer the American priests—"they are not so stern, they understand us better," they say typically. The Peruvian cardinal Juan Landazuri Ricketts remarked, "They (the Peruvians) always ask for the American priests." In the *barriadas* a Peace Corps boy will tell you of the *barriada* dwellers: "I'm afraid they love us, we can do no wrong. They always want one of us to be treasurer because they don't trust anybody else." Equally, when a *barriada* person goes to a doctor, he wants to take an American along "because then the doctors treat us better." I personally experienced many such instances in the shantytowns. In particular I recall one man, on the stinking El Montón garbage dump shantytown in Lima who said, almost starry-eyed: "The United States must be beautiful, eh? The first country in the world. It's a thousand times more advanced."

And I remember the restless Jaime Benítez, rector of the University of Puerto Rico, explaining why Juan Bosch lost the election of 1966 in the Dominican Republic. "I told Juan," he said, with that piercing energy he had, "the poor people in Latin America are not anti-American." But Bosch pegged his campaign to anti-

Americanism and his opponent Dr. Joaquín Balaguer pegged his to the idea that he was the "American candidate" and Balaguer won.

It is no secret that "anti-Americanism" in Latin America is a class phenomenon. It is the prerogative of the middle-class and upper-class man and, in particular, the intellectual, who can afford the pangs and pulls of spiritual misery. The lower classes, the marginal people, with an almost uncanny understanding, seem to perceive quite clearly that their level of individuals are far better off in the United States. They can absorb anti-Americanism, as in Cuba, but they have to be taught it.

Looking at the twentieth-century history of Latin America, it is easy to see the flowering of a reaction against trying to be too much like the other America. For when Latin America went through its own independence struggles in the years around 1810, not knowing itself it attempted to mold its new creole form exactly in the image of the United States. Its revolutions were directly inspired by the American Revolution, its constitutions were based on the American Constitution, its governmental structures were created in the image of Washington's. But as Octavio Paz wrote: "In the United States these principles corresponded to historical reality for they were an expression of the rise of the bourgeoisie. In Spanish America they merely served as modern trappings for the survivals of the colonial system."

By the twentieth century the reaction had set in and the United States, once the inspiration, was blamed for everything. First Mexico found its own way in the revolution of 1910. ("Poor Mexico," the dictator Porfirio Díaz lamented, "so far from God, so close to the United States.") Then Peru in the 1930s produced the first Indo-American ideology, that of Aprismo, the party that was to be the model of the entire spectrum of parties of the Democratic Left. "Anti-Americanism" came into being with a vengeance, and everything was blamed on the formerly admired United States. It was a new form of dependence, crueller than the former.

Partially through Marxist ideology but more largely simply through the traditional position of Latin America vis-à-vis the United States, Latin Americans became almost paranoid in their attitudes toward North America. When the Brazilian dictator and president Getulio Vargas died in 1954 by shooting himself through the head one August day, he left a now famous suicide letter in which he (or possibly someone else, they say) scrawled in typical paranoia: "Once again the forces that are coordinated by the interests against the people have now unleashed themselves over me . . . After decades of domination and exploitation by international economic-financial groups, I made myself the chief of a revolution, and I won . . ."

When another, later, Brazilian president, the mercurial Janio Quadros, resigned, the same spirit—reflecting the Brazilian paranoia that American business interests, which actually control only a small percentage of Brazilian business, were taking over Brazil— dominated his resignation note. "I have been beaten . . . I wanted Brazil for Brazilians . . . I had to face and fight corruption, lies and cowardice, whose only goals are to subject the general needs of the nation to some ambitious groups and individuals from inside and also from outside . . . Terrible forces came forward to fight me and to defame me . . ."

This sense of things being stolen from Latin America by uncontrollable forces from outside today dominates much Latin American thinking both of the left and the right, for it is psychological rather than political, rooted deep in history's swamps. It emerges in the Latin's barely suppressed fury over American investments in the subsoil and expresses itself in the fanatic determination that Americans should not rob Latin America of its mineral riches. The comparison of raping the land is not inapplicable. It is there in the outrageous fishing laws perpetrated by one country after the other, in which the usual twelve-mile limit from shore is extended to two hundred miles; it is part of Latin America's frenetically reclaiming its own.

The newest and most sensitive chauvinistic cry is that North America, by imposing "unnatural" birth control methods, is "stopping Latin Americans from being born." It is simply a new and modern, if more delicate, manifestation of the old complaint —the United States is trying to control, to use, to rape, to abort, to destroy, to change, to deflower, to redefine Latin America.

But the psychological dependence-independence syndrome in Latin America has many and complicated sides; it is a maze that one enters only gingerly. One cannot always find one's way out, but one can wander creatively.

I recall, for instance, a government minister in one of the countries who was off to the United States to study advanced nuclear military strategy. His country was just coming out of the gunpowder age. Yet it made sense to him because "when I go in to talk to American officials, we must be on the same level." When the local Israeli ambassador overheard this he remarked wryly, "Thank God we didn't have their complexes."

Then there was Juan Ugarte, a prominent leftist Chilean journalist who was arguing for the nationalization of the copper mines. "All we want to do is run our own country," he argued vehemently. Then he added, "If you really wanted to help us, why don't you give us money to buy the mines?"

And there was the Uruguayan architect (the lineal descendant of Rodó) who spoke heatedly about the "cold, unspiritual" American architecture and insisted it was not for Latin America. He ended with the curious statement: "We want no inspiration from the United States. To Europe—that is where we will go. But do not send us the cold buildings of Mies van der Rohe and Walter Gropius." Apparently he did not know that both men were born in Germany and that they expressed the spirit of modern European architecture; they moved to the United States only after they were well-established architects.

It is interesting that even in their fury over the United States, the Latins often trust it more than they do each other. One incident during the Dominican revolution of 1965 was particularly telling. Colonel Francisco Caamano, the burly leader of the rebels, was always forced to take a violently anti-American posture. Indeed, the United States had sent in thirty thousand troops to put down his revolution, so there was little else he could do. But when it came to the choice of Brazilian troops, who were allied with the American troops in the Inter-American Peace Force, or American troops to occupy the rebel zone, Caamano, without a second thought, insisted upon the American troops. He knew how they would react, and he trusted them.

Part of the problem is in the difference in the concepts of power —and in particular how this is affected by *machismo*. Latin men traditionally do not like or understand limited power. They strain for unfettered and absolute power, and they use and celebrate it with appropriate displays when they get it.

No one craves power like the Latin man. But the intensity of his craving, and the selfishness of it, keep him from realizing real power in the world as it is. His egotism, his dependence upon woman, which arises from his determination to keep her in her place, his lonely *machismo*—all the things that give him the will to power make it impossible for him to realize power, except in small situations, or to use it well when he gets it.

On one hand the Latin Americans often appear far more self-confident as human beings, for they are raised in a society in which they have a sure and fixed place. They are not buffeted by that restless searching for place and symbol that drives so many Americans. But on the other hand the Latin's impressive power posturing turns out to be sand falling through his fingers. The American man whom he ridicules for drying the dishes turns out to hold in those damp, hesitant hands the greatest power in the world. The Latin knows in his heart that it is the winsome American, with the placelessness of his social equality and his desperate seeking for security and community identity through working with his fellows, who rules. But he does not know why.

Octavio Paz has written: "Would it not be more accurate to say that the North American wants to use reality rather than know it?" And in another place: "North Americans want to understand and we want to contemplate. They are activists and we are quietists; we enjoy our wounds and they enjoy their inventions." And finally: "It seems to me that North Americans consider the world to be something that can be perfected, and that we consider it to be something that can be redeemed."

But unlike most Latins, Paz suspects that all is not well with the supermen of the North, and he states his reservations with: "In the United States man does not feel that he has been torn from the center of creation and suspended between hostile forces. He has built his own world and it is built in his own image: it is his mirror. But now he cannot recognize himself in his inhuman objects, nor in his fellows."

This is unusual, for most Latin Americans, possessing their own superman image of North Americans, believe Americans can do anything; that is why they are so often angry and disappointed in them; they feel their shortcomings must be deliberate, instead of simply human.

It often shocks Americans to discover that Latin Americans consider North Americans a terribly violent people, a sure and swaggering race likely to do anything at any moment. The Latins are wary of them. Latin Americans do not understand the Protestant ethic or the Anglo-Saxon way of life, mistaking order and legality for lack of passion. They do not understand the purpose and fury that fights world wars coolly. Nor do they understand that white men can be poorly dressed and uncultured. This is their reverse racism, for white people among them are always the elite. They talk about liberty but they do not understand the conflicts of liberty inherent in an egalitarian society, where cultural democracy creates a mediocre and even vulgar public life.

When they march off to throw ink and rocks at the American information office (a ritual not unlike the bullfight), they have no conception there are little insecure Americans sitting by their television sets having their feelings hurt and suffering over why nobody likes them. They are rebelling against the giant, against superman, against the case of Nicaragua and Cuba and Santo Domingo and four centuries; and they are rebelling, most of all, against their own dependence and invisibility in the world.

Today more than ever the United States is presenting Latin America with an often desperate dilemma. Not only is the northern power always present, unconsciously bringing about change with its ceaseless gadgetry (the transistor radio is the single greatest catalyst for change in the underdeveloped world) and its manners of social equals, it is also helping Latin America financially. Thus it takes away from the Latin Americans the solace of really being able to hate fully North America.

Not only does the United States demand that Latin America change its society, it demands that it change its very personality. The United States is constantly reminding them that to enter the technically oriented developed world they aspire to, they must give up part of themselves.

They must give up the involved kind of personal pride that keeps men in the twentieth century dueling to protect their honor. They must give up their aristocratic tastes, give up their intricate forms of revenge. They must become impersonal, like a machine. They must learn to judge a man not by who he is but by what he can do. The Latins—at least the modern ones—realize this in their lucid and honest moments, but that does not make it easier for them. Consequently they are furious with the American for being the kind of men they have to become to get what they want. At the same time they fight not to lose themselves and what their people have always been.

Today their ideas and attitudes could be typified by two Latin American statesmen: Prime Minister Fidel Castro of Cuba and President Eduardo Frei of Chile, who could almost be said to represent the two predominant and warring strains in Latin America. Castro is flamboyant, absolutist, theoretical. Frei is grave, practical, compromising. They could also be said to represent two attitudes toward the United States.

Castro is wildly anti-American, and his attitude expresses the feelings of the far left and the far right. He abhors the United States with a cold burning hatred, and he considers it the author of all his country's ills. Frei has said that Castro's Marxism is less Marxism than a "strategic hatred" of the United States. "The most important thing," Castro told me, "is that we are now independent of the United States."

But the Cubans blame everything, including everything they are, on the United States. In his xenophobia, Castro has proved his extreme psychological dependence on North America. Everything he does, even in deciding whether to make ice cream or not, is done in reaction to the United States. He is not free, he has not escaped. He is still in the white heat of love-hate over the United States.

Frei on the other hand was the protagonist of psychological independence as well as economic and political independence, and he speaks almost obsessively—it is a constantly repeated theme—about the Latins' propensity to put the blame for everything on someone else, about their inability to look at themselves and face themselves and what they are.

"We ought to have a word in the world because we have our own personality," Frei has said. "We ought to be independent not only economically but spiritually. If we always look outside for our blame, that is a form of dependence, too. We must look for our own blame to find our own personality."

PART II

THE OLD ORDER CHANGES— THREE CASE STUDIES OF CHANGE

CHAPTER 7

Cuba—A New Society?

"I have found truth." So many Cuban Communists.

In the winter of 1967 a group of top-level "Cuba-watchers" was assembled at a Cuba-watching conference at the Inter-American University in San Germán, Puerto Rico. Participants from the intellectual, exile and journalism communities had gathered for a week-long meeting to discuss the improbable fate of Cuba—why and how it had happened.

At the first session an old Latin American hand, an American writer who lived in Mexico, spoke about the "Cuban character" and managed in a few brief sentences to alienate and infuriate almost the entire Cuban contingent. "After all," he said, "you cannot expect the Cubans to develop a democracy. They are traditionally loyal only to their family group, not to country or to some great cause. They do not prize honesty—look at the corruption that developed time and time again . . ."

By the time he was finished, the exile Cubans were sitting tight-lipped and cold-eyed. Finally Ernesto Betancourt, one of the most able and moderate of the exiles, rose and said with bitter irony: "I think, after listening to our colleague, that we must all thank Fidel Castro. We have heard that Cubans were traditionally corrupt, that they were not capable of being loyal to great causes. Yet under Castro we see quite a different thing. We see the youth very loyal to the cause of Communism, and we see a government that is very honest. Apparently," he summed up, "we owe it to Fidel Castro for what he has done for the Cuban character."

Later another Cuban exile leader, Rufo López-Fresquet, who had been Castro's minister of economics in the first heady year of the revolution, confided how Castro had told him one day, "We are going to bring five hundred thousand peasants into Havana to celebrate the twenty-sixth of July." Rufo said he had broken into the conversation to tell him: "Fidel, you cannot do that. First, there is the matter of sanitation. Where will they stay, what will they eat?

"I did not like to do it," Rufo said, "but someone had to make him think more realistically."

When I asked him what had actually happened to Castro's plan, he shrugged and answered, "They came." Then he admitted haltingly, "It worked out beautifully." His eyes opened wide. "But how was I to know that the people of Havana would take them into their homes?" he demanded. "How was I to know that things would not be as they had always been?"

Much of what happened in Cuba after 1959 is contained in that observation. For over and over again, Fidel Castro was able to do the unexpected, at least partially because he had faith that the unexpected could be done. He was able to see that underneath the phlegm of corruption and runaway sensuality that choked the island there lay a tremendous wellspring of idealism, a self-sacrifice, and discipline waiting to be tapped. The fact that he tapped it is—whether one likes the way the revolution turned out or not and whether one thinks he sold out his early promises or not—one of the salient points of the revolution. Because of the often-voiced cynicism about the ability of "tropical" Latin America (the term mostly given to the hot Caribbean countries) to strive and overcome and sacrifice, Cuba is a particularly interesting country. Because of the enormous and radical changes that have occurred since 1959, it is well to ask of Cuba, "Is it really a New Society?"

The Cuba of 1958 was demoralized and torn apart. For two dreary years, Castro huddled in the Sierra Maestra, waiting to sweep down toward Havana. It was a Cuba on the brink of something new, yet few persons realized it or knew what was gestating. The inner torment of the island was obvious to few people outside Cuba and American officials continued to report that everything was fine. Yet, revolted by the cruelties of the dictator Fulgencio Batista, nearly the entire Cuban people was involved in the resistance. Every historian—whether pro- or anti-Castro—has agreed it was the Cuban people and not just a few guerrillas in the mountains who accounted for the eventual fall of Batista and the triumphal march of Fidel Castro and his men into Havana on January 1, 1959.

The Cuba of that day was a Cuba that, on the surface, was one of the two or three most developed countries in Latin America. American investment made Cuban industry the most heavily capitalized in Latin America. With Argentina, it had the highest per capita income in the hemisphere.

But the wealth was classically concentrated. Seventy percent of the farms were of sixty-five acres or less and they accounted for only 11 percent of the land. Only about 30 percent of all farms were operated by their owners and the remaining 70 percent were managed or worked by people with no ownership interest in them.

While the cities deceptively shone with the sheen of wealth, the countryside languished. An international report in 1950 reported: "The typical citizen is one whose children, if he lives in town, go to school two hours a day 120 days a year for the first few grades only. If he lives in the rural district, his children are more likely to be out of school than in school . . ." The same group reported that an estimated 30 to 40 percent of the urban population and 60 percent of the rural population suffered from serious nutritional deficiencies. Where 50 percent of all urban dwellings had bath or shower facilities, only 9 percent of rural dwellings possessed them.

Still the revolution did not come because of these conditions; the revolution came because of the bestialities of Batista. Eventually he collapsed when an astonishing thing happened that indicated the amount of total revulsion against him: his army simply refused to fight. The Batista soldiers were straggling home as Castro was marching on Havana.

Anti-Castroites constantly point out, in bewilderment, that Cuba was, after all, the "most American" of the Latin American countries, and the most developed. But the nagging and affluent presence of the United States and the highly developed sector within Cuba were only factors (as they always are) which exacerbated difference. The affluence, so unevenly distributed, only reminded the poor of how much there was to have and of how little they had of it. Cuba is the most salient example in Latin America of the first rule of revolution—revolution does not occur in the countries that are most depressed but does occur in countries where a substantial upgrading of life has begun. It happens when people are awakened and when things have already changed, stirring people to further change and giving them confidence it can be obtained.

The American presence in Cuba was always ambiguous. In 1898, after the Spanish-American War finally separated Cuba from Spain (it is significant that Cuba was the last colony to win its independence from Spain), the United States took over the godfathership of the island. Under the Platt Amendment, by which the United States retained for itself the right to interfere in Cuban affairs when it deemed it right to do so, the American military ruled the country for several years until the republic was formed. The United States intervened several times in the years that followed, but the Cuban resentment against the United States does not stem from that per se. It seems to stem more from the fact that U.S. diplomats routinely supported strongmen like Batista, assuming the Cubans were not fit for any other type of regime. The U.S. tourists also turned Havana into their vacation sex capital, where sexual exhibitionists like the famous "Superman" were avidly sought out.

There are as many interpretations of what-happened-to-turn-Cuba-to-Communism as there are people studying it, but the most believable interpretation is that Fidel Castro had no fixed ideology at all when he suddenly found Cuba in his lap. He did have an inchoate idealism about "changing Cuba." It was a question of wanting the old days to return again, and so they felt they had to make certain changes. Haydée Santamaría, *the* heroine of the revolution and a woman who fought next to Castro throughout the revolution, explained to me their interpretation of what happened, and I believe it is the most accurate explanation.

"In the mountains, we knew what we wanted, but we didn't know its name," she said. "It was just a necessary evolution. If we didn't talk about Socialism, we did talk about agrarian reform and housing reform. We knew we had to redistribute wealth, we knew with a professional army there would be a coup the first thing. We knew we had to form a people's army strong enough so no other country could intervene. Afterwards, the most important thing was to maintain power and to make the social transformations. We began to understand where we had to go. We didn't put a name on it, *they* (the wealthy and the United States) did. If we wanted education for the people, that was 'Communism.' If we wanted clinics for the people, that was 'Communism.' If we wanted land for the peasants, that was 'Communism.'"

In Cuba there had been no democratic ideology that might have offered a competitive ideology of modernization to Marxism. The United States, if it did not absolutely oppose Castro, was lukewarm toward social upheaval at a time when the government had been seized by a group of young people who saw their mission in apocalyptic terms. Therefore the interpretation that rings true is that the revolutionary Cubans became Marxists, step by step, and, at least partially, because there was no other place to go. There is no question, too, that Castro's brother Raúl and the Argentine revolutionary Ernesto "Che" Guevara were far more ideologically oriented than Castro himself and that they pushed and pulled him into a Marxist stance. Ernesto Betancourt, who was with Castro on his 1959 trip to the United States, reports how pleased Castro was with his reception, particularly at Princeton University, and how he remarked that he had not known Americans like those existed compared to the Americans he had known in Cuba.

But when Raúl phoned from Havana, Betancourt said, he would remind Castro: "They are saying down here that you are being taken over by the Americans; don't get too close to them." Equally telling, when Castro attempted a rapprochement with the United

States in 1963 through William Attwood, then a member of the American U.N. delegation, Attwood was constantly warned by the Cubans that Che should not be brought into this because he would not approve. It is not idle to speculate that Castro himself came to his totally hardened position against the United States only after Washington rejected every overture he made.

Within a year after he assumed power, the struggle between Fidel Castro and the Old Order was joined. But Castro had the charisma, Castro still held the people with him. And under the umbrella of faith in the maximum leader, he was able to take the consecutive steps that led Cuba—with no previously planned schedule or grand plan—to a Marxist form of modernization.

Cuba was largely an urban country (the estimated figure of urban residents was 57 percent before the revolution). One of the central problems was not farmland in the hands of a few owners, but city property in too few hands. Houses, apartment buildings and land were held in the cities by a relatively small number of owners, who charged exorbitant rents. One of the first things Castro did was to have the state take over all property, divide it up, and arrange for repayments to be made to former owners. This "urban reform," despite enormous tieups and mistakes, worked reasonably well, and within five years everyone was expected to own his own home.

When Castro broke with the United States in 1961 and nationalized the sugar centrals that were the economic lifeblood of the island, he did not do what other countries did regarding agrarian reform—that is, divide the land. Castro did not want a class of small proprietors. He was aware that the Cuban peasants already constituted a rural proletariat that did not worship the land. Instead he instituted state farms where agrarian workers were salaried. "This was Fidel's greatest insight," José Llanusa, minister of education and one of Castro's closest associates, told me five years later. "He saw that we should not divide up the land but rather hold it together."

The first few years were heady and fraught with danger on all sides—mostly with dangers from the "imperialists" of the North that Castro was all too willing to publicize and at times even create. For the youth of Cuba there was the headiness of the massive literacy campaign which sent thousands of young people into the most remote parts of the countryside in 1961 to teach the peasants how to read and write. When two literacy workers were killed by counterrevolutionaries, the literacy revolution had its first martyrs.

At the same time, the Castro government, prodded by that peripatetic revolutionary Che Guevara, reacted in a predictable way, considering Guevara's absolutist, revolutionary philosophy. As Che saw it, wrongly of course, the blame for what Cuba was could be put squarely on the United States for keeping Cuba non-industrialized, for keeping it a one-crop island and an agricultural producer. Che made up a list of the finished products which Cuba imported and shopped around in Eastern Europe for factories to produce them. Unfortunately for Cuba, after the factories arrived Che found out that it was cheaper to buy the finished products abroad than to produce them in Cuba. Like a careless housewife, he had forgotten to price the raw materials.

In those first five years of the revolution Cuba suffered the same total upheaval as Mexico had in 1910 and Bolivia had in 1952. It was a total social overturn—the third in modern Latin American history. The classes were reversed. The peasants and workers became the "upper classes," largely due to their new role in the party. As the wealthy left the island, their houses were taken over for the *becados* or scholarship students who were brought from all over the island to be trained at breakneck speed to become the New Class of the revolution. To replace the technicians who fled to Miami, Castro embarked upon a massive, high-speed program of training new technicians; they progressed as fast as they were able, and not in accordance with any set curriculum or time.

The once private elegant clubs of Havana and the provinces became public "social circles" and the beaches were open to everyone. I went out one Sunday to see the transformation. The Miramar Yacht Club, which used to have seventeen hundred members in all, had ten thousand visitors that day. The brown- and black-skinned Cubans covered the beaches like ants. "They even hold themselves differently since the revolution," said Llanusa, who was with me. We walked from one club to another—from El Náutico to the Casino Español to the Havana Yacht Club while thousands milled around us. "And there were even walls *between* the clubs in the old days," Llanusa said with a disgusted look.

The contrast between the Old Cubans and the New Cubans, the Old Order and the New, became even more dramatically evident a few minutes later when we visited the old race track outside Havana. It was still allowed to run, but with a noose around its neck. Llanusa, tall, lanky, informally dressed, with an open shirtcollar, a minister of education who had never been to college, was the personification of the revolution—its informality and newness. The Cubans at the races wore the long white pleated shifts in the old Cuban style. They had somewhat tired and languid eyes and they snapped their fingers while urging their horses to win. "Look at them, look at them," Llanusa kept saying. It was as if they were from two different worlds. And, indeed, they were.

In the years after his 1961 speech proclaiming himself a "Marxist and always a Marxist," Castro began to solve the international problems of Cuba with specific plans. The "problem" with the United States—both economic and psychological—he "solved" by breaking totally, and he was able to find a new godfather in the Soviet Union. The new godfather was eager to establish a base in Latin America. Land belonging to Americans was simply appropriated. Politically, he separated Cuba from its traditional dependence upon the United States, but allied it with a new dependence on the East. In the style of many of the little countries of the world, Cuba became a pawn between the big powers. But it became a cunning pawn, that new kind of little country pawn that is able, through a shrewd use of its very feminine dependency, to do pretty much what it pleased.

Cuba had become Communist, but it had become Communist in a very special way that is crucially important to the understanding of both nationalism and Communism and their many mixtures in Latin America. The Marxist impulse had been present in Latin America since the end of the nineteenth century, when Anarcho-Syndicalists and socialists infiltrated and eventually took over the labor movements from Argentina to Mexico. Next came the Soviet Communists and the Trotskyites, who still remain in little enclaves to this day. In the 1930s the Soviet Communists took over from the old Anarchists and largely from the socialists. They were better organized and they had a good deal of evangelical inspiration from the USSR. But the parties remained small in all the countries, never got more than a small percentage of the vote and, until 1964 in Chile, never came close to winning any election. Their strength was in the labor movement.

The original Soviet-line Cuban Communist party was one of those in the wave formed in the '30s, and it always slavishly had followed the Moscow line. It had cooperated with the dictator Batista and had not supported Castro in the Sierra Maestra until the very last moment, thinking Castro was a super-romantic and "bourgeois" revolutionary. The Cuban leader forgave or forgot, and even after he officially called himself a "Communist" he was one on nobody's terms but his own. By 1962 he was destroying the old Communist party and building his own indigenous Communist party, using those members of his original 26th of July movement who stayed with him into Communism. His party immediately began to ally itself ideologically and emotionally with the other "little Communists" of the world, like Vietnam. The Cubans felt a strong affinity with the Vietnamese. They were both pawns between the big blocs—and that included the big Communist countries as well as the capitalists.

But if it is interesting to ask how Fidel Castro became a "Communist," it is also interesting to ask how the Cuban people who today consider themselves Communists became such. After talking with scores of Cubans who placed themselves passionately in this category, I am convinced that, basically, they became Communists under the spell of Castro's personality. They were following the all-knowing traditional Latin American leader. And they remained with Communism because of the basic brotherhood and social equality which it offered them.

This came out constantly in the men I questioned. There was the recurrent theme of people being tired of the "old way," of wanting to be modern people. Rogelio Pardo, a young, thoroughly

Marxist student at the University of Havana, in talking about the "New Cuba," first pointed out the absence of beggars and prostitutes. Then he came to the changes in the family: "At home, my mother was always saying, 'Why don't you marry Fulana, she's a nice girl. I've known her mother for years.' That's the way things were. Now we say, 'I don't like her.'"

In Santiago, the second largest Cuban city at the eastern end of the island, I met a very pleasant Cuban Communist, a slim, serious young man named Nicolás Guillén. He was very rational in all his judgments and explored the presence of the Russians with an air of bewilderment, saying, "They are very strange. The Russian sailors get off the ships here and they walk around. They don't talk to anyone. I think it's because of the snow where they come from—there's snow all year round." When I asked him how he became a Communist, he answered: "Well, I had nothing to eat, and I fought with the rebel army and afterwards I went to work and in 1962 they came to my factory and said, 'We want you to choose the best worker, the person who cares most for his fellows, who has the greatest social conscience' . . . and they picked me." He smiled and added: "If what we have now, with enough to eat, and schools and work and a future—if this is Communism, then, yes, I am a Communist."

Another of the Cubans whom I especially liked was Alfredo González, a sergeant in the militia and a waiter at the former Irenee Dupont mansion in Varadero. The mansion was turned into a first-class restaurant after the revolution. Alfredo told fantastic tales about the old days. Every morning, he said, Mr. Dupont used to go out to feed the iguanas that then inhabited the end of the peninsula. They were from three to four feet in length. Later in the day, when the waiters were setting up tables outside, the iguanas would close around them and sometimes the men would have to flee. But whenever Dupont arrived, he related, as though capitalists were something special even to iguanas, the iguanas parted and cleared a path for him.

As to how he became a Communist, González, who was very friendly toward Americans and very complimentary about Dupont, said: "After the revolution, they kept making these laws, and they were good for the people, and then one day they said they were Communist."

Communism appeals to those Cubans who espouse it, but not only for economic reasons. González earned the same amount of money before the revolution. So did a young Negro mechanic I met one day in the cathedral square in Havana. "What is Communism to me?" he asked. "I'll tell you. It's social equality. Before, on Sundays, this square was filled with big cars. All the rich people went to church and prayed. I couldn't even go in and pray. Now they're gone and we all go to the sugar harvest together. This is the first government I've ever had that I would fight for." He, like most of the Cuban Communists, defined everything in terms of his narrow experience in Cuba. He insisted that "Negroes cannot walk on the streets in the United States or sit down in buses."

Cuba today is a mixture of forms. There is still the traditional Latin emotional identification with the leader. Dr. Claudio Palacios Mesa, a Cuban psychiatrist, described the relationship between Fidel and the people in the square in these words: "It was a kind of dialogue between him and the people. Oh, the people didn't speak, but from time to time they would applaud. They would find he was saying exactly the things they were feeling."

This identification sometimes took on bizarre forms. I saw films one day of the first meeting of the party Central Committee which met in Havana in 1966, when Castro suddenly announced that the United Socialist party of the revolution, which had been the interim party for several years, would now be called the Communist party. It was a surprise for everyone—an announcement from on high—but everybody dutifully cheered. Later, at the Bay of Pigs, I asked a little peasant Communist cell leader, Juan Martínez, how he became a Communist. He had been at that meeting and he described it emotionally, saying, "And when Fidel asked us what the name of the party should be, we all shouted 'the Communist party, the Communist party.'"

The obedience to Fidel—and the apparent joy in it—was made evident at the time by the posters all over Havana showing a brave-looking soldier with arm upraised and the exhortatory words: "Commander-in-chief, order us!" When I asked Cubans what this meant, they invariably supplied a variation of "Fidel can tell us to do anything and we will do it."

There is no question that Cuba has gone through a distinct, if ingrown, process of modernization. The society has been ordered, where before it was chaotic. There is equal opportunity for everyone who accepts the basic Marxist philosophy and expounds it. There is the distinct idea of creating New Men, and this is being done through everything from training in Marxism to the gigantic new sports program. But Cuba is a strange, often mystifying place to the foreign, non-Marxist mentality. It is difficult to assess the mixture of idealism and ruthlessness, brotherhood and hatred, constructive and destructive forces and decide what should be credited to Communism and what portion is accountable to Fidel's Cuba.

In the New Cuba, manual labor is idealized, in contrast to the old Cuba, where, as in all of Latin America, it was despised. "Moral incentives" strongly took the place of material incentives because, as Llanusa insisted, "If people are fighting for their country or for the social good, they have to do more. Communism *has* to do something better than capitalism." If it was somewhat naïve, it was also idealistic, and it was an idealism that Cuba had not known in any organized sense before.

Because of this theoretical approach (which is typically Latin), the cost of what Cuba set out to do was much higher than it needed to be. More could have been achieved with less waste, had the Cuban leaders taken a more pragmatic and a less theoretical and less absolutist approach. But as the revolution advanced —stumbled?—into its special form of Marxism, it grew more and more theoretical. Something had to be done because it was *right* to do it. The government sent white-collar workers and managers of offices and factories to work a week or a month in the canefields because it was *right* for every Cuban to share in the manual labor of the country. The fact that during this time the economic life of the country stopped bothered no one. It was Latin theorymongering gone mad.

It was also the exact opposite "solution" to Latin America's problems from, for instance, Chile's. Where Chile was pragmatic ("nationalizing copper would be an ideological decision"), Cuba was theoretical. Where Chile wanted simply to feed and clothe its people and construct a regime of justice and equality, Cuba was intent upon doing it with the right attitude. The cost of such theorizing was that hundreds of thousands of Cubans left, and by 1967 there was a list of more than another million waiting to leave. The entire middle class was destroyed, and the economy still was not on its feet.

In one area at least, Castro learned the hard way the results of such baseless theorizing: economics. By the mid-1960s, after Che's disastrous attempts at rapid industrialization, Castro realized that Cuba had always been an agricultural island because that was what it was peculiarly suited for. At Soviet urgings (the Soviets were horrified by many of the Cuban actions) Cuba returned to monoculture with a vengeance and all industry that was being built was being built around sugar.

Fidel Castro himself is in many ways a continuation of the old style of Latin leader. In many ways he is the *caudillo* and *macho* par excellence—physically powerful, masterful, sought after by women, the holder of all truth, the man who gets up in the Plaza de la Revolución before three hundred thousand people several times a year and witnesses to the truth of the revolution and to Cuba as truth's interpreter in Latin America. He is still the man the poor come to personally, as he roves restlessly around the countryside, seeing personally how every tender little coffee plant is growing and how every tender little Communist cell chief is getting along. He is still the traditional notetaker, and the notes go into his pocket for his secretary Celia Sánchez to empty out later and act upon.

Fidel's style could hardly be compared to that of the Chileans, those "New World managerial types." He abhors the life of administrator and the piece of furniture he hates most in the world is the abominable desk. "Me go to the office?" he declared to me once. "Never!" Then, very seriously, he added, "I think the office is a very unwholesome life. I learned that after the revolution, when I used to go into the office and receive everyone. Of every hundred, ten deserved to see me. I gave that up and went out among the people."

Still Fidel Castro is not an unalloyed "Old Latin" at all. He is a transitional type, for characteristics in him, as in the Cuban revolution, are very mixed. He is a *caudillo*, but a *caudillo* who feels the need to justify his power ideologically. He is very cognizant—and not totally approving—of the terrible reliance of the revolution on him as a person. Many, in particular Cuban exiles, think it naïve to think of Castro as anything other than a traditional *caudillo* with an obsession for power. However, this interpretation is very much oversimplified. He is certainly a man who sees himself as the second Simón Bolívar. But he is also a deeply intelligent man who seeks out and can appreciate ideas and opinions. Still, something else inside him—his ego, perhaps—demands that he surround himself with people who agree only with him.

One Sunday afternoon I went out with Castro on one of his typical trips to mingle with the people, to inspect the works of the revolution and to keep his hand on the pulse of the country. He picked me up in his private car, with the driver and José Llanusa sitting in front. In the back, I sat with him, a huge stack of books between us. He always carries books with him, sometimes as many as a hundred. He likes to be able to pick up something to read, on any subject at any time. We drove out to Santa María Beach, between Havana and Varadero Beach, because he wanted to show me some camping tents they had constructed for vacationers. As always people flocked to him, and for three and a half hours we stood there on the beach while he quizzed them. Was the revolution helping them? Was their housing all right? He joked with them, discussed sharks and the way they swim through the ocean, and urged the people on for the revolution.

While each member of the group clustered around him pushed forward to present his problems to Castro, or to get closer to the leader to listen, he constantly warned them: "No personal favors. We are doing the best we can. What we are trying to do for all is to build a strong economy. It is not so important for a man to have a bottle of cognac as for a child to have a school." Afterwards, as we sat at dinner in his beachhouse, he told me that the people were beginning to understand and asked for a smaller number of favors. "They now think of things as rights that they used to think of as favors," he said. He further talked about the "institutionalization of the revolution": "No one man will be that important anymore, for the revolution will go on its own." He spoke of the changes in the people, too. "They used to have fiestas in the countryside, and at the end everybody got drunk and had a fight," he said. "Now it's different. I think it's an element of the resentment of power. Now they don't feel they have to fight because they are in power—in the militias and the military. They take part in the entire society."

Another thing that has changed dramatically in post-Castro Cuba is the fact that friendships no longer play an important role. Relationships are far more functional. A man is considered for a position because of his capability, although the fervency of his faith in the revolution is also taken into account, but his family ties or whom he knows is of little concern to the choice. (One Cuban complained to me of Castro's doctor and closest associate, Raúl Vallejo, "Why, when he was studying in the hospital years ago, he had no place to sleep. I sent my bed to him. Now he won't do anything for me. They're all afraid to recommend anyone because of the possibility they'll do something wrong.")

Nor does friendship ever serve as an excuse for morality, for the Castro people are almost puritanically moralistic. In the spring of 1966 Castro purged about a hundred of his top aides, most of whom had been in the Sierra Maestra with him. Old friendship— even the fight together in the revolution—carried little weight. Nor had the men been doing anything subversive. They had simply been exercising their Cuban sensuality by staging some spectacular orgies which included, to Castro's dismay, some women members of the party who were supposed to be paragons of Communist morality.

The offenders had often been seen at private clubs, including one called El Torre, located on the top floor of a big old apartment building in downtown Havana. The guilty had all been sent to rehabilitation camps where they planted trees and did other things good for the soul, while they pondered their sins. The clubs were all as quiet as death. The great "high life" scandal was over. There was, however, whispering about the cook of one of the *commandantes* (the highest rank in the Cuban army) who had accompanied his boss to the orgies and told the judge that "before I never had enough to eat, and there I was in bed with four women!"

Castro talked about morality, especially revolutionary Communist morality, constantly. He was fervently creating New Men, and he wanted to control everything about them. He even complained about Cubans' diet choices, but he also admitted that they rebelled at his attempts to make them eat other foods. There is no question to anyone who knows Castro at all that he considers the work of the revolution as very moral. Still there was a mood adrift in Cuba of treating people like products, to fatten and form them; a quest to build the best sample in the world of ideologies.

There was also the curious Cuban collectivism, which was particularly strange for Latin America. Students in the university engaged in "collective study." No one talked about individuals; it was always "the people." But there was no doubt about the sense of brotherhood among the Communists. One Sunday afternoon near the beach at Siboney, the local Communist cell was meeting. They were having a picnic and giving out new ID cards. It reminded me strongly of a club meeting in the United States, with its informality and treatment of everyone as equals and its grave seriousness. When the leader gave out the ID cards, he said, "Be sure you know how to defend them—unto the death, if necessary."

Castro constantly posed questions of morality, in much the same way that students in college soberly ask each other unanswerable questions. One day in Banao in central Cuba, Castro, Llanusa and about thirty of his aides and I were sitting down to a barbecue lunch at one of his favorite model farms and Castro began to talk to me. "If you had to choose between your family and humanity, which would you choose?" he asked.

I demurred. It was such a hopeless question. We had been talking about the morality of journalism, so I tried to bring the conversation back to that. "There are people like me who shouldn't belong to anything," I said, in answer to his earlier statement that everybody had to take a stand. "There are people who should stand apart to see better where the truth really lies."

"You have to belong to the good, don't you?" he insisted, leaning forward eagerly. I nodded. "You don't believe in people dying of hunger? You don't believe in children sick, with no doctors?"

It was typical of Fidel to talk in such a vein, and it was typical of the Cuban revolution to feel it held within its arms all experience and all truth. Yet its morality can be terribly cruel. A visiting Canadian professor described the harshness as he related how a Cuban professor was suddenly taken prisoner. "He just disappeared," the Canadian explained. "He was in prison for three months and no one asked why. The other teachers said that under the last regime they used to make mistakes but now they don't. Nobody visited him and his wife was ostracized. I tried to argue with the other professors, 'This is a man you worked with.' But nobody would talk about it."

The Cuban revolution is also terribly egotistical, believing as it does that it holds the only revolutionary experience for Latin America. Partially this is based in the absolutism of the traditional Cuban, and partially it is based in the singularity of the Marxist belief. When I asked Cubans how they became Communists, it was common for them to say, "I found the truth."

Here was a continuation of the medieval idea of the unity of all truth. They did not believe in a pluralistic society or in the relativity of knowledge and truth. Like traditional Latins, they see objectivity as another creed. They talked a great deal about "solidarity" with the other countries of the world, but it was a qualified solidarity which lasted as long as other countries agreed completely with Cuba. When incidents of disagreement developed, then the Swiss ambassador was a "fool," the papal nuncio ought to be "shipped home," the Czechs were the new Yugoslav revisionists, and the Canadians might trade with them but they were "still capitalists" and one ought not to forget it.

Along with this singleness of thought there is now among Cuban Communists a passionate feeling for the land. This is typical of all the new Latins, for one of their major characteristics is their fervency to reclaim the land, and particularly from foreign ownership. This is indicated in the passion attached to reclaiming contracts wherein subsoil investment is held by foreign companies; it has about it the characteristics of a man protecting his woman from rape by an intruder.

More than any other people in Latin America the Cuban Communists have ingeniously used public manpower to plant and prune the land. In Santiago and other cities they have planted rings of trees around the cities to "refresh" the climate. As Nicolás Guillén, the local party propaganda chief in Santiago, said: "The people plant the fruit trees—thirty-two thousand of them. Then they come to take care of them." And the harvest? I asked. "The agrarian reform office does that and then sells the fruit back to the people. They plant them and take care of them and then buy them back, and they are happy."

Castro himself is a zealot when it comes to a concern for the land. When I was a guest for supper at his beachhouse at Santa María, we wandered out to the front of the house at sunset and he showed me the neat and beautiful rows of pines they had planted in the sand between the house and the sea. Only a few nights before there had been a storm, and a number of the branches had been torn from the trees and were lying on the beach. "How monstrous, what the storm did," Fidel said, picking up a branch. He said it with intense feeling.

But if Cuba is in many ways different, in many ways it is still the same. The more rigid East European Communists constantly complain about the Cubans' playfulness. How could a "serious Communist" take the graduating medical school class on a hike to Pico Turquino, the highest peak in Cuba, and then invite the diplomatic corps to come up in helicopters? When his pack was strapped on his back for the trip, the Romanian ambassador reneged, thinking it was a parachute. The foreign Communists also complained about the barely clad showgirls in the Tropicana nightclub before the clubs were closed in 1968. The girls wriggled just as they had in the old days under capitalism, even if now they were singing ideological lyrics ("Now is the time to be free of Washington, Jefferson and Lincoln"). And the foreign Communists complained endlessly about the messiness of everything, and the waste. "What I could do with all the wood they waste on carnival," an East German confided to me.

The Cuban route to modernization was not to spread out power, as the Chileans were doing. Their idea was to centralize power even more than it already was centralized. Cuba had become the most centralized, the most socialized government within the Communist bloc. There were no Soviets, no parliamentarianism, no multiparty system such as still existed in Eastern European countries and even in the Soviet Union. "To us these things are fictions," Carlos Rafael Rodríguez, one of the major Communist ideologues in Havana, told me. "We think of ourselves as being in the avant garde."

Nor were there any apologies about the total subservience of the intelligentsia to the cause of Communism. Here there was no place for an individual conscience. "Individual conscience?" Lisandro Otero, editor of the magazine *Cuba* and one of the young Castroite intellectuals, asked. "It depends upon what kind of conscience it is. If it is counterrevolutionary, there is no place for it. We don't have to give the right to anyone to go above the system. We're in a period of dictatorship to destroy all of the past. In this period, there is no room for a dissident conscience." Juan Felipe Carneardo, director of the Castroite wire service Prensa Latina, put it another way: "There is a socialist objectivity and a capitalist and bourgeois objectivity. Abstract objectivity does not exist."

The Cubans' traditional Spanish individualism carried over into their insisting, between 1965 and 1967, on forming their own indigenous Latin American Communism and, in effect, reading the Soviets out of revolutionary strategy in Latin America. The ideological break had been brewing for several years, as the old-line Soviet Communist parties in the hemisphere had increasingly balked and disagreed with Castro's violent approach. The Soviet Union was seeking diplomatic and commercial ties throughout Latin America and its Latin parties took the line that the eventual revolution could best be served through political action and united fronts.

But Castro continued to look at himself as the second Bolívar, and the idea of the long-range, nonviolent revolution was unthinkable to him. So in the winter of 1967 he formulated his own anti-Soviet, indigenous Latin American Communism, and published his ideas in a book written by a young French Marxist, Jules Régis Debray, called *Revolution Within the Revolution?*

Debray was the French counterpart of Castro. A freethinking, freewheeling, eclectic Marxist, he turned his back on the big Marxist blocs as well as the capitalist blocs. The "Debray philosophy," which was really the Castro philosophy, snatched revolution out of the hands of the old Soviet parties and put it squarely in the hands of the "revolutionary armies" in Latin America—armies patterned exactly after Castro's original band in the Sierra Maestra. It was a call to guerrilla warfare on a massive scale. At the same time Castro was increasing his support for, and organization of, the guerrillas of the hemisphere.

What was crucially important about the new philosophy, too, was the fact that throughout the book runs the theme that morality and goodness and revolutionary fervor and the real Latin America lies in the countryside, in the peasantry. The strategy is for the movements born in the countryside, as was the case with Castro, to swoop down on the corrupt old cities (where, not incidentally, the Soviet-line parties are based) and transform Latin American society for all time. It is another attempt to seek out the "real" Latin America, and it is related to concepts such as Father Vekemans' idea that the continent is colonized around the edges with the rest of it existing in marginal form inside.

Castro himself was a champion of the idea that the marginal form is the authentic form and that this is what must be strengthened in order to take over the corrupt old society. Yet perhaps no one personified all these conceptions—eventually he gave his life for them—so dramatically as Ernesto Che Guevara.

Castro always considered the revolution would transcend Cuba; he always sought its historic purpose in its universality. He hoped to devise the model for the "continental revolution" in Latin America. But to Che, who was hailed in Havana after his death as a "citizen of Latin America," the oneness and unity of Latin

America was a passion that permeated his entire life and existence.

As a student he had wandered from Argentina to Bolivia, where he watched the impassioned faces of the revolutionaries who took over in the revolution of 1952. He was in Guatemala for the fall of the pro-Communist Jacobo Arbenz in 1954; Che watched land which had been given to the peasants go back to the wealthy landowners, and he seethed with indignation.

When he met Castro in Mexico, where Castro was assembling his invasion crew for Cuba, Che immediately joined up. He had come upon his life's work.

To the dissident mind, Che quickly became a hero. Irreverent, charming, dreaming of a "new world," Che personified, more even than Castro, the new revolutionary. A violent man, he believed you had to destroy the old system with the gun in order to create a new one. A very human man, he once wrote to a woman who had asked him if they might be related: "I doubt very much that we are related, but if you are capable of trembling with indignation each time an injustice is committed in the world, then we are comrades, and that is more important."

Eventually Che decided he must act on the imperatives that molded his entire life, that the time had come to extend the mystical Cuban revolutionary experience to other lands. In 1966 he suddenly disappeared from Cuba. Che with the ironic eyes, Che with the flippant manner and the burning revolutionary passions—one day he was gone. Castro, noticeably moved, announced that Che had gone to "other lands" to liberate people by implanting revolution.

Every early act that Che performed testified to his belief—one of the very basic ideas of all the New Latins of all political beliefs—in the oneness and potential solidarity of Latin America. He chose Bolivia for his first attack because Bolivia was the most centrally located. It would be easy—so he thought—to overthrow that suicidally unstable little country with its 179 revolutions. He then planned to move on to the countries that bordered it. Today Bolivia; tomorrow, Argentina, Paraguay, Chile.

But from the beginning nothing went quite right. The new— the passion for unity, for "one America," for respect for the individual—was constantly impinged upon by the old: autocratic control, lack of respect for national characteristics, a certain crazy, bizarre quality that seemed to permeate everything.

The guerrillas moved in and out of Bolivia as if they were tourists. Tania, the Argentine girl who was the only female guerrilla, worked in the foreign ministry for a while and roomed with the foreign minister's secretary. "I knew she was a radical girl with free ways," Foreign Minister Walter Guevara commented later. "But so what? There are many like that."

Che set up camp in the mountains and forests on the east side of the Andes, and he remained in the camp, reading, while Bolivians were "recruited." Some of the recruits thought they were going to Cuba; others, to the Soviet Union. When they found they were guerrillas, they were stunned. A number fled, and told the Bolivian officials everything.

Che never took the nationalism of the Bolivians into account. The Cubans were in all the positions of power and told the Bolivians what to do. Che's men held the Bolivian experience and the Bolivian will in such low regard that they walked through the mountains with no security and no scouts, falling into ambush after ambush.

It was an overconfidence that bordered on the profligate that killed them. A few months afterwards, I sat in the prison in Camiri, a hot little oil town in the area where Che had been, talking with Ciro Bustos, the Argentine artist who had been arrested with Che. "The biggest problem was Che's vision of the revolution as continental," Bustos said, "so he didn't see the drawbacks of choosing Bolivia.

"He underestimated Bolivia—the army, the will, the nationalism. He simply didn't expect the army to fight as it did. Then there was the fact that the Cubans were a drawback." He shook his head. "There were too many Cubans."

By the time Bustos was analyzing the failure of the "continental revolution"—the "second Latin American war for independence" —Che had been dead for several months. On October 8, 1967, he was captured by Bolivian Rangers after weeks of wandering hopelessly through the forests. Che had written much earlier that the support of the peasants was necessary in any guerrilla movement but they had reacted to him with empty stares and cryptic parables. "They are impenetrable as rocks," he wrote in his diary. "When you talk to them, it seems that in the depths of their eyes they are mocking you."

About 1:30 P.M. that afternoon, near the remote village of La Higuera, Che suddenly found himself face to face with Captain Gary Prado, a tall, hawk-nosed leader of ninety Bolivian Rangers. "I am Che Guevara and I'm worth more to you dead than alive," the guerrilla leader said. A few minutes later he added: "We didn't know the Rangers were going to be here. Everywhere we go, there are soldiers."

When Prado ordered his men to cover their flanks, Che said with his bittersweet smile, "Don't worry, Captain, this is all over."

A soldier, Tito Sánchez, said jubilantly, "The chief has fallen, Captain; with this, the guerrillas are finished."

The comment revived Che. Looking steadily at the soldier, he said: "Don't be naïve, my friend. The revolution does not have a chief." Then, turning to Prado, he said, "Very soon, Captain, these same soldiers that you now command will be shooting at you."

The next day Che died—killed with a gun and a machete by a Bolivian sergeant, one of the men he hoped to "liberate." But the legend grew. His body was carried by helicopter to the nearby town of Valle Grande. An almost pure Spanish town, with women wearing black shawls over their heads even in the morning sunlight, Valle Grande has a sad desolate air about it. Swathed in whitewash and restless dark shadows, it seems itself to be a town in perpetual mourning.

There the body was laid on boards laid across washtubs in the open laundry house of the hospital, and all day long the people of Valle Grande filed by to see who had been Che Guevara.

Anyone who saw the body maintains that it had a strange aura about it. The eyes were open. The resemblance to Christ—the long hair and beard, the mystical expression, the comparison of riding on a mule during his last days—caused many peasants in the area to develop a deeply superstitious feeling about Che.

In La Higuera, where he was killed, the villagers feared there were more guerrillas who would return and take vengeance upon them for the death. Soldiers preserved locks of his hair in memory. Windows all over Valle Grande displayed the strange grisly pictures of Che in death, as the townspeople fed the cherished legend with their own dark Spanish curiosity and superstition. The body disappeared—secretly buried by the Bolivian army to avoid any "cult of Che" from arising.

The Che story should have ended there. But it didn't end, and most probably it never will end.

To the restless young idealists of Latin America, Che was the consummate hero. In razor-sharp contrast to the bloated, egotistical men of the Latin American past, Che was a knight of the future. He represented the ultimate sacrifice—the sacrifice of one's self for others, for Latin America itself.

But in truth Che's revolutionary movement—his revolutionary impulse—represented things that were both very old and very new. He was a man who dreamed of the very best for Latin America and often attempted to reach it with the very worst elements in Latin America.

At the heart of it all, however, is the Cuban experience, and it points up a great deal. Why Cuba went to Communism is an interesting question, but it is not the crucial issue about the Cuban experience. What Cuba and its road to modernization shows is that the Latin American people are receptive to being formed, and that they can be formed in a variety of ways. The revolution points up a country that was dramatically ready for change, despite its outward patina of sluggish, sensual tropicality; and a country existing without a rival democratic ideology of modernization to confront the impact of Marxism. For Marxism took over by default. It also shows that many young Latins are willing to sacrifice themselves for the concept of Pan Americanism —Latin unity—and not only nationalism.

Cuba today is the exact opposite of Chile. Cuban Communists have engaged in a war to the ideological death. Chile represents European political thought in an attempt to form a democratic, egalitarian, pluralistic society whose evangelical inspiration is radical Christianity. Cuba represents the hot, tropical, super-

Spanish traits, and proclaims the singleness and unity of all truth and the centralization of all power—but at the same time the equality of man and the dignity of work. Which one, if either, will "win" in Latin America is a question that will remain unanswered for a long time. What is important is that they represent two dramatic new approaches to change and modernization and prove the continent's essential readiness and search for change.

At best the Cuban experience is baffling. At the seminar in Puerto Rico the Cuban exile leaders lambasted Castro during the sessions. They could not find one word of approbation for Castro's Cuba—children were without milk, people were in concentration camps, land had been stolen.

But in the evenings, as they stood with drinks in their hands, the expressions were quite different. Two of them confessed that, could they do it again, they would not have left Cuba. One of the top exile leaders added, "If I gained power, you know what I would do? I would erect a statue to Fidel Castro. I think he is the only one who could have taken care of our problems with the United States and modernized the country."

CHAPTER 8

Chile—Is Peaceful Revolution Possible?

"We do not like dogmatics." Gabriel Valdés, Foreign
Minister of Chile.

Santiago de Chile is a gray city, so unlike the hot, bright cities of
the Caribbean and "tropical" Latin America. It is thoroughly un-
derstated. Men talk and act without flamboyance; they rarely
wave their arms and they take pride in being called "the English-
men of Latin America." The Chilean women are notably pretty,
and the men take pride in that too. Chileans have had revolutions,
at times, but they prefer not to talk about it—it embarrasses them
a little. In short the Chileans are admirably, tiresomely, predict-
ably legalistic—they believe in the rule of law and correctly as-
sume there will be order. And outsiders often ask in puzzlement,
"Are they Latins?"

Election day, September 4, 1964, was typically Chilean. But
alongside the obsessive order there was another, un-Chilean element: it was fear. For though the country is restrained, it ordinarily
is also happy, and that day there was a cold rigid fear that
shrouded its usual celebration of electoral propriety. The fear had
eaten into the body of Chile for weeks and it was, for Latin America, a weird and unseemly feeling—there was a good possibility
that a convinced Marxist would win in a free election.

For weeks the fear had slowly crept over the country. There
would be quiet at a party and then someone would start laughing

almost hysterically and saying, "But it couldn't happen here, but no, but no . . ." People started hoarding. A Chilean industrialist leaned forward across his desk and said deliberately to a foreign visitor, "One . . . has . . . to . . . realize . . . that one may have to leave, and we are . . . prepared for this." Then, humanly, "But I already escaped from Fascism in Europe once"—wistfully— "only to leave again?"

The Marxists were enraptured and confident. The Apocalypse had come, and they would be voted into power. At the night rallies in the gray streets of Santiago, red flags appeared and there was an air like the '30s in the United States when socialism was expected to triumph.

If Chilean history could have been halted for a moment on that day, in a historic frieze, the study of the country would have revealed many interesting social currents. But basically and most importantly it would have provided a cross section of Latin America as a whole, changing for all time and changing in the way that many feel all of Latin America will change in the next twenty-five years.

The popular gendarmes, who in Chile are like "fathers" to the people and take care of them, unlike the more predatory Latin American policemen elsewhere, were stationed on every street corner all day. Santiago was quiet, and Chileans went dutifully if tensely to the polls. I went out that day to the *callampas*, the shantytowns around Santiago, for I wanted to gauge the mood. Everywhere change was in the air.

In the Callampa Club de Polo, a scattering of houses on the riverbed near the mountain range and immediately next door to the aristocratic polo club from which it took its name, people stood in the early spring sun and talked.

"That's the polo club," one said to me, with a gesture of his arm. "They have everything—tennis, polo. Here, children play with dirt. We don't have a doctor, not a school. When we call an ambulance it takes two or three hours and by the time it gets here the person's dead."

In contrast to other *callampas*, Club de Polo had decent little two-room wooden houses. They were neat inside, with pictures from magazines tacked to the walls and embroidered things strewn about. "We try to arrange them as nice as possible," one young housewife said. "You have to eat less in order to pay the fifteen *escudos* a month (about five dollars at that time) rent." The average salary was three *escudos* or a little over a dollar a day. Most families had from four to eight children.

Like most of the *callampas* and most of the marginal towns all over Latin America, they were on the outskirts of the city. This particular community lay close to the two stark ranges of the Andes that enclose Santiago like two long black arms. In the center of the city, it was sunny and light; on either side, there were always the shadows. One man—one of the dark but jaunty Chilean types who seems to have so much more spirit about them than the "oppressed" elsewhere in South America—with barely controlled anger pointed his finger at the polo club.

"You see that fence," he said. "Inside that fence there is a little stream that used to be ours. The fence used to be on their side of the stream. Then they moved the fence and even took our stream."

When I asked him what he wanted of life, he looked up at the foothills of the mountains, which at that time of year look as though a lacework of snow has been stretched over them, and said with a strangely romantic symbolism: "We don't have any way to get to a civilized neighborhood. We always have to be in the shadow of the mountains."

Everyone voted that day—rich, poor, old, young, aristocrats, those in the shadows, those in the sunlight—for Chile was like that. Not far from the Club de Polo I picked up a very old, very wrinkled and very poor man and took him to the polls at the Escuela Militar del General Bernardo O'Higgins, named after the liberator of Chile in the wars of the independence. He walked nonchalantly into a polling place where most of the people were obviously well-to-do, and did it without, apparently, the slightest reservation. "We're all together," he said as he waved good-bye, "not rich in one place and poor in the other."

The last tableau in the frieze came later that night. From about 5 P.M. on, when the polling was over, a hush settled over Santiago. There was no one in the streets. Dr. Salvador Allende, the Marxist candidate and a serious doctor who looked very bourgeois indeed, waited in his red-bannered headquarters in a scabrous old building downtown, while his lieutenants milled about in exuberant spirits. A mile away, on the broad Alameda Boulevard, the other party headquarters, the Christian Democrats, middle- and lower-class Catholics and social reformers, many of them of a very radical cast, waited in equally high spirits. They were correspondingly convinced in their own apocalyptic way that their man, the lean, hawk-nosed, deep-eyed Eduardo Frei, would win.

About nine o'clock the word began to spread, first by word of mouth from the polling places, then by radio: Eduardo Frei was winning. The first Christian Democrat president in Latin America? Then Eduardo Frei was pulling far ahead; then far, far ahead. Chileans began to pour into the somber downtown areas. The streets are lined with gray buildings that all resemble banks. It was an atmosphere that can only be described as delirious.

In his offices, Allende's men grew incredulous, then angry. Allende's teenaged daughter, Maria Isabela, a pretty brunette biology student, began to weep. Senator Salomón Corbalán, coordinator of the party, said gruffly, when it was suggested that Allende go to Frei's house to congratulate him: "I'm opposed to it. This is not a football match." Outside on the street the more radical Trotskyite youth of the party began to shout for "revolution." But Allende, dignified, went to the balcony and told his followers to accept the election results "calmly and with dignity."

Soon the streets of Santiago were transformed into carnival, as massive feelings of relief poured out onto the sidewalks. Young people rode around in trucks, twisting and blowing New Year's noisemakers and wearing colored hats. They danced in snakelines down the Alameda. On the scoresheet outside Frei headquarters the figures mounted and mounted until it became clear Frei had won an absolute majority, almost unheard of in Chile.

About ten o'clock, Eduardo Frei, gaunt, spiritual-looking, emerged on the balcony of his simple little house in a suburban neighborhood and, too moved to speak, simply acknowledged the tumultuous applause of the crowds who had gathered there all evening. Downtown, Renán Fuentealba, chairman of Frei's party, read a victory statement calling on Chileans to join in achieving "the transformation of our political democracy into a real social and economic democracy."

And the next day Frei himself, at a victory press conference, gave his interpretation of what had happened. "I believe this country elected various things simultaneously," he said slowly and surely. "The people voted between democracy and a totalitarian danger, but it was not simply this. They did not want to keep living under the present modes. They saw that the present forms were very limited. In consequence, they voted in favor of democracy, but a democracy that extends itself to the majority. In one word, this country wants change, but it does not want to sacrifice liberty. If anyone thinks we are going to continue things as they are, they are mistaken."

That election night in 1964 could have been an ordinary election; it could have been, had the world not changed. But the world had changed and the election was not ordinary. Within one electoral period, Chile had moved from a balance of political elements that had existed since the nineteenth century to a choice between two revolutionary ideologies that offered a total change in the country's substance.

From the 1800s on, Chile, like most of the Latin American countries, had been ruled by groupings of parties which usually called themselves conservatives, liberals and radicals. One had taken over from the other consecutively, and each time a little more of the populace was integrated into the body politic. At one time the titles had meant something—at one time the radicals had been radical, for instance—but not by 1964. By that time, the radicals represented only a small portion of the ownership classes. The conservatives, formerly the stronghold of the Catholic hierarchy, were even out of style with the newly liberalized, conciliar hierarchy. The cardinal himself supported land reform. Yet somehow no one quite realized that the outward "reality" of those three parties, and the classes they represented, no longer was real.

It took an unsung little local election in the town of Curicó, early in 1964, to stun the country into the awareness that the earth had moved. In that election, the two "out" parties, the Marxist coalition of socialists and Communists called the FRAP, and the Christian Democrats, suddenly became the "in" parties. These two parties of the left—one Marxist, one Christian—emerged as the only real contenders. The masses of Chilean people had come to the fore and were finally conscious of their existence.

The Marxist candidate won in Curicó, causing such political upheaval that the radical candidate for president, who everyone had formerly assumed would win, dropped from the race, his party collapsed. The word quickly traveled around Latin America that something big had happened in Chile.

Actually had anyone looked carefully and not relied upon traditional gauges, he could have seen the changes coming for some time. There was an element of inevitability about it. Chile, first of all, was the one country where change had historically come about peacefully, where people had always reacted rationally in times of stress. The Chileans believed in law and not in palace coups, something that grew out of their nineteenth-century experience. Chile was more Central European in outlook and less pure Spanish than the rest of Latin America. The fact that Chile absorbed large immigrations of German, Hungarian, Basque and other non-Castilian blood was a major fact, for instance, in the Vatican's decision to choose Chile as the first country for its "Catholic revolution." It was not unalloyed Latin; it was malleable. "Of course, Chile is the first country to attack," one of the leaders of the "Catholic revolution" told me once. Because it's the least Latin? "Of course!"

The ensuing waves of immigrants—men who did not share in the Latin's traditional singleness of motive and dominance of ego—settled Chile. The country became known as "little Europe" and in the European holocausts of this and the last century, refugees poured into Chile. Frei himself was the son of a Swiss immigrant. Parsimonious, a devout husband and father of seven, simple to the point of monasticism in his habits of living—there was little of the traditional Latin in him. Many of his top men were not Latin. Radomiro Tomic, the man groomed to be his successor, was of Yugoslav descent. Even Frei's Marxist opponent, Dr. Allende, though he had a typically Latin reputation for a fondness for the ladies, had few of the other traditional Latin traits or weaknesses. Honest, dedicated, serious, intelligent—even his enemies described him in this way.

Still if Chile did not have the acute traditional political problems of the other Latin American countries, it did have its economic and social problems. It was a political democracy but not a social democracy. Economically 30 percent of the population existed outside the national market, a major factor of marginality. The economic life of the country was totally controlled by extended family groupings to which no outsider need apply. The idea of an "impersonal" American corporation simply did not exist, and the Chilean conservatives' traditional anti-Americanism really stemmed from a resentment of egalitarian and open practices. In each family grouping there was someone who owned a bank or headed a bank, and often he would also hold ministerial rank in the government. The customary rate of interest banks collected was 18 percent, effectively cutting out any newcomers to finances.

Socially 20 percent of the Chileans were private servants and more than 50 percent worked in service capacities. Thirty-seven percent of the population received 8 percent of the wealth; 19 percent received 47 percent; and 10 percent got 45 percent. The country was far more urban—around 60 percent—than the rest of Latin America, a fact which partially explained why its politics radicalized so rapidly. People were hungry, United Nations surveys showed. Life expectancy was less than forty years, and though Chile had been a food surplus country until 1940 it began importing food because of the inefficiency of the *fundos* or haciendas; by 1964 it was importing $140 million in food a year, using up any capital that might be invested for internal development.

Physically Chile was one of the Latin countries whose sheer beauty made up for a lot of other deficiencies. In the North is the Atacama Desert, the driest hills of sand in the world. The Atacama was once described by a group of scientists from the California Institute of Technology as having surpassed all their expectations "in its similarities to what we expect to find on Mars." Chile took the Atacama, then rich in nitrates, from Peru and Bolivia in the War of the Pacific in 1883 and made a fortune out of it. Today the old mining camps sit along the roadside as ghost towns. At one, Pampa Union, the old Sevillana nightclub stands like a bombed-out shelter in the desert.

In central and southern Chile the country is one of the most stunning places on earth. Volcanoes, snow-covered all the year around, stand above turquoise lakes. The land grows thick green grass which is reminiscent of the Austrian Alps. The villages are Germanic-looking, reflecting the German emigration at the turn of the century. About two-thirds of the way down Chile the roads end and one of the great wildernesses of the world begins, with a spattering of towns and pockets of people isolated in a majestic mountain fastness. At the very bottom is the remote and barren island of Tierra del Fuego, the last and loneliest place on earth.

Perhaps partially because of this beauty Chileans are deeply patriotic. Even though several hundred thousand of them have had to emigrate to neighboring Argentina to work, they have clung to their Chileanness. One of these explained, typically, "It is not Chile's fault that she cannot give me work."

But both the Frei people and the Allende people felt it *was* Chile's fault; they believed it was time for the *rotos* to enter Chilean society. *Roto* means literally "torn one" or "broken one" and it is the term given to the peasants and to the poor in Chile. The fact that there is a "Day of the *Rotos*" observed throughout Chile in which their values of humility and stalwartness were celebrated no longer seemed enough to the new leaders.

The two new movements both really began to take form in the 1930s and both claimed they could integrate the masses into Chilean life. The Christian Democrats were formed when Frei, then a young senator, took a group of young reform Catholics out of the conservative party, then the bastion of Catholic political power, and formed a new party which was first called the Falangue. Inspired by the teachings of Jacques Maritain, the French layman-philosopher who outlined the twentieth-century philosophy of the involvement of the individual Catholic in the modern political milieu ("As concerns the revitalized democracy we are hoping for, the only solution is of the pluralistic type"), the party early stressed the importance of ideology. "We believe very much in ideology,"

Father Renato Poblete, a Jesuit who works closely with the Christian Democrats, says. "There must be content in organizations, or else they will become Communist. Anyone who holds the same principles can belong. It is not confessional at all. The Church has a concrete doctrine, but it's not going to tell the Christian Democrats how to do it. It only asks the Christian Democrats to hold the doctrine." This was a long way from the theoretical absolutism of the traditional Latins.

Just as the party was getting started conservative priests appealed to Rome, warning the Vatican against the radical ideas of Frei. But Frei was upheld, some say personally by the pope. Frei only worked harder and never changed his position, always stressing that only Christian Democracy was really "new" for Latin America. "Just as there is a rightist reaction that is atrophied," he said, "so there is an atrophy in the extreme left. Our only solution lies in the rational economic development and in the equitable distribution advocated by the democratic left."

The Christian Democratic philosophy was always carefully spelled out for the people, and the party stressed that it would not, as had so many other Latin American parties, change or give up principle with time, because it had its roots in the Catholic social doctrine. It believed not in man for the state, as does Marxism, but the state for man. It believed in cooperativism and free association. It believed in curbing monopolies and, where possible, "communitarianism," a vague concept that as far as anyone seemed to know meant that workers own their own factories. It believed, as in Marxism, that the interests of the entire community—the *bien común* the Christian Democrats called it—preceded the interests of the individual. Frei ran third in 1958.

In the 1940s the Church hierarchy itself began to change. Since it was changing not in the vanguard but in the wake of the laymen's activities in the party, it is generally considered that the party transformed the Church. Here is another example of the spontaneous reform impulse on the part of individual Latin American men acting outside the organized sectors.

Alberto Hurtado, a Jesuit, was one spiritual force that began to force change in the Church by involving the Chilean priests in social causes. By the time he died in 1952, the cardinal consciously sought out a priest to take his place, and he came upon Father Roger Vekemans, the Belgian-born son of a Marxist father. Father Vekemans is tall, handsome and, by anyone's account, brilliant. Lacking neither confidence nor ideas, he could soon be seen about Santiago with his long cigarette holder, shaking his shaggy head in glee as he threw himself into the study of Latin American society with rare energy. There are other priests who have had substantial influence in the Chilean scene. But if the object is to isolate any *one* force, any *one* intelligence, any *one* brilliance, it must be Vekemans'.

One of the first things Father Vekemans did after he was transported across the sea to carry on the Catholic Church's new offensive in Latin America was to form the *Centro Bellarmino* or Bellarmine Center, where he brought together various highly qualified priests in a dark old building on a corner of the Alameda, to think. A "brain trust," he called it. Others, less charitably, called it a "nest of radicals." Nonetheless, it certainly was a major force for social change in Chile. Father Poblete, one of the brain trust, explained: "The revolution is not only political but cultural and religious. Some group had to have the time and capacity and scope to analyze signs of change and to see what the Christian answer to these things is."

The Bellarmino group, named for Robert Bellarmine, the early head of the Jesuits who concerned himself with the Church in the world, was not intended to remain simply at the thought level; nor did it. It wrote the letter for the Catholic bishops, published in 1961, in which they called for land reform. It published a monthly magazine, *Mensaje* or "Message," in which everything from birth control to the right of property was exhumed from the depths of traditional silence. When it published a special and especially provocative issue on "Revolution," the government withdrew its ads but *Mensaje* and its devil-making went irreverently on.

Father Vekemans then moved to the next step—the *inevitable* next step, in the Christian Democrat scheme of things. He formed an organization called DESAL or the Center for Economic and

Social Development of Latin America, which then proceeded to the business of developing "intermediate organizations." In many respects this organization is the most crucial thrust of the entire Christian Democrat (and thus Roman Catholic) idea for change in Latin America, for it is the means by which the lonely, alienated individual is brought into the mainstream of Latin American life.

"In classic Latin American society," Vekemans says, "you find the dichotomy between the state and the atomized dust, and nothing in between. Nothing in between the state and the individual. The individual takes no real part in decisions, for he is living in a formal democracy. We want our people to live in a real authentic democracy where all the decisions are participated in by them. A country like Chile is changing," he concludes, "from a hierarchical society to an open society, from a closed society which prefers passive responses to an open society which demands active ones."

The idea was to create (from the unrepresentative formalism of democracy in a country like Chile) a "real social and political and economic democracy" by establishing the pressure groups that provide the give and take of a democracy. They were willing to borrow from any quarter—co-ops from the Swedish system, savings and loan associations from the United States, agrarian leagues from the Belgians, even kibbutzim from Israel. And so Vekemans and DESAL set out to organize the "new fabric of society from the bottom up." They organized labor unions, mothers' groups, community groups, and peasant federations. Self-help was a holy concept. "Nothing is donated," Vekemans said, "no charity at all. In our idea, charity is worse than Communism."

At the same time, the German Catholics had begun looking at Latin America and, through a unique governmental arrangement in West Germany by which the government matched in foreign aid all money given by the churches, German money began pouring into DESAL. Outside financial assistance totaled $26 million in 1964; by 1966 it was $80 million, including Belgian, French and even American AID money.

The Chilean Christian Democrats were concerned with abolishing authoritarianism and paternalism, and Frei pointed out: "The

central tenet of Christian Democracy is the belief that we are witnesses to the crisis of a world exhausted, to the death of paternalism, and to the birth of a civilization of work and solidarity
with man as its center, rather than the pursuit of monetary gain
that has pervaded the bourgeois society." They were also imbued
with new ideas regarding the traditional relationship of Latin Americans to the United States.

Frei in particular was deeply concerned with the Latin American
complex about the United States, and about the "dependence"
of the Latins in blaming their condition on North America, as if
they had no will of their own. He kept stressing that they had to
open a triangular relationship, between Latin America, Europe
and the United States, in which Europe (which never had the
emotional connotations to Latin America that the United States
had, not being a sibling) would act as the escape valve for Latin
America's paranoia about the States. He made it clear that the
Latins had to accept their own blame, look at themselves and what
they were and change if they could not live as they were in the
modern world.

Father Vekemans, sitting in his bustling little office in Santiago
as the money poured in from all over the world, went even further.
He formulated an entire philosophy of how, if he was to enter the
modern world, Latin American man himself must change. He
said flatly that the Latin American could not gain what he aspired
to—modernization of his societies—being what he was. It was a
fault, as he saw it, of the traditional Latin man's reliance on the
testimony of the all-knowing leader, rather than seeking scientific
proof on which to act. He explained that the Latin Church must
change and become less Latin centered. In analyzing the Catholic
influence, he observed: "It seems obvious that the different
Catholicisms of this region, Dutch, Belgian, northern French,
northern Italian, Swiss and Bavarian, have managed because they
share a frontier, to make the synthesis between genuine Catholicism and the motor values of social progress: science and technology."

Nor were men like Vekemans acting alone. His actions were
part of a conscious and deliberate Catholic effort, which reached

to the inner sanctums of the Vatican, to form a new postconciliar Catholic Church in Latin America and to revive the fading power of Catholicism. It was the Catholic Church re-entering politics in a new, modern, and revolutionary way, for the old methods had clearly failed.

There was the brutal realization that if Latin America could not be saved for Catholicism and Western civilization (it is, the Christian Democrats keep stressing, the only part of the under-developed, uncommitted world that is Western) both might well fall. And there was the impatience of the young (50 percent of Chileans were under twenty-one years of age) with the old formal-isms of the Church. A poem published in the university magazine makes the point of dissatisfied youth:

> We don't want saints of stone, who have never seen their mother, who have never fed at their breasts.
> We want living saints with blood, who have lived the wretchedness, the dirtiness, the vileness, the desperation, the suffering.
> Who have in their hands wounds ulcerated and infected with the work of the harvest.
> Living saints!

There was really only one basic aim to the "Catholic revolution," as it can legitimately be called since it aims at a total change in structure. It was to prove that for the first time in history revolu-tion could take place peacefully and nonviolently. A sensible rev-olution. "If we look at the history of Europe, the rupture with the Old Order was always violent," said L'Abbé François Houtart. As secretary general of the International Federation of Catholic Institutes of Social and Socio-Religious Research in Belgium, he is behind much of the sociological research directed toward changes in Latin America. "Now we know more, we have longer experience. We are in a better position to do it in a peaceful way. But there must be structural changes. I think it can be done in Chile, but I am less sure about some of the other countries. It is theoretically possible to change society peacefully. I hope it is practically pos-sible."

But the Marxists in Chile were equally convinced that *they* were the New Men and the wave of the future. Within their coalition, there were two groups: the more radical socialists and the Communists. In following a Soviet line the Communists were actually far more moderate. Allende was a socialist and leaned toward Cuba and Peking. He had come close to winning in 1958, but he lost the election by thirty thousand votes, a loss widely attributed to his alienation of the more conservative women's vote. He and his men were dedicated and modern in point of view, but there were other difficulties.

Allende, dapper and somewhat vain, was fascinated with the Cuban revolution. He counted Fidel Castro as one of his best friends. He traveled regularly to Havana where, as one of those Latin "tourists in socialism," he ensconced himself in the old Hilton, now the Hotel Havana Libre, and enjoyed the pool while he suffered over the problems of Latin America. All this earned him a great deal of criticism at home. Chileans are fiercely nationalistic and think of Cuba as unattractively "tropical." As the elections approached, a rabid campaign was launched that drove him to the wall.

If Allende believed in Cuba, the opposition posters proclaimed, then he believed in "the wall" for his enemies. Posters went up all over Santiago showing a priest standing by while a Cuban was being executed. Castro's sister Juana, who had abandoned him, went on the air warning the Chileans against Communism. Victor Raúl Haya de la Torre, Peru's grand old man of Aprismo, added his warning. Throughout the entire country, there was a feeling of a fortress beseiged. Nothing could save Allende.

Nor did he help himself. Asked the day before the election whether he believed that a one-party state would be good for Chile, he sat in his office in the Senate and told me very thoughtfully: "No . . . not right away. It would take preparation. It would take a while." Later he told me in Havana that he considered the 1964 election proof that democracy could not work because he had not been elected.

Many of the "new wave" of Latins—and this included Marxists as well as Christian Democrats and many democratic leftists—saw the Chilean election as symbolic of what must eventually happen everywhere.

The prevalent idea was that by the 1950s Latin America was nearly ready to integrate all the "outs"—the peasants and urban workers—into society. But the old parties of the democratic left had gone as far as they could. They had no ideology and therefore had shown themselves singularly open to corruption. So, the argument went, what was needed was for man himself to be reformed. This could only be done by a movement with an ideology, and there were only two movements of ideology, Christian Democracy and Marxism. Latin American man was waiting for one or the other to pick him up, pick him up out of his nothingness and make him a citizen of a country and a total man.

Both insisted there must be an absolute change in the structure of the society. Both would—through conscious efforts—raise the lower levels to the top and equalize society by taking from those who have to give to those who do not. Both believed in social equality—enforced social equality. But perhaps the greatest difference was in the Christian Democrats' pragmatism, their relativism. They were nontheoretical; when they talked of agrarian reform, they did not mean "right thinking"—they meant growing more food.

Eduardo Hamuy, Chile's most prominent sociologist and a proponent of the left, insisted that the Christian Democrats were really the "new men," for they were technically oriented, "modern" men. "It's a traditional society moving toward a modern society," he said one day, using his hands generously to describe the shifting of forms. "Now Allende is more of a traditional man than Frei, who is more modern. The Christian Democrats are men trained with modern tools. They have modern minds and they use modern tools to handle social realities.

"The difference between traditional leadership—which is ideologically formed leadership with specific ideas about reality—and modern leadership is the way they use their tools. The modern leader has a rational attitude, he has the facts, he verifies things, he wants evidence about it. Copper is such an instance. The traditional man wants to nationalize copper and that is an ideological statement. It has meaning in an ideological framework. Modern leadership says, 'We don't want to nationalize the mines because it's not good business for us.' They're very cold and impersonal.

"I've taken many interviews," continued Hamuy, who made a specialty of polling, "and the people are worn out with the left. The Christian Democrat movement is something new. They are new political technicians. They are the most pro-American, the most New World managerial types. If there is one distinction between traditional and modern leadership, it is efficiency."

What the Christian Democrats have done since they came to power in 1964 is very much in line with this interpretation. They set out to transform Chilean society, and in many ways they did it. They hit out in all directions but landed first on the copper problem—a "problem" because copper, Chile's main "crop," was 90 percent owned by American companies and provided no less than 60 percent of Chile's foreign exchange. With the cooperation of the copper companies, Frei first avoided an ideological decision ("Copper must be nationalized because it is *right*") and worked out a compromise that was desirable for both sides. The mines were "Chileanized." The government bought up to 51 percent of some, 25 percent of others. Both business and government agreed to invest profits to make Chile the No. 1 copper producer in the world.

It was an extremely important agreement, for it was typical of a new approach to relations with the United States. It recognized interdependence and it recognized that anyone must pay his own way, but it also demanded participation on a self-respecting basis, the opposite of Marxist approach, which demanded total sovereignty, even at the cost of national suicide.

Education was completely reformed, and in such a way that class distinctions would eventually be eliminated. Chile had established an educational system which served to form an elite, in the French style. Under it everyone was trained in a classics curriculum, despite the fact that only 2 percent entered the university. As one American educator said of the system, "It produced educated failures." Now vocational training was instituted and became a key to social mobility. A massive campaign was begun

to enroll every student in school and during the first year of the
Frei administration, 186,000 additional students enrolled, some in
carabinero stations, instead of the usual thirty thousand new
pupils that annually entered the schools.

Plans moved ahead for an agrarian reform that would make
small landowners out of a hundred thousand farm families and
break up the big estates, so suicidally unproductive. Plans were
formulated to break up the monopolies. Peasant wages were
brought up to urban wage standards. Tax structures were revised
to redistribute income.

A massive organization of the "marginal" groups had begun.
The Christian Democrat government formed a government or-
ganism, *Promoción Popular*, which set out—in tandem psychologically with Vekemans' DESAL—to organize intermediate groups.
In the first year and a half of this movement, six thousand mothers'
clubs, fifteen hundred neighborhood councils, four hundred rural
clubhouses were formed and sixty thousand persons were enrolled in leadership courses.

But all did not go unrelievedly well. In February of 1965, a little
over a year after Frei took power, I was traveling with the Frei
group to the southern town of Valdivia where Frei had gone to
dedicate some *Promoción Popular* projects. By then Frei was
looked upon by his supporters as half president and half saint.
Indeed, he had a certain priestly look about him, with his piercing
deep-set eyes and his manner of holding his hand up, as in a blessing. In a large meadow that surrounded the outskirts of a cluster
of wooden houses where marginal people lived, he walked through
their exhibits—so strikingly like a county fair in the Midwest, with
quilts, homemade toys and foods. Men and women beamed at
him, with an obvious faith in what he represented to them. In
another area, as he dedicated a school, an elderly woman ran to
him, kissed his hand fervently, and said, "Don't forget us, Mr.
President."

But it wasn't all as easy as it appeared. At one point, the
minister of economy, Domingo Santa María—like so many Chileans a strikingly handsome man—said softly to me: "It's a hard
road. We're between the Communists on one side and the rightists

on the other side. One has the organization; the other has the economic power. We represent the common man, and he is loyal to us. That's why we organized him—he has no organization, no pressure groups."

The Christian Democrats continued to press for Latin American unity. For a while they tried to bring Castro back into the fold, but it didn't work. In February of 1965 Castro began bitterly attacking Frei in a barrage of verbiage. He called Frei a "pseudo revolutionary," a "middle-class reformer," a "prostitute." Frei refused to answer, but from then on pan-Latin Americanism existed without Cuba.

The Chileans' obsession with unity—the leitmotif of the New Latins—dominated everything. There was a meeting of Latin intellectuals in Arica, in the northern Chilean desert, to discuss cultural unity—what was it, after all, to be a Latin American? The Chileans pushed economic unity, while the more "sophisticated" Argentines and Brazilians stood coolly to the side. Just as the Marxists pushed their theoretical unity of the "peoples" who must be trained to see where their future lay in Marxism, the Chileans pushed their unifying concepts on concrete levels.

But the greatest revolution of all was in mental outlook, the psychology, the revolution taking place inside man. In 1964 Chile had moved to the brink of social change. It was possible the Christian Democrats might fail—they certainly were immediately beset with problem after problem. Within a few years, the movement would lose the radical young Catholics. Many of them would seek a strange new unity, with the Castroite "New Marxists." People would begin to say that "Frei has failed," that Frei was only a "Latin Kerensky" who presided over the death of experimental radical democracy.

By the next election the greatest threat was the group thought to be dead and buried—the *momios* or mummies of the old oligarchy and landholding classes. They arose out of their sarcophaguses with their pale old *momio* candidate, Alessandri, and threatened to win back the government.

And it was not illogical when one thought about it. Frei had attempted to make a revolution without using or inventing an external enemy—something most revolutions depend upon. He also was trying to make a revolution while keeping his actions constantly answerable to the electorate—something few revolutionaries ever have done.

In the beginning people were caught up in the passion and enthusiasm of change. But then the bills had to be paid, as in any country where capital is to be accumulated for future development. And once the sacrifices begin to come there are moments when almost any people will vote a revolutionary regime out—if it can. In Chile this was complicated by the large 40 percent of the populace that was middle class; it was this class which largely was being asked to make the sacrifices to bring up the lower classes, and they rebelled.

But none of these factors was really important. For it was not a question of any one political movement, it was a question of people coming of age. It was a question of the moment when the world changes, when the old distinctions fall away and a new form is in the process of creation. No one really thought that even a victory for the right would mean more than a rest period of one presidential administration; no one thought that a conservative president could or would rescind the changes.

As one observer noted, "The history of reform is that the reformers go, but the reforms remain." To a great extent what Frei had done was to do so much and to raise expectations so high that he could not fulfill them. "And now these expectations may destroy him," another observer commented.

The prevailing and continuing mood of Chile was demonstrated to me dramatically a few weeks before the elections in 1964. I was visiting the town of Talca in central Chile. This had always been *the* town of the *fundo*-owners—the big landowners—who invested their money in land as a hedge against inflation and because they liked the prestigious life on the land. In the old days, they used to say "Paris, Rome and Talca," such was their presumption. They lived on the *fundos* then, surrounded by their *roto* peons, whom they treated with proper paternalistic attachment.

In the evenings they went to the elegant Club de la Unión, the watering spot of central Chile, with its big central room filled with leather couches and arm chairs.

That night in August, I sat in the club. It was very quiet. There were holes in the couches and the large chandelier hanging down from the ceiling had loose wires and dangling sockets. There were few guests—everybody lived in Santiago by then and came out weekends only.

A swarthy man stopped by our table, chattered amiably about the *rotos* taking over and left. My host, a wealthy businessman of the town, shook his head and said, "An Arab—we never used to let them in the club."

The third man at our table brought out a bottle of whisky at that point and motioned to the waiter. "I've brought my own bottle," he said to us. "Hope you don't mind, but all the other whisky is watered down." There was the depressing feeling that everything was falling apart, disintegrating before our very eyes.

When they discussed the coming election, our host leaned forward eagerly and asked, after a discussion of the current presumptions of the *rotos*, "Do you think we might stave it all off with profit-sharing?"

But it was too late for profit-sharing. The *rotos* were coming and things would never be the same again; they were symbolically marching on the Club de la Unión. Chile in 1964 was the meadow in Runnymede as the barons shifted from foot to foot and scratched their heads. Chile in 1964 was the White House when Jackson was elected and the frontiersmen danced on the table.

CHAPTER 9

Inca Renaissance in the Andes

"Though I weep like the rainstorm, though I grieve like
the snow, I will not find my mother, I will not find my
father." Old Inca song.

To examine Peru's human and social development since World
War II is to look at one of the most dramatic examples of social
and cultural change in Latin America today.

It is not the kind of convulsive revolutionary change that shook
Cuba in 1959. Nor is it in any way similar to the change in Chile,
where a new ideology of peaceful revolution marked the first step
toward the transformation of an old society. Peru represents the
kind of unconscious and spontaneous change that is sweeping
many areas of Latin America and is, to a great extent, more total
than violent revolution. It is similiar to the moments in history
when something within them prods large numbers of people to
move on and out and around. In so doing they change their lives
and change their worlds.

When you look at the 13,000-foot-high *altiplano*, the high plain
of the Andes where the Inca civilization flourished five centuries
ago, at first it is difficult to see any movement at all. The *altiplano*
is as still and empty a place as the world possesses, a land of sand
and snow with llama packs running ahead of the rain.

Here the last twenty generations of Incas have lived as though
stunned by the shock of the Spanish Conquest. Along the bleak

roadsides the Quechua-speaking Indians stand like ancient brown statues in the spotted sunlight, their cheeks swollen by the wads of narcotic *coca* leaves which they chew to relieve the pains of cold and hunger and history. It is all so quiet, so abandoned and mysterious; it is as if time had stopped at the fall of the Inca empire.

But such is not the case. Today the descendants of the Incas, both the pure-blood Indians and the mixed-blood *cholos*, are awakening—politically, socially and psychologically—with such renewed cultural energy that the phenomenon could be called an Inca Renaissance.

For the last fifteen years the Indians have been pouring down from the *altiplano* to the coast, where they have transformed the formerly aristocratic creole cities like Lima. They are mestizoizing —culturally mixing—the formerly pure Spanish culture of formal plazas, formal class structures and formal manners.

The major Indian language, Quechua, which anthropologists once claimed had nearly died out twenty years ago, is now spoken by more people than ever before in its history. It has become so stylish to learn Quechua—more Peruvian university students now study it than any other language—that in 1964 the national culture magazine of Peru, always very "creole," published its first poem in Quechua.

Politically the change is even more dramatic. Peruvian politicians of a new and innovative mind—later followed by young revolutionary military men—began looking around in the early 1960s for effective ways to develop Peru. To their astonishment they found that many of the old Inca forms of social organization were still intact—the community work groups, for instance, and the reciprocal aid groups. For the first time in Latin history politicians began adapting developments to these old social and political structures instead of trying to destroy them.

But the changes were not confined to the coast. All over the *altiplano*, new Indian political organizations began springing up to challenge the old aristocracy, which always controlled political life from Lima. These new Indian peasant leagues and peasant parties immediately took over mayoral posts and local councils in several key areas. In Bolivia the Indians had already won so much freedom and influence during and after the revolution of 1952 that Bolivia could be called with some legitimacy an Indian state.

Perhaps the most dramatic change occurred when the Indians gained enough psychic security to leave the *altiplano*, where they had always lived and to which they had, over the centuries, become physiologically adapted. In the mid-twentieth century, in the grip of an adventurous spirit totally unknown to them since the early expansionist days of the Inca empire, they spilled out along the coasts of Peru and into the fertile eastern jungle regions in Bolivia. In the process, they became *cholos*—citified, deracinated, Westernized Indians—and, if only by their sheer numbers, they began transforming everything they touched. Anthropologists and sociologists almost unanimously affirm that they will transform a large portion of Latin America in the future.

What makes all this particularly dramatic in Peru is the precise clarity with which the "two cultures" of Peru have always been separated. It had been a schismatized society, divided as by a chasm between the desert coast with its big cities and Spanish culture and the mountainous *altiplano* with its thin air and stout Indians. The creole and Indian cultures have always existed apart from each other, one living in the colonial past with its eyes on Europe, the other living lost in time and seared by grand memories of its Inca past.

Lima was always the classic creole city, where the upper classes self-consciously collected Inca vases but printed all the books about the Incas in English, for the tourists. On the coast the creoles constructed a way of life that was aristocratic in taste, hierarchical in structure and sleepy in spirit. Creole was the term given the Spanish born in Peru after the Conquest. It meant an ordered way of life, a genteel disdain for manual labor and an appreciation of such things as the slow creole waltz that is typical of Lima.

Creoles are class-conscious and time-unconscious, and the stories that foreigners tell about them always have a "typically Latin American" element of the absurd about them. An American was traveling by Peruvian plane to the northern fishing boom town of Chimbote one day, and Chimbote was fogged in so the plane couldn't stop. The pilot suggested that he make the round trip to several northern cities and, if the weather cleared, they would stop at Chimbote on the way back later in the morning.

The American, eager to get his business in Chimbote finished, thought he should get off at the next stop and take a cab back to the city. "No, no," the creole pilot insisted, "come with me." "And if it's foggy when we return?" the American persisted. "Why then you'll be back in Lima with your family for lunch." That, the American asserted, is purely creole.

Indian society had none of this engaging whimsy about it. Indian society was always a serious business. The Indians lived lives riven with difficulties and always threatened with misfortune. They had to prevail over the *altiplano* itself, stunning but devilishly difficult to live with. Its broad barren valleys and purple mountains are dotted by floating clouds that suddenly erupt in flamboyant rainbows and convulsive showers. Its thin air provides a brittle clarity of vision that often transforms colors into strange and eerie shades. But its beauty is deceptive, for it also exacts its toll from people who live there.

Balanced like a slate between the two black ridges of the Andes, the *altiplano* shaped the life of the Indians more than anything else. The extraordinary height, with the thin buoyant air that goes with it, forced the Incas to develop more red corpuscles to withstand the cold, and larger lungs to compensate for the lack of oxygen. It also forced them to excel, to build a culture which Arnold Toynbee classifies as one of the world's great civilizations.

Historians say that the very barrenness of the land—its very prohibitiveness—prodded the Incas into their astonishing accomplishments. They had to use every foot of land, to terrace and burrow and organize and work together, if they were to live there. Rock by rock they built roads that connected the entire empire. And with reason and persuasion they gradually brought all the tribes of Ecuador and Bolivia under their sway.

But it was in no sense a Western empire. Its dominating characteristics were absolute discipline, perfect obedience, and total, hierarchical organization.

The empire, which was called Tahuantisuyo, was divided into four quarters, each governed by the equivalent of a viceroy and further divided into provinces ruled by Inca administrators. The major social unit was the *ayllu*, the traditional Indian family group whose chief was responsible for all the acts of his clansmen. The total empire was broken down into groups of ten, each headed by a decurion; and these groups were organized into groups of fifty "souls," then one hundred, then five hundred, and finally a thousand. One Inca was supposed to have said, "the care of one thousand persons is quite sufficient to occupy one man alone."

There was no appeal from the absolute power of the emperor. He traveled in a gold palanquin throughout the lengths of the empire and wore his specially woven clothes only one time. Status was fixed from birth, and punishment for disobedience or crime was severe and immediate—usually death. If someone stole from the state or church lands, his entire *ayllu* might be wiped out. Yet, typically too, nobles were punished more harshly than the peasants. The decurion was compelled to report any juridical misdemeanor occurring within his group of ten within the hour or the decurion himself was doubly punished—for the failure to perform his duty and also for keeping silent.

Over the centuries the Incas created their own myths and legends, many of them strangely similar to those of other cultures. Up the mountain from the town of Sicuani, near Cuzco, there is Lake Langui. The people who lived near the lake thousands of years ago, the Indians say, were very evil. One night they were having a party when the gods approached in the form of a beggar. Only the young princess was kind to him and he warned her to leave before the city was destroyed. He also warned her not to look back.

But leaving the city as the Inca Armageddon approached, she could not resist looking back and she was turned to stone—a stone, the Indians say, which still stands near the lake. They also insist that debris from some strange city at the bottom of the lake still comes to the surface now and then.

Nor have the Indians in any way forgotten their past. Near

Cuzco, Indian women still wear black, in mourning for the last Inca emperor, and some believe he is still imprisoned in a tower there.

Remembering all too well the conquistadores, they are deeply suspicious of foreigners. In one village two foreign anthropologists who had been working there without any problems one day inexplicably found their house surrounded by Indians they had thought to be their friends. The Indians accused the Americans of being *pistacos*, a slang word which the Indians interpreted to mean a foreign witch who kills Indians in order to take the oil from their bones to make the atomic bomb.

A sadness and mourning for what was, coupled with feelings of hopelessness and despair in the face of history, is a major element in the psyche of the Indians today. Anthropologists note how much the Indians sing of lost parents—"I will not find my mother, I will not find my father"—who have abandoned them. Given these feelings, it is all the more surprising that today the Indians are breaking away, opening their lives to new forms, and asserting themselves in the world outside the *altiplano*, a world riven with disequilibrium.

But the truth is that despite their despair, despite the oppressive sense of fatalism, the Indians never quite gave up. They continued to cling to and to live within their own forms. They adapted their gods to the new Catholic religion. They continued to use the *minca* or family mutual-help groups and to observe the *mita*, the Inca form of service to the community by which they built roads, schools and community buildings. Those who were not tied to the haciendas continued to live within five thousand indigenous communities which held their own land and elected their own traditional leadership.

The re-evaluation and subsequent idealization of the Indian that had started in Mexico with the revolution of 1910 barely touched Peru, until Victor Raúl Haya de la Torre formulated an Indo-American philosophy in the '30s. But although he had great influence, because of the opposition of the military he was never permitted to come to power. Whereas in Mexico it was forbidden by law even to erect a statue to the conquistador Hernán Cortés, in Lima the bones of Pizarro—their authenticity is disputed—lay in state in the cathedral with his viscera lying alongside in slimy jars.

A number of forces occurred simultaneously in the late 1940s and during the 1950s, all contributing to change. One of the greatest catalysts was the transistor radio—suddenly the poor Indian in the sierra was walking about with a transistor glued to his ear, listening to a host of foreign propagandists, all trying to woo him. The Maryknoll priests of that energetic American Roman Catholic mission society were thrown out of China when the Communists came and the pope said, "Go to South America." Modern-minded, egalitarian in their habits and impatient of hierarchy, the Maryknolls spread out across the Andes forming radio schools, small industries, model farms and peasant leagues. Anthropologists came, sociologists came. A middle class was growing that in seeking its rationale was extending itself to politics.

By the election of 1962 every one of the seven presidential candidates campaigned in the villages for the first time in history, talking about change, about the new Peru, and about such untouchable subjects as land reform. One of these men was Fernando Belaúnde Terry. He became president in 1963 and symbolized an entirely new way of looking at Indian society.

Belaúnde was an architect, a handsome man and an aristocrat. He dressed impeccably—his hair always lay back like a fold of black velvet. He looked like a perfectly turned-out drawing room type. Yet—amazing for Peru—he considered the Indians as people.

Belaúnde had done some impetuous things in his life, and to Americans they sometimes looked a little bizarre. But they didn't hurt his *macho* with Peruvians. In 1962, for instance, when the military annulled the presidential election because they would not allow the hated and controversial Haya de la Torre to become president, Belaúnde resisted the decision and took to the streets with his followers in the southern city of Arequipa.

They tore up the cobblestones, made them into barricades and sat behind them all night. As the darkness grew colder and colder, his followers gradually drifted home. By morning the revolt died out simply because nobody was left, and the angry city fathers insisted Belaúnde pay for the damage.

His election to the presidency in 1963 signified, much as did Chile's election a year later, the taking-over of the middle-class reformers. It marked the ascension to power of a new class—doctors, professors, engineers and lawyers—which was neither aristocracy nor proletariat nor peasantry but which seriously intended to change things. It also marked the debut of the Indian.

Until he was overthrown in 1968, Belaúnde told the story—he told it incessantly—of how in the campaign of 1962 he traveled all over the country, finding roads, schools and community buildings everywhere. Whenever he asked where they came from, he relates, he was told *"El pueblo lo hizo"*—the people did it.

He was discovering belatedly what the anthropologists who have webbed out across the Andes with their research grants and their head measurements and their Rorschach tests have known for years—that the Indian villages, far from being hopelessly somnolent or unstructured, were dramatically alive and had continued to use the old Inca forms, like the *minca*, to create for themselves everything they wanted. Self-generating and spontaneous, this work never caught the eye of the authorities in Lima simply because those authorities had formerly despised and ignored everything Indian.

Under the Inca structures there had existed first the *ayllu*, which was a patriarchal group supposedly all descended from a plant, an animal or mineral which they venerated. Each *ayllu* worked together caring for its own lands and caring secondarily for the lands set aside for the Inca and the sun. Each person had one *tupu* of land (between 3600 and 4825 square meters, compared to 1800 square meters per person today) and took part in the two types of community work, the *minca* and the *mita*.

The Indians worked under the ancient Peruvian "Law of Brotherhood," which according to Garcilaso de la Vega, the descendant of both Incas and Spaniards who became the Conquest chronicler of the Incas, "ordered the citizens of every village to help each other in plowing, sowing, harvesting, building houses and other similar endeavors, working without pay of any kind."

After he took office, Belaúnde resolved to encourage the *minca* and to build his community plans around it. He promulgated the law of *Cooperación Popular* or "Community Action," calling it "the cornerstone of my platform" and noting that "from the very beginning I have always proclaimed that this law is fundamentally based in our deep historical traditions, and a vigorous Peru can, and will, be built upon it."

This was revolutionary in a profound sense for a country like Peru: revolutionary psychologically because it indicated a public respect for the formerly despised Indian ways; revolutionary politically because it gave representation to the Indian communities; and revolutionary socially because it signified that the Indian could be considered as possessing some social worth.

The way the law worked, the Indian communities could come to the *Cooperación Popular* offices with projects (sometimes they came with impractical requests, such as a swimming pool or a plaza). There, conferring with the officials, they would decide what projects would get government aid. At its height in 1964–65, the value of national capital produced through this communal work project totaled some $60 million and included 2600 kilometers of roads, 3700 community buildings and more than 250 irrigation projects.

The program brought college students, most of whom had never been near an Indian in any human relationship, into the sierra to live in the villages and supervise or stimulate the programs. At one point one-fifth of all the university students in the country had applied to *Cooperación Popular*. These hopeful figures—and the amount of work accomplished—decreased toward the end of Belaúnde's term, when his political opposition cut down the allocated funds because it feared Belaúnde would use the popular program for political capital. But this was not important because the impulse remained and it showed how much the country had changed.

"You can say that on one hand there's a real interest on the part of the professional politicians to take advantage of the Indian structures," commented José María Arguedes, one of Peru's finest intellectuals and former director of Casa Cultura, the national culture office, pointing out the dichotomy. "It has created a re-evaluation on the part of the Indians of their own structures, as well as renewed academic interest. But it has also awakened the reaction of the extreme right to destroy it."

Belaúnde's intention to strengthen the old forms to a point where a synthesis of Spanish and Indian would emerge in a "new Peru" continued, despite the opposition. "The solution," he said, "lies in the possibility of fusing these two forces, one surging from within the country and the other coming from without, in order to create a genuinely Peruvian hybrid economy for the inevitable transition to the modern world." He spoke of it, too, as a "transition from the mutual aid of the ancient system to the contractual and monetary regimen of the modern world."

Another of Belaúnde's actions was to institute municipal elections for the first time in forty-two years, something that immediately stirred a political awakening in the country. For part of Peru's problem was the extreme centralization of the country that came as part of the Spanish heritage.

With about twelve million people in Peru today, an estimated 50 percent could be classified as *cholos* (it must be remembered this is largely a cultural and not a racial term), 35 percent as pure Indians and 15 percent as creoles. Under a system of extreme centralization of political powers and in a country where illiterates do not vote, it has naturally been the small 10 or 15 percent of creoles in Lima that controlled everything. The wealth of the country poured in from the countryside and stayed in the capital; in one typical year $15 million was allocated to government services in Lima and $20 million went to all the rest of the huge country.

The people reacted immediately to the revival of municipal elections. In the Puno region around Lake Titicaca, where Indian life is at its most conservative, a peasant league of between fifty and eighty thousand Indians was formed. The instigators were two local merchant brothers, the Cáceres brothers, who had a sensitive ear cocked for the hour of change. Their appeal was directly to the pure-blooded Indian peasants, who elected them to Congress. In municipal elections their leagues took about one-third of the mayoral posts in the Puno section. This case is typical of what happened elsewhere.

Another aspect of the dramatic awakening in the Andes was the insatiable land hunger, which in the 1960s translated itself into an insistent and violent demand for land. There were some five thousand *comunidades indígenas* or Indian communities, which still held land in common. But about a third of the Indian population worked as peons on the big haciendas. Until midcentury it was common to see Indians hitched up as oxen, plowing primitively worked fields in front of the magnificent and productive terraces which their Inca forefathers created. Working also as shepherds for the *hacendado's* roaming alpaca and llama herds, the Indians had to pay with one of their own animals if one of the owner's was lost.

Each part of the system supported the other in a carefully woven whole. The Indians were often paid, not in money, but in the narcotic *coca* (cocaine) leaf, which kept them in a passive, accepting state. It is one of the many curious things about Peru that *coca*, which keeps at least half of the population in a constant somnolent state, is a state monopoly. The leaf is grown in state plantations on the eastern side of the Andes and stored in state storage houses in the villages.

To complete the social fabric, company stores owned by the *hacendados* kept the Indians in debt. And bleak statistic piled upon bleak statistic. In most sierra villages 80 percent had tuberculosis; 50 percent had syphilis; the infant mortality rate was 50 percent and higher. Of the inhospitable sierra lands, approximately 350 *hacendados* owned over half the area and 23,500 owned about 17 percent of it. On the coast, 70 percent of the farm land was in estates of more than 247 acres and was in the hands of 2 percent of the landowners.

Organized by Trotskyites and peasant dissidents of every type, the Indians began to walk in and take over the land they claimed was theirs "from Inca times." These land invasions reached a height in 1964 and 1965 when the valleys of the Andes were ablaze with haciendas burning and people marching. In one period of six months, officials estimated that 150,000 persons had invaded five hundred plantations throughout Peru and occupied more than two million acres of land. About sixty-five deaths and between two and three thousand injuries resulted.

The most dramatic land invasion area—the land invasion became the favorite technique of the budding revolution—was around Sicuani, a town of colored houses and crooked balconies on the lonely little railroad line that chugs from Cuzco to Puno and back. For months the curious little Andean class war had been gaining heat. Trotskyite-led, the increasingly restive Indians in the quiet valleys around Sicuani several times had marched into town, shouting such slogans as "Kill everyone who wears a tie." By cutting the electricity and blocking the rails, they cut off the town, leaving the creoles in a state of panic.

Then on February 4, 1964, a group of several hundred Indians, with women preceding them, carrying wet rags hidden in their shawls to protect the group in case of tear gas, invaded land they claimed was theirs from Inca times. It was one of those beautiful, quiet, high Andean valleys, with the coal gray mountains ringing it and protecting it while the sacred river of the Incas, the Vilcanota, ran beside it.

The police came. Someone threw a stone. To this day no one knows how it really started, but the police chief fell to the ground with a gash in his forehead and a wild orgy of shooting began.

Within minutes seventeen lay dead and forty-one were wounded. The police threw the bodies, the dead mixed with the living, on railroad flatcars stacked like cordwood, and carried them into Sicuani. Whoever had fired first—it could have been the police or it could have been the Trotskyites who stayed to the rear—had used dum-dum bullets and whole portions of bodies were blown apart. "It was exactly like a war," said one of the stunned American nurses who worked in the local hospital.

The hills rocked with the sound of gunfire that winter, and the sky was filled with the smoke of burning haciendas. All strange, new happenings that announced "change." On Christmas Eve a wealthy *hacendado*, Miguel Luna, raised his gun in his elegant hacienda house on the outskirts of nearby Urcos as several thousand Indians attacked with stones and guns. Within minutes seven Indians lay dead and the others fled screaming. The gentlemanly looking Luna, who keeps a beautiful colonial townhouse on an old square in nearby Cuzco, was held in the Urcos jail for two months—one of the first occasions in Peruvian history that a *hacendado* saw the inside of a village jail.

"We'd be fools if we weren't armed, because they're going to kill us," Luna told me after his release. "They had threatened me for weeks. I asked the police, the governor and the army for protection and they wouldn't give it. I only did what anybody would do."

The forms were always mixed, the social changes in the Andes always had strange twists to them. In the library of his house in the mountains near Sicuani, a judge who was considered a liberal-minded man, showed me how he kept books on Marxism hidden in other jackets on his shelves. "An educated man has to know what they said," he explained. In the next breath he was muttering the age-old belief of the creoles about the Indians: "I don't think the agrarian reform will work. The Indian does not understand agriculture. The Indian is an animal who works without thinking. He is semi-savage."

It was always confusing when attempting to sort out the strange trinitarian mixture of Communism-Christianity-Paganism that was stalking the Andes in those times of change. Many were radicals in the sense that Christians were radicals in the early ages of Christianity.

In one small village, remote and alone on a mountainside, were men who had fled the aftermath of the Sicuani invasion. When a trusted American priest, Father Joseph Malone of Sicuani, went up the mountain to visit, the villagers would watch. If someone were with him they rang the churchbells to warn the "wanted" men to hide.

To Father Malone it was obvious these Indian men were not "Communists," as the local authorities had charged. Many were Catholics, others were Evangelicals. Previously they had rented a pasture below the village from the local *hacendado* for $1600 a year. But when the land invasions began the owner drove them out and put DDT on the pasture to kill their animals. Then, charged by the police with being Communists, they hid in the mountains where the Incas had always hidden from any authority they had not instituted.

One townsman, Teodoro Choque Suyo, was taken to jail for taking part in the "Communist invasion." As they dragged him across the plaza of Sicuani he cried out: "I am in good company. Christ went to prison too. And so do I go, with good heart."

After a while Belaúnde was able to put through an agrarian reform and the land invasions stopped temporarily. With their needs represented, or at least believing that to be the case, the Indians resorted to law. Every day in the big gray National Archives in Lima you could see the Indian leaders shuffling in in their sandals to look up the four-hundred-year-old deeds which the fussily legalistic Spaniards had provided to indicate how the land passed from the Indians to them.

But the land invasions . . . the expansion of the political spectrum . . . the re-evaluation of the old Inca structures and the use of them for development . . . the Inca Renaissance in culture and language . . . are only part of the story of change in Peru, a country still looked upon from outside as frozen with old and unchanging forms.

Change is coming about in conscious ways and in unconscious ways, among Indians and *cholos*. Many of these programs eventually failed to be the answer on any large scale to Peru's nagging problems of cultural and spiritual underdevelopment, but that was not important. What was important was that wherever the Indians and *cholos* got the chance—and even in areas where they didn't—they showed an extraordinary desire and readiness to change their old feudal ways of life.

And at the heart is the cultural change that has come about through the great movements of people: the Indians leaving the mountains, moving to the coast, and becoming westernized. The greatest change is that involved in the transformation of a man from an Indian to a *cholo*.

Anyone who knew Lima twenty years ago, anyone who was familiar with Pizarro's aristocratic "City of Kings," would be as-

tonished to see the changes today in this city. It is still dotted with
the dinosaurian grand plazas and aristocratic churches and palaces
of another age, but today at dusk on the narrow downtown streets
of Lima the predominant stroller is neither old nor aristocratic.

The *cholos* are roasting chicken livers and pieces of beef hearts
on sticks—*anticuchos*—over little black coal stoves and selling
them for a few *centavos*. Along the throbbing Jirón de la Unión,
Lima's busiest street, wild entrepreneurs hawk rope bags, plastic
covers, toys that make the sound of wild birds, cheap leather
pocketbooks, magazines, and a thousand knickknacks that roll,
squeal and turn somersaults.

They live around the city in jerry-built shacktowns that have
sprung up overnight, every night, since the early 1950s. By the
late '60s, half a million *limeños*, or about one-fourth to one-third
of the city's population, lived in these *barriadas* of the *cholos*.

In the *barriadas* the *cholos* are both competitive and imaginative. A common sight is a home generator which a *cholo* uses to
rent electricity to his neighbors. "The sheer achievement of these
barriadas is astonishing," John C. Turner, a British architect who
is a specialist on housing in Latin America, observes. "They surpass in area and population the second city of Peru, Arequipa, and
not one house is more than fifteen years old."

The *barriadas* began forming after World War II, when the Indians began migrating to the coast—away from the stagnation of
the sierra and toward the sea and the modern world. At first these
immigrants—for they were immigrants to a new society—moved
into the centers of the cities, into the *callejón* or big apartment
slum. Then they organized themselves and began moving out to
the government land in the deserts around the city. They were
surprisingly well organized, and they depended upon each other
and worked together in a country where mutual distrust had always been the rule.

At night there would be only the empty sand, looking so
astonishingly like the Sahara. In the morning there would be an
entire city of several hundred mat houses, usually with a Peruvian
flag flying, all standing bravely against society. There were many
killings, as police were sent out to dislodge them, but in the end

Lima capitulated to its *cholos*. In 1961 the *barriada* law was passed giving squatters legal title to the land.

On Sundays the *cholos* held their *coliseos* or fairs and danced to the whining, repetitive *huayno* songs, whirling their handkerchiefs as they shuffled in circles. The *huaynos* were Inca songs from ancient times and Dr. Arguedes points out that "in 1930 to sing *huaynos* in Lima was as strange as wearing feathers." But by 1966 the favorite-selling record in Lima was *Longplaying de Huayno. Huaynos* were being composed by *limeñan* composers who only a few years back composed only the circumspect *criollo* waltzes. "Where before it was a disgrace to compose *huaynos*, today it is an honor," Dr. Arguedes explains. A few years ago they were on the radio only at 6 A.M. By the mid-1960s they were on every station, all day. Even the *huaylas*, an Inca dance of magic, had become a popular dance.

It was all part of the choloization—the cultural democratization—of Lima and the coastal cities. "Twenty years ago Lima was a Spanish city," commented Dr. José Matos, head of the Department of Anthropology at Lima's San Marcos University. "No more. Today it has an Indian flavor. The whole atmosphere has changed."

Cholos tend to be astonishingly democratically oriented; probably this stems from the democracy within the Indian communities, where every voice is heard. Long before the municipal elections were held in 1963, they were electing their own mayors in the *barriadas* and electing them spontaneously and without outside help or hindrance. They also learned spontaneously how to picket and protest. On almost any day in the early 1960s, you could see a *barriada* delegation walking downtown to the Lima newspapers with huge banners that stretched across whole streets, demanding water or sanitation or representation in the *barriadas*.

This generation is largely interested in their homes and in establishing themselves on the coast. The next generation, say the anthropologists, will be revolutionary. They prize manual labor and are competitive. They are egalitarian.

It is clear that the restless *cholos* carry within themselves new, indigenously American values which they are introducing to the historically Europe-oriented coast. They constitute another example of what is indigenously, natively, naturally Latin American —not European or North American, but Latin American. And in this they are related to Castro's experiment, to Frei's, and to many others.

What was especially telling was that even when the Peruvian military overthrew Belaúnde in 1968 and took over the government, the same basic concern with the social, cultural and economic integration of the country continued. These officers, mostly from the rural, lower and middle classes, were of the same generation and of the same ideas as Belaúnde's men. For these new commitments to the marginal men, to social justice and to national development cut across all lines—they involved the new military men as well as the new-style politicians.

Father Vekemans has said that Latin America is only "partly colonized," that urban colonials still look to Europe and to the States for guidance and inspiration, and that in the steps of nationhood these countries have developed the backbone, without the skeleton or the tissue.

Until mid-twentieth century this was more true of schizophrenic Peru than of almost any other country on the continent. But now the Indians of the Andes are moving and striving, forcing the old "colonists," whose eyes and hearts have been somewhere else, to look at indigenous Latin America and finally to mate with it.

PART III

THE NEW LATINS

CHAPTER 10

The Revolt Against Authoritarianism

"Death to all Spaniards, even though indifferent, and life to the creoles, even though guilty." Simón Bolívar's "War to the Death" announcement, 1813.

Like a hard, steely thread running through the fabric of Latin American life, authoritarianism has toughened and often deformed the weave. But it has never been the only clothing for the often contradictory and always struggling society of Latin America. Running parallel to the presence of and respect for authoritarianism, there has always been a strong revolt against it; in the same breath, you find Latin man praising it and cursing it. And perhaps nowhere is the struggle—the struggle to rise above the strict authoritarianism of the past and to arrive at some new "solution" involving individual responsibility—more dramatic than in Colombia, and there nowhere more fascinating than in one small *barrio*.

The *barrio* San José on the outskirts of Bogotá was one of those typical marginal towns that have drawn, in the last fifteen years, like threatening nooses around the body politic. Dusty and disheveled, with half-finished stucco houses and people to match, it belonged to the modern wanderers who are pouring from the Colombian countryside to the cities.

Somehow in formal Bogotá, such a proper town, it seemed more outrageous than elsewhere that towns like San José should exist. In Bogotá men wear homburgs. In Bogotá the beautiful museums of the independence wars are preserved in impeccable condition. In Bogotá the Catholic hierarchy has "kept up standards" with only barely bloodied head, and refused to bow to the cries and carpings of those who would liberalize the church. Bogotá, in everything, represents *respeto*, so important in Latin American life and meaning more than "respect," meaning a mystic order and the maintenance of place.

How strange, then, San José. Stranger still were the lines of curious people who were looking about the half-destroyed house and placing candles on a spot in a dusty adjoining field.

The house was where Efraín González, one of the "heroes" of *la violencia* or "The Violence" was killed in 1965 and a symbol of one of the weirdest phenomena in Latin America today. It was also an example of the revolt against the authoritarianism of the past that is one of the startling realities of what is now happening in Latin America.

Efraín González, only thirty-three years old, was a wiry young man from Santander del Sur, and he had killed five hundred persons "at least," the hero-worshipers around his house told me the day I was there. He was one of Colombia's "great" bandits, which is to say one of the world's great killers, and this was the house where fifty soldiers finally got him in the spring of 1965. He took five of them with him, his last gift to the world.

I had heard about the house, and how the poor Colombians had made it into a shrine; how on the first Sunday after the bandit was captured there were so many cars near the spot it was practically impossible to get through; and how the people continued to come. I drove out there one cool afternoon to see if it were true, and it was. There was a line of people waiting to see the house, which was simply four bare ceilingless walls with gaping holes in the front. Children were peering through the holes. "Is there blood, there should be blood," one sang, in a singsong dirge.

In the field in front—at the last he had run out through the fifty soldiers and into the field—women were putting candles on the spot where he had fallen. Some were crossing themselves. In cafes nearby, people were writing "Viva Efraín González" next to "Viva Fidel Castro."

"He was a man of great courage," one elderly man said, stopping as he passed the "monument." "I myself admire him, even though he was a conservative and I am a liberal."

"It was the form in which they killed him," a cabdriver offered, as if in explanation. "It was so unequal. Why, they had to use mortars to get him. Many admire his valor in the face of so many soldiers." Then he pointed out the historic scene to me. "You see" —his swarthy finger traced the flight—"he ran from the house, to there, in the field and there he dropped." The finger dropped to where it was pointing at the ground, where there was a candle flickering in the wind.

Efraín González was one of the reasons that two to three hundred thousand Colombians, between 1948 and 1964, died terrible, grisly deaths. Violence is nothing new to Colombia, just as it is nothing new to all of Latin America. But in scope and horror there is nothing to surpass *la violencia*, about which Colombian President Alberto Lleras said in his inaugural speech of 1958:

"We descended, savagely and suddenly, to monstrous extremes. We saw with amazement how there had been a reserve of savagery in our people which defied entire centuries of Christian preaching, of civil order and of advanced communal existence. More of our compatriots have died in this irregular war than in the indispensable battles for independence . . . The most humble people suffered martyrdom . . . The entire nation must prepare itself for a long and arduous endeavor, which might require the alteration of most of our customs, our concepts, and our capacity to endure difficult trials."

There was always bitter violence etched into the country's psyche, as deep as the fold of the brain. Banditry and vendetta, almost Sicilian in their barbarity, have haunted Colombia since its inception. In the War of a Thousand Days between 1899 and 1902, Colombians managed to kill more than a hundred thousand of their compatriots. Total destruction of the enemy, in the purest Spanish style, has always been the rule in Colombia.

The most recent violence emerged out of the fight, common to Latin America, between liberals, representing the masses, and conservatives, representing the landed, seignorial class. Though

the liberals were in power until 1946, they were able to do little
about fulfilling the wants of the people—indeed, their promises
and intentions only increased and frustrated them.

An addiction to violence as a means of solving problems is not,
of course, uncommon in Latin America. The Bolivian tin miners,
one of the most violent peoples in the world, have a game in
which the players all stand in a circle passing a stick of dynamite;
the one who runs first is disgraced. But what marked the Colombian experience was the fact that, after 1946, violence never fell
below critical proportions in any part of the country. From 1949 to
1953 it was country-wide, ranging to the period 1958–60, when it
was possible to lift the state of siege in all but five departments.

The year 1946 was the watershed because of Jorge Eliecer
Gaitán, the messianic leader of the liberal party who promised
radical reform to benefit the masses. A great orator and enormously
popular leader, Gaitán lost the election of 1946 to the ultra-
conservatives when his own party split over his radical programs.
By 1948 the country was in turmoil, and it was just then that the
Ninth International Conference of American States was scheduled
to meet in Bogotá.

Violence permeated the atmosphere, and the meeting opened
in an atmosphere of barely suppressed tension. A worker was
arrested while trying to place a bomb in the capital, where the conference met. Handbills attacked the United States, the conference and the aristocratic delegates "who dined in state while the
people went hungry," and there were rumors of a bomb plot
against U.S. Secretary of State George C. Marshall.

Then on April 9, as Colombians were milling through the streets
of Bogotá at lunch hour, Gaitán was shot on the street near the
capital. His enraged followers kicked and pounded the assassin
to death, and Bogotá exploded in one of those dark days in Latin
American history which has come down to us under the name
bogotazo—three mad days of rioting, burning, looting and killing.
Mobs marched on the president's palace and, repulsed by the national guard, rushed the nearby capitol, shouting for the death of
the arch-conservative, Laureano Gómez, and for the end of the
conference. The liberal-sympathizing police turned arms and am-

munition over to the mob and for three days Bogotá was in a state of revolution.

The *bogotazo*—where a young visiting Cuban student leader, Fidel Castro, observed the holocaust—was brought under control, but Colombia was embarked on one of the darkest periods of world history. Had it happened anywhere except Latin America, the world would have been stunned; as it was, being in the area that is not real to most people, few know today the horror of *la violencia.*

The fury of class bitterness spread to the remote rural areas, which in Colombia are unusually isolated and remote from centers of power. Politicians in Bogotá urged their followers on, from the safety of the capital city, and conservative and liberal villages wiped each other out. Villagers were herded into buildings that were then dynamited and burned. The common weapon was the machete, and the ritual of hacking, mutilating, and dismembering became a way of life. In the House of Representatives in 1949, several conservatives drew pistols and fired upon the liberal members, who shot back. One deputy was killed on the spot and another was fatally wounded. The pictures of *la violencia* became more and more brutal, as it gradually changed from political vendetta to a savage, pathological banditry.

In the later years, bandits grew to adulthood who had known nothing but the violence. There was no longer any political excuse. Bandits would stop a bus, line up the passengers on the side of a cliff and shoot everyone. Their favorite victims were pregnant women. The ones who died quickly were lucky. Others were victims of an operation peculiar to the Colombian bandits wherein they cut a hole in the person's neck and pulled his tongue out through it. The Colombian sociologist Orlando Fals Borda has described the terror antiseptically: "The conflict passed through successive stages: (a) a stage of directed conflict and (b) a stage of total conflict, or conflict of annihilation."

There was an element of the phenomenon that was particularly fascinating. In 1951 and 1952 the violence extended to creating little pockets of guerrilla fighters which, through the influence of the Colombian Communist party, set up five autonomous "little

republics." They did not recognize the Colombian state and felt
no consciousness of nationality. A primitive form of agrarian reformers, they were besieged in the wild mountainous regions of
Colombia where no one could get to them.

I visited the major "little republic" in 1965. It was called
Marquetalia, and it had just been taken over by the Colombian
army in its new campaign to "pacify" the little republics. Marquetalia was particularly important because it had been the lair
and kingdom of the worst bandit, Manuel Marulanda, popularly
called Tiro Fijo or "Sure Shot."

The republic of Marquetalia was born in 1952, but really was
activated in 1960 when Tiro Fijo, who had been a local bandit boss
living more or less openly, attacked a group of soldiers and killed
nine. He fled into Marquetalia and took it over, along with his
Communist ideologue, Isauro Yosa. His pictures show Tiro Fijo,
long considered the most terrible and brutal of the bandits, to be
an unprepossessing man with a flat face and slit eyes. But there
were more interesting pictures to come out of Marquetalia—the
common pictures of the bandits, posed in their favorite stance,
with their caps on and their guns ready to shoot.

With the extremely rugged terrain and the absence of any
federal authority, it was easy to establish Marquetalia. There were
only a few Indians there, chewing the narcotic *coca* leaf, so the
"Communists" took over the mountains and valleys. The settlement grew to about three thousand persons. In the "town" of Marquetalia, which was actually just a cluster of houses, there were
also barracks for a guerrilla force, which came and went in patrols
throughout the mountains.

Organizationally, they had a military chief and a political chief,
who indoctrinated the people in a primitive form of agrarian
Marxism. Land was held in common. Orders, money and arms
came from the Colombian Communist party, which was jealously
proud of its little republics. It was only when the Colombian government eventually decided to move against the republics that the
Communist party adopted a violent line against the government.

Marquetalia must have been a strange place, at best. The
farmers raised oranges, avocados, papaya, sugar, coffee, bananas

and yucca. There were some cows. There were also thirty to forty "tax collectors" who collected six *pesos* a month and a share of the harvest from surrounding farmers on pain of death for failure to pay.

Every once in a while someone ventured from outside into the republic. Father Heli Ramírez, the priest from the nearby town of Planadas, walked in one day in 1960. "When they tried to indoctrinate me with Communism, I changed the subject," the priest recalled. "They allowed me to say a mass once and all the women came, but none of the men." In 1962 a male nurse, named Pedro Antonio Ardino, went in as a government employee, during a brief time of truce with the central government. "I saw two or three meetings where they were teaching Communism," Ardino related to me in the nearby town of Gaitania, where by then he was head of the health post. "There were about twenty women and the numbers of men always changed. Sometimes there were twenty, sometimes two hundred. Then, suddenly, the mood changed and they thought I was a spy. One night they came after me and shot eighteen or twenty times. I ran away into the forest and finally made my way out."

In 1964 the Colombian army, one of the few really professional armies in Latin America, started a major campaign against the bandits and, in June of that year, it moved into Marquetalia. "Action Marquetalia" was justified by the fact that Tiro Fijo's men were growing more and more pugnacious. As well as attacking villages and killing villagers, they were shooting down planes. Three battalions were deployed in the action and Colombian soldiers spent two months walking up the canyons, often cutting new mountain paths as they went. Tiro Fijo's strange band of "agrarian Communists" abandoned Gaitania, the last little town they had held just outside Marquetalia, and let it be known they would fight at a narrow gorge at a spot named Juntas. "No soldier will cross Juntas," they told the townspeople.

But a dual attack by Colombian soldiers and helicopters supplied by the U.S. aid mission broke the resistance, and the bandits fled into the mountains, burning most of the meager buildings that had been Marquetalia as they went. Of the estimated three

thousand persons in the "independent republic," most went to
Río Chiquito, another republic nearby. Some "came out" to regular
towns, and about 120 were killed. Tiro Fijo lived on and was soon
to turn into a Castroite, since he was, one might say, ideologically
unstable.

But the lore of the bandits and their weird attraction for the
Colombian people lived on. I was standing on one of the dusty
streets of Gaitania, a tiny town on the side of a mountain, when
a nine-year-old boy came along and led me down past brightly
painted wooden houses to show me where Jacobo Prías Alape,
alias Charro Negro, one of the other bandit bosses, had died at
the hands of rival bandits. "He came out of that house," the boy
said eagerly, pointing to bullet holes in a bright blue wooden door,
"and he walked a few feet before the men over there shot him. He
staggered and fell. Then the men came over and cut his throat
with their machetes." Of such is legend woven in the country of
la violencia.

Perhaps the world ignored the violence so completely because it
happened in Latin America. Perhaps, too, it was because it was so
unfathomable. But some observers drew themselves out of the
shock long enough to attempt to analyze. Some offered the
traditional Latin American self-hating "curse-of-racial-mixture"
idea—that the ethnic mixture of the country caused it to have a
"low boiling point." Others suggested it was a desperation born of
generations of political promises with no real concomitant change
in the people's lives. Still others found Spanish individualism
(each man a law unto himself) and *machismo* (the cult of opposition unto the death) to be the causes.

In the 1950s several sociologists, most prominent among them
the young Protestant, Orlando Fals Borda, and a Catholic priest,
Germán Guzmán, analyzed the violence for the first time, at first
hand. They traveled to the violence areas and talked with the
bandits, and the two of them issued the study which became the
classic work on this strange, very Latin American phenomenon.
What they found was that the violence was a revolt against the
excessive authoritarianism of the past, a seeking for revolution . . .

"The violence is the outlet for a frustrated revolution—you can't compare it to anything else," Fals Borda said one day, sitting in his office in the National University of Colombia in Bogotá. "It's a new type of violence. It became respectable to use violence. But this went out of bounds. It became something new, amorphous, much more dangerous."

But the "revolt" against the authoritarianism of the past— based in one class and in one exclusive outlook toward life in which the masses of people did not share—was not only evident in Colombia, it was coming to the fore all over Latin America. Wherever they had a chance—and often against enormous odds— the masses of Latin voters voted for liberal reforms in preference to either autocratic dictators or autocratic Marxists. In all the de- mocracies, democratic organizers were concerning themselves with community organization and with the "forming" of the people, with teaching them how to assert themselves in society and what channels to march through on the way up. Still another expression of the change was a spontaneous turning away, on the part of the people themselves, from the old forms of the past. This took the form, to give only one example, of a turn to Protestantism and in particular to the unstratified Pentecostal cults. It also took the form of mass movements to the cities and to the "new places" where people could throw off the shackles of the past—social and psychological.

A third reaction was the spectacular, often suicidal, and desper- ate way of the guerrilla movements and the ritual demonstrations. This was the way of the angry young students who would overturn the world with their bare hands. When threatened these young men became suicidal. When in power they most often became the new authoritarians.

The first such example, the community development idea, really began in the 1940s and 1950s with the rise to popularity and to power of the new leaders of the Democratic left. It is difficult to trace exactly where it started, but probably it was in Puerto Rico, that half-Latin, half-American island that served as the fore- runner and proving ground for so many of the ideas for social change that later were to appear elsewhere. In the flurry and verve that hit that island after Luis Muñoz Marín became governor and the United States decided to turn it into a showcase for democratic change, democratically oriented, super-idealistic social workers went out to the villages to spur the villagers on, literally, by doing nothing.

Their conscious idea was to break the dependence upon outer authority that had kept the islanders passive and obedient in the past. First the islanders, wanting a new road or bridge or community building, would invite the social workers to come, expecting them to do the job for them, just as the central government had always been the source to which the poor went for favors.

Instead the social workers simply came and did nothing. Eventually the villagers began to realize that they wouldn't get anything that way, so they began to hold meetings and themselves decided how to get the bridge or road. The idea was to break the hold of the authoritarian past in one generation, to internalize authority. By and large they did it, even if it caused natural disruptions in society.

Puerto Rico pioneered, too, in self-help housing, something that then appeared in South America, and in a particularly dramatic form in the new Venezuelan industrial complex in the backwoods, Ciudad Guayana. In order to integrate slum families, without too great a sense of upheaval, into the new modern Puerto Rico, they brought the huts from the slums to land outside of San Juan and placed one hut on each lot. Then the government provided technical aid and loaned the people the money and gradually— some in individual family working groups, some in community groups—they built their own homes.

The entire idea of community development—developing the individual marginal man in Latin America so he would have the confidence and ability to live as an independent person—grew in Venezuela under Rómulo Betancourt's democratic regime, in Peru with Belaúnde's ideas about development, in Chile and in other countries too. The Chileans in particular, holding their almost apocalyptic view of the importance of "forming" the marginal people and organizing them to form their own destinies, were insistent that, although in the first stages of organization there might necessarily be some paternalism, in the last analysis it must be the new individuals who made the decisions about their lives.

Perhaps the most interesting attempt to "form" people and to awaken them took place in the barren northeast of Brazil in the early 1960s. Natal is a white, sun-baked town that sits in the sun on the northern coastline. It is such a strange and poor little town that the best place for visitors to stay is in the local hospital, whose nuns are as efficient in registering guests as any check-in desk at a big hotel.

But something began happening in Natal when the local bishop, Eugenio Sales, began a vast program whose theme in Portuguese was the word *concientização*. This term, untranslatable in precise terms, roughly means "to make people conscious" or "making people aware politically and socially." It was a fully integrated program, with radio schools, the formation of trade unions, community action groups and even some curious little booklets for teaching literacy that soon became a *cause célèbre*. For the booklets were designed not only to teach people to read, they were also designed to teach the peasants their rights in a world that was all too imperfect. One lesson was called "The peasant wants justice in his work." Another was entitled, "We fight for justice, truth and unity among men." And a third, "We are fighting to construct a new society."

Two groups—one revolutionary, one gradualist, part inside and part outside the church—began contending for control of *concientização*. "For one, it was the means to wake up the wretched, lethargic masses—part of a pedagogy of revolution," Henrique C. de Lima Vaz, professor of philosophy, Federal University of Belo Horizonte, Brazil, has written. "Its natural outcome, as its proponents saw it, was nothing less than a revolutionary transformation of society from the ground up. An alternate group . . . wanted to use it for the social integration of the marginalized groups, whose underprivileged status was thus placed in the foreground. Basic education, these reformists hoped, could give these depressed groups the means to catch up with and be integrated into the body of society."

But the proponents of change, one kind or another, never got a chance to see which group would prevail. When the military took over the country in 1964, the literacy booklets went underground. Although Catholic in inspiration, they were seized as subversive literature, and only a few remained in hiding, to be drawn out on special occasions to show to visitors like me.

To the Marxists the formation of the "new Latin American man" must be done with equal care, with conscious deliberativeness. For they all agree that man *must be formed*; that Latin American society has only the human shell, none of the human substance. But it is part of the Castroite rationale that man does not himself realize in the early throes of revolutionary fervor what he is doing. It is telling in this respect that eight years after his revolution, Fidel Castro was still formulating the ideology of his revolution.

And how did he explain away such a lengthy period of gestation between the act and the birth? In his twenty-sixth of July speech in 1966 he asked the people, standing for hours in the hot sun in the Plaza de la Revolución to hear him talk: "Did you understand it then?" and they shouted, "No!" And he asked them, "Did *we* understand it then?" And they shouted, "No!" And then he answered, "We know now that *man must gain consciousness of what he is doing through the fight and not before it . . .*"

Here is the main difference between the liberal democratic approach and the Marxist approach. The democrats believe to a great extent in giving to the people the tools for self-expression and self-realization and largely letting them use them for what they seek. The Marxists believe man must be formed *in a specific way* and in a specific philosophy and for specific ends: theirs.

Democratic community organization, in various forms and with various intent, has been carried through by a number of groups in Latin America—the Peace Corps, national community development corporations, the CIA-backed International Development Corporation, to name a few. But the unifying and important thing in all these efforts was that everyone involved in the field reported the same thing—that the Latin American poor, the undigested marginal people who had heretofore taken no real part in their society—were enthusiastic about the possibility and that they had quickly given their energies to it. Nor, despite centuries of obedience, were they simple rubber stamps of the programs.

In Santo Domingo, in the Dominican Republic, the local government-sponsored community action program had, as the jewel in its cap, a project by which some two hundred acres of land had been reclaimed in the southwestern desert-like Azua section, an area of empty, barren sand. The project had taken twenty-nine families, organized them, bought a well, and the farmers did well raising watermelons.

The day I visited the project we circled round and round the watermelon patch, with the vast desert and the blue sky in the background, looking for Eugenio Díaz, the president of the association. We finally tracked him down on a back road at the far corner of the path and he jumped lithely over the fence. As the organizer talked to him, Díaz stood there with a set and stubborn look on his face.

"There is one other thing," he said with unmovable determination to the organizer, who was by far his superior in class and education. "We're quitting." The organizer looked as though the world had shaken. "You promised us we'd get our own land," Díaz said, "and we didn't get it. We're tired of working it together and, if it isn't resolved, we quit." This—in a country where Rafael Trujillo, the dictator who controlled everything, had only been dead for five years.

Nor should it be simply assumed that there is no base organization in Communist Cuba. In the many union, peasant federation and Communist party meetings I attended, I had a very definite impression that the Cubans felt strongly they were taking part in their society. Nor were they shy about expressing their feelings, even in opposition to something the government had done. Once on a trip through Cuba's remote Sierra Maestra with the minister of health and several of the top men in Castro's government, we stopped by a thin woman of about forty who had three of her eight children on her horse with her. She informed us she was the woman—we had just heard about her in the *bohio*, a few miles back—whose husband had recently died in a new hospital nearby. The villagers were plainly unhappy about the hospital and indicated they thought it was a good place to go to die, but that was about all. She showed not the slightest deference to the minister of health when he identified himself. "It's a bad hospital," she said positively, "and he wouldn't have died had he gone to another one."

The fact that power is passing (wherever the impulses of the majority of the people are respected and translated into power) to political parties which represent the needs and will of the masses of people is too obvious to be stressed. In every election in the last twenty years, "popular" candidates have been elected when the elections were fair, sometimes even against tremendous odds, when the electoral machinery was controlled by the military or the landed classes. The willingness of the marginal Latin American not only to consider but enthusiastically to embrace birth control, is another aspect of the revolt against the dicta of the past. So is the mass movement of people from the old traditional parts of Latin society to the "new places," the physical, social and psychological frontiers where the old norms do not hold.

An important element in these places is the change of tens of thousands of Latin Americans to the Protestant faith, a change that effectively demonstrates the loosening of—and revolt against—the old social ties. It was in the most advanced countries, not surprisingly, that the numbers of Protestants were largest. In Chile converts constituted about a tenth of the population. In particular the Pentecostal sects, with their unstructured organization, gained strongly. In Brazil by 1967 there were 2,600,000 Pentecostalists, marking a gain of 1,100,000 in five years.

Emilio Willems, the European-born sociologist who is a specialist on Protestantism in Latin America, found that Protestantism appeals most to those Latin Americans who find themselves removed from their customary milieu and are forced to confront new and unusual circumstances. "When undergoing a dramatic experience of change," he wrote, "Latin Americans often reject traditional Catholic values. In particular, they seek to escape from the authoritarian, hierarchial features of Catholicism and are attracted by a religious faith that stresses equalitarianism. As a result, they often find Pentecostal sects more to their liking than some of the older and institutionalized forms of Protestantism."

The third major reaction against traditional authoritarianism is the far better known one, the one that acts itself out nightly in the television commentaries, in moments when Latin America is sputtering and erupting. It is the violent demonstrations of the students against constituted authority, and it finds its ultimate expression in the entire guerrilla complex, in the idea of the idealistic young taking up arms to overthrow traditional, corrupt society.

Guerrilla warfare is nothing new, either in Latin America or in the entire Hispanic world. The name originated in the Spanish war for independence between 1808 and 1814, when the term *guerrillas* was applied to the bands of Spanish peasants who fought the French occupation armies. Guerrilla warfare was also carried on to some extent during the American Revolution and to a great degree during the Civil War. During the Spanish-American War, the Cubans formed guerrilla bands, as they would do under Fidel Castro sixty years later.

Guerrilla warfare of various types (which Latin America has known since the wars of independence) has continued sporadically in various countries during this century, but it reached its apex in Cuba in the 1950s, as Fidel Castro and his apocalyptic group of urban unemployed and peasants formed what was to become the classic guerrilla experience of this century in Latin America. The Cuban experience of forming a peasant army that would sweep down from the mountains onto the corrupt city was one that Castro would then try to use as a form to ignite revolution elsewhere in Latin America, whether it fit the other societies or not. But the important thing about the Cuban experience— and ideas of the young revolutionaries who look upon it as their archetype—was what developed during the 1960s as their philosophy and ideology toward traditional society.

The heart of this was that traditional Latin American society was corrupt and, most important, that this corrupt society was personified by the city. The corresponding idea was that the peasantry and the mountains represented purity and goodness and that the only answer was for the mountains—and thus the guerrillas

—to overtake and reform the cities. It should not be missed that what they meant by this basically was a revolt by the "real" Latin Americans, that is the peasants and marginal people, against the elites who in this interpretation and others never really were Latin Americans but actually belonged spiritually and psychologically to Europe and the United States. The "real" Latin Americans were in the countryside and the mountains; the simulated Latin Americans were in the cities.

The important element of this, in terms of the greater revolt taking place in Latin America, was that what the Castro philosophy really was saying was that the authority of the past—based in the creole elite—was without basis and that the "authority" of the marginal groups of peasants and urban workers must be substituted for it.

Soon after Castro swept down from the Sierra Maestra and took over Cuba, guerrilla movements began to spin off from the Cuban archetype like sparks off a fast-moving wheel. The Venezuelan National Liberation Movement became the second best-known one and, true to the different Venezuelan character, was far more desperate and brutal. The Central University of Caracas, a huge, sprawling campus of modern buildings in a parklike setting, became a school for crime in the service of the one Marxist ideology.

I went to the mountains of Guatemala in the fall of 1966 with the Guatemalan guerrilla movement, which in many ways is the most typical of the young Marxist movements that were developing across Latin America. There I was able to see the kinds of young men who were in full revolt against their societies and its rigid, vapid authoritarianism.

In many ways, Guatemala was a classic case, almost as good an example as Cuba had been only a few years before. This exquisitely beautiful little country lies just below Mexico. But where Mexico went through a total revolution in 1910 and is one of the most developed countries on earth, Guatemala still lies in its feudal slough. There is the classic and frozen mixture of the Indian-Spanish, with about 45 percent of the population pure (Mayan) Indian and about 35 percent *ladino*, the term given to Westernized mixed-bloods in Guatemala. It is the 10 percent of mostly pure Spanish blood that controls everything.

Guatemala may be Latin America's most beautiful country. Its *tierra fría* or "cold land"—the words used to describe the highland mountain regions—has a magic, misty quality about it that is breath-taking. But underneath it are all the tormenting problems of classic Latin America: a military cast which looks upon itself with puritanical righteousness as the arbiter of the country's political differences; a miserably poor rural population whose relative and absolute income moves steadily down instead of up; and a small landowning caste, one of whom gives statues of the humble Peruvian mulatto saint, San Martín de Porres, to his peasants to keep them sweet-tempered.

Guatemala had tried since 1944, when the dictator Jorge Ubico was overthrown by a massive popular democratic movement that included both students and military officers, to find some way to modernize itself and to create for itself a workable, reasonably representative government. In every election that has been held, the Guatemalan people elected democratic candidates and modern-minded men of the left. They did it again in March 1966, even though the military totally controlled the election machinery and had planned to impose its own candidate.

However, each time the elected candidates were overthrown by the military when the military decided they were going too far with reform. There was the added entanglement that the United States supported the military in its machinations, which led to the most xenophobic anti-Americanism in the hemisphere. And so many of the young, restless at best, soon came to the conclusion that democratic and evolutionary change (or even democratic revolutionary change) was no longer possible. They began to feel that the only answer to overthrowing the authoritarianism of the past was a movement that incorporated absolutist tendencies and, though they did not think of it in this way, a movement that would substitute a new authoritarianism, but of the masses.

When I made contact with them, they first hesitated about taking me to the mountains with them. They were ensconced in the Sierra de las Minas, a rather remote and barren mountain region to the east of Guatemala City, where small peasant villages had been largely isolated, even from the authority of the central government. So since 1960 the guerrilla movement had grown there, giving Marxist indoctrination courses to the villagers and using Castro's by-then Latin American strategy of forming the peasant army, and at the same time waging a war of demoralization through terrorism in Guatemala City. It was a dual tactic, but with the authority centered in the mountains, where Latin man could renew himself.

I waited for four weeks in Guatemala City to hear from the guerrillas. Sometimes I would hear nothing for a week, then they would turn up again one afternoon. During the time of waiting, several other incidents occurred. The police started following me one Sunday morning and hung around the street corners by my hotel waiting for me to lead them to someone. But being Latins of the old style, they were no great threat. They went home every day for lunch and dinner and were easy to lose by darting in and out of the market.

Finally they stopped trailing me and at that point I received a threatening letter from a rightist terrorist organization which called itself the White Hand. The letter, couched in the most vulgar suggestions, had a hand etched across it. It obviously was tied up with the police; it also was typical of *macho* politics. As has happened to other foreign women writers working in Latin America and irritating certain political factions, their threats to me were all vulgar and sexually oriented. This is the only manner in which this type of Latin man can conceive of a woman. They accused me first of being the mistress of the former dictator, a rightist, who they said had given me money and cars. In the next section they accused me of being aligned with the guerrillas (which also was untrue— I hadn't even been able to contact them). Most of all, I resented the slur on my taste—the former dictator was a very unattractive man.

Then suddenly one afternoon the guerrillas appeared, saying simply, "The time is now." We were off at 10 P.M. that night, driving three hours through the darkness and a siege which the government had imposed in order to capture the guerrillas, to the

Sierra de las Minas. For three nights we walked over mountain ranges, slept on the ground, ate tortillas and beanpaste, and talked.

The twenty-nine guerrillas in our unit were mostly young. They came from all classes, though most were or had been students, and they had modern ideas about changing their society. "The Guatemalan constitution says a woman is subservient to her husband," César Montés, the leader of the guerrillas told me in disgust one day, as we both rested on the side of the mountain. "Can you imagine such feudal concepts!" They all wanted to create a "new society" and they felt driven to do it on their own, without help from anyone. This sometimes led to unconsciously ironic utterances. When I asked César one day whether they got money from Cuba he said in a wounded voice, referring to the fact that the guerrillas made a great deal of money through kidnaping wealthy people and robbing banks: "You've heard about our kidnapings and robberies. You know, we're self-supporting!"

All of the guerrillas were interesting as types, but the Guatemalan guerrilla who called himself "Miguel" was the one who interested me most. He was dark-haired and handsome and moved with an urbane air. Having studied at one of the finest European universities, he often conversed with me in German. The others wore khaki shirts and hats, high boots and faded blue pants, but Miguel wore a cocky straw hat and expensive Continental sweaters, shirts and trousers. He carried a suitcase as he tramped through the forest and in it he had his books: Karl Marx's *Das Kapital*, a book on Lenin and one on psychology. He read every chance he got. His manner was engaging, and he laughed and joked a good deal. I watched for a chance and as he perched on top of a rock in the morning sunlight one day I asked him, with some wonderment: "Why are you here? Really."

"I come from a good family, a comfortable family," he began. "We had some properties. I never lacked anything. But the boys I grew up with—they really were poor. They had nothing—no shoes, nothing. It all seemed so unfair to me, that I had everything and they had nothing.

"You see, we all believe now that democratic revolution here is impossible. This way is closed. We had a revolution here in 1944 and two progressive presidents, but always they were overthrown by the military . . ." He shrugged, but in the happy manner he had of doing everything. "Gradually I came to believe this was the only way."

He leaned forward. "After the 1944 revolution, under the progressive presidents, illiteracy dropped. But they were overthrown, and now it is higher than ever. We aren't going forward, we're going backwards. We know we have chosen the right path. Violence is the only path here." He repeated, with greater emphasis: "We know we are right.

"They present us as crazy men, as adventurers. This is not true. We like nice things, we like beautiful things, we like comfort. I—I like to dance, for instance. It is because we love good things that we do this. We want them for everyone."

I asked him if his family knew he was a guerrilla.

"Not exactly," he said shortly.

"What do they think you're doing when you're in the mountains?"

"You know how students are . . . You go here and there, work in politics . . ." He shrugged. "They think I am looking for work somewhere in the country . . ."

A few minutes later he was saying, his voice angry: "Here in this country the mentality is unbelievable. You know, the landowners still advertise in the papers 'A large *finca* (hacienda) to sell with 200 hectares and 300 Indians.' They have no humanity at all." Miguel was killed about a year later.

All of the guerrillas I met were, like Miguel, driven by a sense of outrage about things-as-they-are-and-always-have-been. They wanted to change things and the only way they could see to do it was to totally destroy the Old Order ("The rich never voluntarily give up power," they said over and over). Marxism offered them the only coherent, fully integrated, total ideology by which to transform their societies from feudalism to modernism, and they embraced it like a lonely man who finally found a willing woman. That they would form another authoritarian structure does not concern them—they believed it would be a genuine authority because it would be of "the masses of the people."

On the larger scale there is still, of course, the question of who will win. There is still a possibility that the aristocratic authoritarianism of the past will simply be replaced by a new military authoritarianism or proletarian authoritarianism. What there is no question of is what the masses of Latin Americans want. They have shown over and over that they favor some type of natural democratic development, and in many places they have spontaneously organized themselves in order to have it.

CHAPTER 11

The New People in the New Places—
Democracy Among the Marginal Men

"Neither the feudal loyalties characteristic of the hacienda system nor the more subtle controls of the kinship group find much chance to survive in the impersonal and atomistic society of the city and the rural frontier." Emilio Willems.

"Every time a road is built, nothing is the same." Father Raymond Conrad, priest and advisor to Dominican peasants who spontaneously went out and built themselves a road.

In the beginning they settled along the shorelines that kept them closest to the sea and closest to the Spain and Portugal of their birth. For several centuries they clung there, like children afraid to leave a father's door, like crabs hovering in the foam after the waves had crashed.

The cities faced the sea, not the interior, which not unrealistically was perceived as an infernal place of dark jungles, inhospitable peaks and windblown savannahs. And the early Latin Americans of the first few centuries in the New World strung themselves and their progeny out like long uneven necklaces along the jagged coastlines of their strange new continent.

This is still the pattern perceived by outsiders today, and to some—but only to some—extent it is true. For in addition to the beads of cities and peoples along the coasts there is the enormous group of Latin Americans of the shantytowns and the interior—the often marginal Latins—the unconsciously uprooted and the Latins who consciously uproot themselves and carry themselves somewhere else, thus changing their ways of life and thought . . . the new towns . . . the new places.

It is these Latins that the new political movements appeal to and aim for—it is these Latins who begin the movements. It is these Latins who form the new modern ideologies, these Latins who are giving the new forms and the new substance to Latin life. It is this group that the new leaders are coming from. And largely it was movement that made these people something new.

Movements to the interior, like Brazil's profound "interior quest" launched by the famous pioneering brigands, the *bandeirantes*. But also, particularly today, movements of people to the cities.

In Latin America as in all history, it was movement that changed and reformed and molded men and made them into something new as they put aside and forgot the past and built new futures. But it is another peculiarity of Latin America that here few have perceived the breadth and profundity of movement that has been going on—it is still seen as a static continent shaken only by palace revolutions and the sensuous contortions of the cha cha cha.

Yet, look. In 1925 the urban sector of Latin America comprised about 33 percent of the population. In 1945 it had reached 39 percent, by 1955 it was 45 percent, and by the 1960s more than 50 percent of the people lived in the cities. Not surprisingly the most massive migration occurred since World War II.

Poor Brazilians from the drought-ridden *sertão* in the northeast were piling in trucks and traveling the brutal six-day trip to São Paulo, where special stations had been set up to find work for those of them who lived through the trip. Peruvians from the *altiplano* were walking down to the coastal cities while Bolivians were riding trucks down newly cut roads to colonization projects in the eastern jungles. Chileans were crossing over into Argentina for work, Venezuelans were trekking out to their massive new industrial complex at Ciudad Guayana, and Colombians were devouring themselves alive in *la violencia* because there was no place for them to go to seek change.

An important sociological report by the Catholic Church on "The Church and Social Change in Latin America" in the early 1960s stated: "If we take our figure for urbanization, the number of people who live in cities of a population of a million or more, we arrive at the conclusion that in 1955 a larger proportion of the population lived in such cities in Latin America than in the United States. It changes the image of Latin America as an essentially rural and tradition-minded continent."

Other statistics clearly establish that Latin America is the region of the world where the population flow from rural to urban areas is occurring at the fastest rate. Eduardo Frei has said, "This means that population masses invade the urban centers and surround the cities with belts that under a variety of names typify the social reality of direst poverty, marginal settlements, and subproletariats."

The importance of both the move to the frontiers and the move to the cities is similar—it is the move, the change, that frees men. As the Catholic Church report defines it: "An entire new society and culture arise and the majority of the basic social institutions are transformed." It keeps talking about those two concepts: "A new society and culture."

Emilio Willems, the German-born sociologist who was formerly with Vanderbilt University and is a specialist on cultural change in Latin America, writes that "the cities as well as the recently settled rural areas of the South (in Brazil) are relatively free from the strictures of the traditional social order. The new class structure is the product of considerable social mobility: neither the feudal loyalties characteristic of the hacienda system nor the more subtle controls of the kinship group find much chance to survive in the impersonal and atomistic society of the city and the rural frontier. If a man wishes to join a group of religious dissenters he may do so without feeling impeded by what his family and compadres may have to say about his decision."

Gilberto Freyre, the Brazilian sociologist, has written in the same vein. "In Brazil," he said, "the 'moving frontier' has meant the creation of ways of life and new combinations of culture . . ."

This new man is less bound by the strictures of the past. He is more egalitarian, more cooperative with his fellows. He seeks new types of leaders—*his* leaders—and sees new perspectives. He is in almost every respect a new man, a man who both creates the new places and is created by them.

What emerges in the process involved in creating the new people of the new places is not unlike what emerged when a similar process took uprooted lower-class men from Europe and made them into that New Man, the American. In both cases, one of the most interesting outcomes was the fact they created their own new social and political structures. And today in every "new" community, in every country, among every racial and linguistic group, there is evidence of a spontaneous self-organization on the part of these Latins that is the rule and not the exception.

You find some kind of vigorous and working grass-roots organization in the *barriadas* of Lima, the *callampas* of Santiago, the *favelas* of Rio and São Paulo, the shantytowns of Caracas, the half-breed towns of Amazonia. It exists often in contradiction to the historic idea that the poor in Latin America are hopelessly wedded to the strongman leader. It is the new juxtaposed against the old, and in most cases the forms are still mixed. But in most of Latin America it indicates there is a self-generated authority to build on that could well lay the basis for truly representative and democratic societies in the future. You find this innate sense of self-organization everywhere—even in unusual places like Rio's samba schools.

Every year, during carnival in February, Rio de Janeiro is transformed into a throbbing, swinging, jostling, heaving, ecstatic, orgiastic mob. The wide, usually aristocratic streets of downtown Rio become the parade grounds for a different form of Carioca than the resident of Rio who usually roves there. The streets fall then to the *sambistas*—the men and women of the *favelas* and the *morros* and the poor towns on the mountainside who take over the city, and their organizations are the "samba schools" which actually put on carnival.

But what is particularly interesting about carnival is not only the chaos and turbulence of the carnival act itself, it is the intricacy and correctness of the organizations that put it on. Each "samba school" has a charter or constitution—long documents with endless lists of officers and the excessive detail common to countries under Roman Law. The "school's" objectives are carefully listed: to promote and expand Brazil's popular music form and to provide recreational, social, sporting and cultural activities for members. Most schools have four organs: a general assembly, where all dues-paying members take part; a board of directors; a deliberative council; and a financial council.

Membership rules are strict and the school can suspend members "who have committed acts detrimental to the guild's interests." The director of social events can refuse admission to anyone who "may appear dressed in clothes which are incompatible with certain social occasions" and can expel anyone who is "discourteous or behaves rudely or ungraciously."

As to membership, there are proprietary members or shareholders, contributing or regular members, honorary members, benefactors, and members of honor, like the president of the republic and his ministers. Meetings are always held late at night and they use the expressions of the British parliament, like "Your Excellency" and "My Illustrious Friend," in addressing one another. Meetings tend to be very emotional. A man was once expelled from Imperio Serrano, one of the big schools, for bad behavior. When the other members saw him sitting in a corner, weeping, someone shouted that such cruelty was intolerable, that it was the others who should be punished for such inconsiderateness. The man was carried out in triumph.

In addition to their own internal organization, the samba schools are organized into a General Union of Schools of Samba of Brazil, which receives subsidies from the state to encourage carnival. It is not surprising that in Brazil this kind of spontaneous grass-roots organization has revolved around a cultural event like carnival, since Brazil is the country that has the surest cultural (if not political) sense of itself. Brazilians know what it is to be a Brazilian—far more than the citizens of the Spanish-speaking countries know what it is to be a member of their country. There is a well-developed, rich and intricately textured Brazilian music, literature and art.

In the Spanish-speaking countries, on the other hand, the impulse is largely toward self-generated organizations which aim at political and economic power through unity. Sometimes they are traditional (in the American sense) community organizations. Sometimes they are cooperatives. But they all have one thing in common: the people who do not take part in the formal society of Latin society have formed their own "real" and working societies.

On the outskirts of Santiago de Chile, there is a typical cooperative housing organization, the Cooperative Yolanda Díaz Pérez, named after a social worker who was instrumental in helping organize the cooperative. The streets are dusty, but in little patches there are neat wooden houses, many of them surrounded by gardens, even with roses. The co-op was formed through the spontaneous efforts of the people; the social worker was *asked* by them to help them. They put their money together in order to build their houses and the Sunday morning I visited the neighborhood they were having a meeting in the little wooden clubhouse they built for themselves.

The slogans on the walls were typical: "That which you do today your sons will appreciate tomorrow. Cooperate!" "Why do we have nothing? We want to do everything!" "The new world will be a better world." "Don't think of yourself, think of your children. Cooperate!"

The meeting was impressive, for these were simple people, the people of Latin America who supposedly hate and distrust each other and cannot, the story goes, be made to work together. They were discussing their mutual work plans and, indeed, that very morning the men had been out straightening the roads and building sidewalks. "You are the only ones who can decide," the president said to the people, sitting there on the hard wooden benches, as they discussed problem after problem, "so I present it all to you."

Much the same sort of meeting goes on in the Lima *barriadas*, where the people have carried down with them, from the mountains, the cooperative habits of the Indian communities, where each man has a voice. A few years ago one of these neighborhoods, Huascarán, just like many neighborhoods in the United States, got involved in an interesting little urban renewal battle with the office of the National Housing Board. Huascarán looks much like all the other *barriadas*. Along with about half of the population of Lima, the residents of Huascarán live in adobe brick huts huddled along bleak and dusty streets. They have lived there, most of them, since they banded together and left Lima on July 9, 1950, invaded this land and built their homes—another expression of the desire of the urban poor for homes of their own.

After a number of battles between the *barriada cholos* and the police, in 1961, as has been mentioned, the government finally recognized the right of the *barriadas* to exist. The people were given the land on which their houses stood, but the government also charged itself with setting standards for the *barriadas*. If these funny little neighborhoods were to remain and to become permanent, respectable communities, then some order had to be brought to this helter-skelter development, and according to the government's "standards," some of the houses were just too big.

The situation of the sober and serious city planners, moving into dusty free-spirited Huascarán to try to make some sense of it all, led to some comical scenes. At one point a delegation from the *barriada* went down to the offices of the big Lima newspaper *La Prensa* to complain about the state making them live in smaller houses. It was a "crime against private property," these consummate home-dwellers insisted.

The idealistic, hard-working young architects of the housing board, meanwhile, moved their files, maps, cards, measures, desks, and tables into a room in the big community building which the people of Huascarán had built. One day at the height of the squabble, Rafael Mesías, leader of the brigade that was trying to inject sense into Huascarán, spread out a map of the community and tried desperately to explain what they were doing. "These broken lines are the houses that exist," he said, pointing to a disorderly array of unusual shapes and sizes. "The red lines are what are going to be the lots." The neat red lines were overlaid on the chaotic broken ones. "You see," he continued, as if it all *must* be made simple, "here are five houses and they will be one house." Then he pointed out one house that would be five houses. "In many cases, the people will have to reconstruct their houses," he summed up, a little wistfully.

Once this brigade of lawyers, architects, social workers and census-takers (blue cards for men, pink for women) studied the community, they began marking it for change. They went out with paint brushes and painted white lines over the walls, roofs and ground to designate where streets, parks and sewage would go. In no time at all Huascarán's mud houses were a maze of large white stripes. It looked as if a series of intersecting baseball diamonds had been painted over everything in town.

Meanwhile, every day the villagers gathered at the door to the office, their faces troubled and their eyes accusing. "But my house is completely built," an old Indian man dressed in a white suit told David Flores Vásquez, a housing board lawyer, at the desk inside. "Why should it come down? Why? Why?"

To outsiders, and particularly to middle- and upper-class Peruvians, places like Huascarán look like miserable slums, seedbeds of crime and disorganization. To the people in them, they are pride itself. Like all the marginal people, they are joiners and avid, almost pathetic believers in the efficacy of organization. They are happy with their homes and with their organizations. They cannot understand why the housing board insists upon cutting up their little town, all in the interests of a uniformity that exists nowhere else in Peru.

Padres de Familia del Barrio Huascarán is the local community organization, on whose letterhead was written "Founded on July 19, 1950, legally recognized July 14, 1953." This organization was then affiliated with the Frente Unido de Defensa de las Barriadas del Peru (United Front for the Defense of the Peruvian Barriadas) which met on Tuesday nights to discuss and act on common problems.

These organizations, which were present in the *barriadas* throughout Peru, were not formal or ineffective groups. The people took an active interest in the meetings, where the exchange was lively and opinionated. They elected their own leaders, long be-

fore President Belaúnde put through the municipal election law
in 1963, and the large numbers of people they could get out voluntarily to go in delegations downtown showed the obvious solidarity they felt with one another and the special organizational
relationship they had with one another. They also worked communally in the *barriadas*. It was common to see the men and
even the little boys out working and sweeping the streets.

Evangelista Batiquín, the president of the association, explained:
"We take our recommendations to the housing board. And they
listen." Taking visitors on a tour through the *barriada*, followed
by thirty to forty people, he demonstrated his pride in the area.
"Here will be the Malecón Drive," he said, his arm sweeping out
over the dirty Rimac River, where little boys were splashing in the
filth. "We hope for a park here," one of the women added shyly,
"and a school of two floors."

Another interesting phenomenon that has been happening
spontaneously in every country in Latin America in recent years
is the gathering together of people, villagers and some urban residents, to build whatever they needed. It is important to posit this
against the egotistical behavior of many in the middle and upper
classes. This "gathering together" has particularly been centered
in building roads and this is not unsymbolic: it shows the villages
are opening up; it shows the people want to move, to go places.

In one case in a whitewashed parish house on the Dominican
border with Haiti, an American priest, Father Raymond Conrad, at
first tried to discourage the peasants from building a road. But
they wouldn't give in. "They got the idea themselves," he said,
"and there they were, out there with picks and shovels and singing
in chorus."

He smiled a sly smile. "The road has already been used," he went
on. "Campaign caravans have used them and others will come.
The villagers were so pleased. When we originally talked about it,
I told them the ambulance would come in some day and take out
the sick . . . that the peanut people would come in and take out
the peanuts to market . . . and that they'd be able to make their
own wagons . . . and I'd bring in barbed wire. I didn't tell them

the priest could come out then to say mass, but it was in the back of my mind."

This was only five years after the death of the Dominican dictator, Rafael Trujillo, who had robbed these peasants, the most backward in Latin America, of their initiative for thirty-two years. Nowhere more than in the Dominican Republic were people so inured with the idea of bringing everything to the *"jefe máximo."* As the priest commented in conclusion, "It's slow, but it's up from paternalism."

The stories of roads could go on indefinitely. But the most important thing about this sudden spontaneous building of roads is that it is a saga of sorts; it represents, on the part of people historically rooted in fatalism, the spontaneous assumption of a measure of responsibility for their lives and futures. It is a striking out at society, a reminding that "we are here and we want to go places."

In the original colonies, as one historian put it, the colony "sat down" in the static Spanish square. Historically Latin American cities were laid out in an exact grid plan, and grouped around the central plaza were the symbols of authority—the cathedral, the archbishop's house, the presidential palace and usually some military building. But in the new places this pattern is shattered.

Out in the newly colonized eastern jungle regions of Bolivia, there is a Wild West kind of town, Caranavi, whose center is a bustling, unruly, arrow-straight street that is typical and significant. "Look at these towns," the Bolivian diplomat and publisher Julio Sanjines pointed out once. "There are no squares with the cathedral and government buildings. Here there are main streets, for people are moving on and not stopping."

The movement goes both ways—the countryside reaching out toward the cosmopolitan city and the ingrown, static city reaching out to the "real" values of the countryside. In the last ten years, for instance, Latin America has witnessed the conscious building of many "new places": some of them, like Brasília, spectacular; others, like Venezuela's Guayana, powerful. And these, too, have exerted a profound change on the human beings involved.

Look at one telling example. Maria Antônia, a small and handsome Brazilian woman, sat in her living room in the housing block where she lived in Brasília, the dramatic new capital of Brazil. Wife of Ramiro de Pôrto Alegre, a Brazilian physicist, she had lived all over the world and was an unusually worldly Latin woman. She wore a trim and fashionable slack suit as she relaxed in an avant-garde leather strap chair and gazed out the huge windows at the ordered landscape of Brasília.

The scene before her eyes, with large stolid housing blocks, looked very much as if some giant child had taken his blocks and scattered them carelessly across the red mud plain of central Brazil. For centuries—part of their semimystical "interior quest"—the Brazilian had dreamed of moving their capital inland, of reclaiming the interior. Then, in the late 1950s, using President Juscelino Kubitschek's verve and architect Oscar Niemeyer's spectacular modern style, Brazília was born and tens of thousands of Brazilians had to uproot themselves and—God forbid!—actually go there and live.

"The first thing I heard when I came," Maria Antônia said, smiling an ambivalent smile, "was about the 'Brasília neurosis.' It apparently hits most of the women. This is when a doctor is called first thing in the morning for a woman who just hasn't been feeling right, and what does he do? He sends her home to her mother for a few weeks." She curled up in the modernistic chair. "Most of the couples here are just married. They're not used to being alone. Without their mothers. There is nothing to do—no nightclubs, a few films. I never felt it because I was used to living apart from my family. But the others!" She threw her trim arms up in a gesture that seemed to say, "What to do?"

"The worst thing here is the dust," she went on. "It is everywhere. But it's an ideal place for raising children. Brasília is one huge backyard—they can run everywhere. You can let them free here. It's not like Copacabana Beach. It's hard to get maids, and most women work, so they have washing machines and they train the children to make their own beds. You have to have a car. Housewives can't get by without cars."

Then she shifted to what happens to Brazilians who were uprooted and brought to an outrageous place like Brasília. It was an analysis that applied not only to Brasília, but also to many of the "new places" where the past is forgotten and a new kind of man emerges. "I feel this is not Brazil at all," Maria Antônia said, with an energetic, obviously considered approach to her subject, her handsome, dark eyes shining. "There is a sense of community here. We have PTA meetings—and they are not very natural to us. There is a club for teenagers. People feel bored. It is like the U.S.A. They are lonely for their families and they make up for it by clinging together. I cannot but feel it is artificial, but what else can one do?

"This is what is going to happen elsewhere in Brazil. This is just the first place. When you have your mothers and sisters around you, you feel safe; you don't need other people. But here there are people from everywhere. Piauí—I never met anyone from the state of Piauí, and here I met one. There are people from Goiás. This building has many from Bahia, and they make Bahian food. We have a Festival of States and everybody brings food from his state. There's even a name for people born in Brasília now. It's Candango. That used to be for people born in the North. Now we call everyone born here Candango.

"I've never seen so many people going to church as here. I think they go to church to get a community feeling. Protestant churches, too."

In closing she said something remarkable for a Latin American, whose family feelings have always been very exclusive: "We're all like one family here."

The feeling of uprootedness is not simply a figment of Maria Antônia's imagination. It comes out in every conversation with Latin Americans recently moved away from their traditional homes to one of the "new places." On the one hand, for the more adventurous young, there is a sense of excitement and of being pioneers. In a country like Cuba, where revolutionary change has taken the place of traditional mores, they have made it a matter of pride to penetrate into the "interior" and grapple with it; revolutionary fervor has taken the place of the security of the parental wings. But there is among most others a sense of being adrift and alone, so often an important element in social change.

One tall and lanky young man in Brasília who was a tour guide poured out his heart to me one day. He was twenty-two. He had one friend, Gus, the owner of the tourist agency for which he worked. "I'm all alone here," he said to me, with a look that could break a heart. "My mother is in São Paulo. I have Gus, but it's not like having a mother. I have to work for every penny here. Mother would let me get by.

"Of course, it's good for me," he acknowledged, but without conviction. "But I wish it could have been done more gradually. My aunt dared me. She said, 'Why accept your mother's money? You should be on your own now.' I said I'd do it. I thought, 'Maybe my mother will turn me down.' But she said, 'All right, then. Go ahead. You'll be back.' Then, of course, I couldn't go back. I was trapped. It's awfully hard," he summed up.

For all of these reasons, Brasília is something astonishing. In the sunset, looked at in a sweep, rising out of the empty red mud, Brasília is a grand gesture of classic sorts. It is an epic dare, and one finds oneself acting like a dreary twentieth-century mole who has just discovered his first frontier. It is also a challenge to what the Brazilians and the Latins have always been, to the sensuality and corruption of Rio and the other Latin Babylons, and to what young Latins can become.

Little by little, the Brazilians tend to remain in the city. Forced by inflation to give up Rio-hopping, they are beginning to dig roots. The air bridge has been discontinued. Roads are going across the continent and connecting Brasília with other new places, even with Bolivia and Peru. Little by little, the government is moving there. Out of necessity if nothing else, the Candangos are getting to know their neighbors, a word seldom used in Brazil before.

In Venezuela's Ciudad Guayana on the Orinoco River, the experiences were not dissimilar, although here there were conscious attempts made at egalitarianism and the integration of the marginals who began flocking there at a rate of a thousand a month.

The great Orinoco River flows out of Venezuela like a brown snake, emptying into the Caribbean just below the oil-rich island of Trinidad. For centuries it had been a lonely giant, flowing on its way with little interruption from nature or man's hand. By the mid-1960s Venezuela had built the huge Orinoco Steel

Mill and, nearby, was working the famous 2631-foot-high, 7½-mile-long ridge Cerro Bolívar. When the Venezuelan president came to dedicate the new bridge across the river at Ciudad Guayana in 1966, an old woman of the area embraced him. "Why are you so happy about the bridge?" he asked her. "It's not the bridge," she said. "It's because I've never seen the other side of the river before."

But the Venezuelans did not want Ciudad Guayana to develop like the free city around Brasília. They brought in city planners from the Massachusetts Institute of Technology to lay out the form of the city and social workers to deal with its internal structure. A housing program was worked out that was not unlike Puerto Rico's program of self-help housing. The land was already divided up before the people came, and each family got three hundred square meters on which they were allowed to build a shack before building a house.

Social class became irrelevant in Ciudad Guayana. Engineers were living side by side with workers in the same developments—an unheard-of thing in class- and status-conscious Latin America. Helena Vargas, an attractive young social worker who was working with the project, insisted there was "a community sense here." "Everybody helps," she said. "Here, nobody was actually born." There is a Rotary Club and every kind of social service. Prostitutes are rehabilitated in a program which stresses learning other work and which is strikingly like Cuba's. "This is a country on the road to development," said Mrs. Vargas, a typical young Latin American of the new stripe. "It's going to develop some kind of communitarianism." Why is *she* there? Her eyes sparkled. "Because it is very exciting to be here."

Every "new place" is different—a blend of marginal men seeking stability and brotherhood, the interior quest, the particular brand of Latin utopianism and pure economic development.

There is the utopianism, rooted deep in Latin history, of a little community outside Bogotá, "Minuto de Dios." Founded by a very knowledgeable priest, Father García Herreros, known for his popular radio programs, Minuto de Dios is a proud little theocracy in which perfection is sought. Residents work for the community once a week; they do not drink; they are obliged to attend meetings on Saturday night at which the zealous priest lectures them on proper Christian behavior.

"The problem of Latin America is collaboration," the priest commented to me, as we walked up and down the orderly little streets. "People want to collaborate, but they don't have the organization."

Father García Herreros is very ecumenical. Minuto de Dios has a John XXIII Street, but it also has a Karl Marx Street and a Martin Luther Street—"because we'd still be paying salaries of two cents if it weren't for fear of Marx and there would never have been a Vatican Council if it hadn't been for Luther." He paused. "I'm sure both of them are in heaven," he added briskly.

Not all the "new places" had this ordered optimism about them, however. One, Cuiu Cuiu in the depths of the Amazon jungle, was a clandestine gold-mining camp which consisted of two rows of little board- and thatch-roofed houses facing a dirt street. The day I visited, barefoot children moved but did not run, their hair damp in the exhausting heat of the day. Adults leaning against the sides of doors had that dull malarial look in their eyes as they gazed at the town's four cemeteries.

After arriving by bush plane from Santarém, which is on the Amazon, I found the young American post-debutante Pamela Painter, whom I was seeking. Tall, willowy and beautiful, Pamela was gold-mining with a crew of five half-breeds. We sat in her "camp" for a time while I interviewed her, and that night we decided, since there was nothing else to do but listen to the Voice of America, Radio Peking or the Voice of Nigeria, to "go to town."

This meant following a weaving path through the jungle, skirting open *burracos*, balancing on the single log that crossed the river and was covered with red ants, and climbing a mud path. At the edge of town the sheriff was waiting. "Leave your gun," he commanded. This was a new ruling, designed to cut down homicides. (There were two hundred people in town, fifty in the cemeteries.)

On the main (and only) street, we sat in one of Cuiu Cuiu's

several booming nightspots, and here you could see the "new people" of Cuiu Cuiu, this strange new place. It was an open, thatch-roofed building and men stood around the outside watching the girls—mostly thirteen- and fourteen-year-old prostitutes who come from the bigger Amazon towns and sometimes make hundreds of dollars a night. The men made money and spent it. When they had a lot they went to Belém or Manaus, rented the biggest suite in the hotel and drank and whored for several weeks. Then they came back and panned more gold, which was flown out clandestinely to secret airports in the Guianas, from which it was transported to Europe. Even here things were expensive. Beer cost $1.25 a bottle and a banana about forty cents. Storekeepers made from 200 to 300 percent profit, with everything flown in.

There was an oddly old-fashioned feeling about the whole business. People would dance the jungle two-step in wide circles, arms cranking in 1890 style in the hot damp night. No one smiled and only rarely did anyone speak. Many of the men kept their hats on while they danced.

Here as nowhere else, one felt the sadness, the lostness, of Cuiu Cuiu—and of many of the marginal people. These miners, small, undernourished, ambitious descendants of the Indian-Negro-Portuguese mixture of the Amazon races, had only themselves and their dreary work in the jungle. There was no church, no priest, no school, no marriage, not even a consigning to God when a person died.

One could not help feeling that without the solid gold talismans of the miner's pick and shovel which they all wore around their necks for luck, they would not know who or where they were.

Just as the Latin Americans always have swung pendulously back and forth, back and forth, between dictatorship and democracy, between authoritarianism and self-generated authority, so has the history of their interior and their truly new places wavered between an interior quest that was purely and ruthlessly materialistic and one that was utopian and idealistic.

Cortés, conquerer of Mexico, put the first impulse clearly when he said that he had "come for gold, not to till the soil like a peasant." And even in the early days of the discovery, man after man went into the interior, always searching for gold.

Expeditions crossed and recrossed the north of the continent searching for El Dorado, "the gilded one," for the credulous Spaniards had been told by the Indians that there was an Indian king—legend placed him in Colombia or Peru—who once a year was generously sprinkled with gold dust and then immersed in a sacred lake. In the end the legend won; a half dozen expeditions went out and perished in the jungles and El Dorado was never found. Probably, however, there *was* an El Dorado. Probably it was the tribe that lived around what is now Lake Guatavita not far from Bogotá. For we know today that the king there did paint himself with gold for an annual celebration and that they did throw small gold figures, many of which have now been found, into the small, round lake.

But nothing could disabuse the conquistadores of the idea that fabulous riches—even more fabulous than the already stupendous riches they had already found in the Inca empire—lay beyond the black barrier of the Andes. In 1540 Francisco Pizarro, the conqueror of Peru, appointed his brother Gonzalo governor of Quito and sent him on an expedition to the east, to what they called the "land of spices and gold." Gonzalo set out with two hundred Spaniards, several thousand Indians, herds of swine, dogs, and llamas, and supplies. For eight months, encouraged by the Indians they chanced upon that fortune lay ahead, they pushed on, until most of the Indians were dead from the cold and the jungle and the supplies were gone.

Unaware that they were camping on one of the streams leading to the Amazon, Gonzalo sent his lieutenant Francisco de Orellana downstream with fifty-seven men and some boats to search for food. Eventually Gonzalo, thinking Orellana was lost, led his motley crew back to Quito in August 1542.

Orellana, meanwhile, unknowingly was drifting down the greatest river on earth; he was discovering the Amazon. In August 1542 he and his men were attacked by large and apparently belli-cose Indian women whom the Spaniards named "Amazons." The Spaniards fired back, killing many of them. They were totally unaware that this was an annual spring mating ceremony of this particular tribe, which was led by females.

All the women wanted to do was carry the foreigners off to their huts and afterwards they would have been rewarded with the gold amulets the women traditionally gave their lovers. Instead the Spaniards left many of the women dead. They sailed out the mouth of the Amazon and three months later landed in Santo Domingo. In Spain they announced their discovery of "The Amazon," encouraged Spain in its rivalry with Portugal for the interior of the continent, and spun tales of gold, cinnamon and mammoth women. Orellana eventually returned to explore further, but his ship overturned in the mouth of the Amazon and the entire expedition drowned. From that time on Portugal gradually extended its sway over the Amazon basin.

Still all of these were only forays into the interior—there was no "new man" pushing into the interior to stay and to develop—and they continued forays, often brutal, for three centuries. By the seventeenth century, Brazil was still an empty land. As with the Spanish settlements, it clung to the coast.

Then suddenly in the seventeenth and eighteenth centuries the "interior quest" began. Along the coasts the settlers had created societies like the ones they had left in Europe. But on the frontiers, life was different, freer, more experimental and open. Farmers and missionaries pushed up the rivers—up the Amazon, up the Uruguay and Paraguay to Mato Grosso, up the San Francisco. The Jesuits took the wandering Guaraní Indians of Paraguay and settled them in *reducciones* which were the precursors of Father García Herreros' theocracy and Fidel Castro's utopian Communism. The gauchos—half-Indian cowboys—tamed the new settlements.

But the most dramatic—and the most predatory—were the famous *bandeirantes* of Brazil, who took their names from being members of a *bandeira* or military company. Racially the *bandeirantes* were hybrids. They were the result of the promiscuity that was rife when the Portuguese arrived without women. Father José de Anchieta, an early Jesuit who educated the Indians near what is now São Paulo, wrote at the time that "the women go naked and are unable to say no to anyone but they themselves provoke and importune the men . . . for they hold it to be an honor to sleep with the Christians." As for the Portuguese, they were "begetting offspring with procreative fervor."

Half-Indian, half-Portuguese and, their biographers uncharitably insist, half-savage, the *bandeirantes* sallied forth out of São Paulo to open the interior. Their opening of it was a rape. Following the rivers and armed with rifles, waterbags and manioc flour, they hunted Indian slaves. Organized in bands of anywhere from fifty to a thousand men, they would be gone for a year, occasionally stopping to plant and harvest crops. No place in the interior was too rough for them, and everywhere they established settlements and built roads. But mostly they enslaved the Indians.

The *bandeirantes* soon came up against the Spanish Jesuits who had concentrated the Guaraní in *reducciones*. In 1629 alone the twenty-one mission villages in the region of the Upper Paraná were attacked by a *bandeira* of nine hundred *bandeirantes* and two thousand Indian allies. Twenty-five hundred Indians were captured, of whom no more than half reached the slave markets of São Paulo.

The epic of the *bandeirantes* affected all of Brazilian history in profound ways. Profits from the slave trade poured into Brazil, laying the base for the industrialization of today. Portuguese power in the interior was enhanced at the cost of Spain. The myth of the *bandeirantes* grew and grew and, as it grew, it was cleaned and polished until today the term *bandeirante* in Brazil is almost synonymous with "pioneer" in the United States.

Time and time again, strong-willed eccentric religious "saviors" arose in the interior, just as they did on the American frontiers. One of them was Antônio o Conselheiro (Anthony the Adviser), who called himself simply "the Prophet." He appeared in Canudos, a remote region of the north of Brazil, in 1877 and, dressed in a blue linen garment, leaning on a staff, his beard blowing, his hair falling to his shoulders, his eyes filled with a fanatic magnetism, he soon became leader of the ragged hordes of the Northeast.

On an old estate in the countryside, he settled with his followers, building the old church there into a new church that looked like a mysterious fortress. The Prophet knew he would eventually have to defend himself there. Once, Arciniegas tells us, the Capuchins asked permission to preach there and were given it. But after a while the people dragged them out, shouting, "Why should we listen to the poor Capuchins when we have a prophet right here in Canudos?"

Eventually the government equipped a military expedition to crush the experiment at Canudos. Four times the Prophet and his people drove them back. Finally a large national expedition of several thousand men attacked and was successful. Approximately six hundred of the Prophet's men surrendered, only to be beheaded. The Prophet was found in front of the altar, dead of starvation.

The utopian streak, always present in such men as the Prophet, evinced itself in ways almost as bizarre and colorful as the acquisitive gold-seeking streak. One of the attempts at a self-determined utopian experiment was the flight of plantation Negroes in Brazil to the interior of the northern state of Alagoas.

There they organized a para-socialist dictatorship called the "Republic of Palmares," named after the great forest of palm trees in which they set up a fortified stronghold. The ex-slaves had a king and an organized government and historians say they pooled the products of their work, stored their crops in a community granary, and distributed food evenly. Arriving in 1631 the Negroes held out in their city of straw shacks until 1697 when, after numerous failures, the *bandeirantes* from São Paulo were able to destroy the community of some twenty thousand Negroes who, the historian Hubert Herring says, "were carrying on their business and government in a capable manner."

Nor was Palmares the only example of early Negro cooperativism; there are many others. In the beautiful town of Ouro Prêto in the south, where mineral wealth flowed out to the world of the eighteenth century, Negro slaves organized with unusual effectiveness to procure one another's freedom. Led by a man named Francisco, a large number of slaves in the mines bought their own freedom—and then the next man's. Eventually the free Negroes wound up owners of Encardideira Mine. They further organized themselves into a brotherhood of Saint Iphigenia and celebrated in a giant merrymaking spectacle that was as much African as

Christian. Unlike those in the United States, the Negroes of
Brazil worked for abolition on a massive scale.

Chico Rei, an African "king" sold into slavery in the state of
Minas Gerais in the eighteenth century, purchased freedom for
himself and his son, then worked with other freed Negroes to liberate not only his own kin but the slaves of other tribes. He became
known as the "first Negro abolitionist in Brazil," and in Ouro Prêto
today there is a church known as Chico Rei's church.

The impulse to self-generated authority, to self-government, to
cooperativism, and to a change from the authoritarianism of
traditional Spanish-oriented Latin America differs from country to
country. But the important concern is that it is present in one
form or another everywhere. In Brazil it has taken more peaceful
and evolutionary ways, because of the more prevalent Brazilian
paternalism. In Peru it has been particularly influenced by the
Indian strain in the people, which makes communal effort obliga-
tory. In Chile it is molded by the intense sense of legalism of the
people; in Venezuela by the lack of any aristocratic tradition. In
Bolivia, Mexico and Cuba there is the added push of great revolutions which did a great deal to free the people from past psychic
burdens. Even in countries with as little community sense and as
great hierarchical sense as the Dominican Republic, there is the
custom of the peasants helping one another with their crops.

Even authoritarian Paraguay was not immune to the infection.
One of the earliest illustrations of the urge toward self-government
occurred there in 1762, when the *comuneros* (roughly "those who
live communally") revolted against the strictures of Spain. One of
their leaders, Fernando Mompax, talked about the power of the
community in any republic, city, town or village and insisted that
it was more powerful than the king himself. He said the commune
might justly resist and cease to obey the law or the governor, even
if it be issued by the prince, if the people did not like him. On
Saint Augustine's day that year the common people grew so an-
noyed with the members of the town corporation (the town
officials) that they destroyed the staircase in the town hall, making
them all prisoners on the second floor. As the *comuneros'*

communal militia entered the city, cries of "Death to bad government!" went up from the crowds.

Time and time again in those years, Europeans, too, looked at Latin America and projected their utopian yearnings onto the rich, green, exotic continent. The Paraguayan missions, manned by the Jesuits, made such an impression on writers like Montesquieu that he believed Plato's Republic had been built there. Montaigne conceived the idea of the noble savage when he saw a group of Guaraní Indians from Paraguay arrive in Rouen.

At one point in his writings, Montaigne discusses the impressions of one of the Indians: "He said that in the first place, he found it strange that having seen how half the people had enough comforts and more, while the other half were emaciated by hunger and poverty, he could not explain to himself how the needy half could bear such injustices, nor why they did not seize the others by the throat and burn down their houses." It was a very easy step from this to the concept of the noble savage. It was also easy for Voltaire to send Candide to Paraguay and the Guianas in order to find the unstained purity of the indigenous race, and for Byron to dream of visiting South America where "the people are as fresh as their New World, and as violent as their earthquakes."

European ideas about the social contract early infiltrated Latin America and enormously influenced the strivings toward representative government. In Uruguay the gaucho José Artigas, who led Uruguay to independence, talked to the ranch workers about the Contract, and they understood. Rousseau's ideas were written into the Uruguayan constitution. In Chile in 1764, two years after Rousseau's book was finished, the ideal republic was sketched out by two Frenchmen who dreamed of exchanging the monarchical regime for a republic and placing its government in the hands of a "sovereign Senate." The entire idea was so intoxicating in Latin America that the very publishing of the Social Contract was banned. In Mexico a circular announced that: "Those ideas in Rousseau's Social Contract in The Spirit of the Laws by Montesquieu, and the works of other like-minded philosophers who hold that each private person with his own share of independence, which he may use at will, may concur in the election of the prince,

are proscribed because they contribute to the freedom and independence with which they seek to destroy religion, the state, the
throne, and all property, and to establish equality, which is an
impracticable and chimerical system, as France herself has proved
by her example to us."

Things have a way of becoming bizarre to the ultimate degree
in Latin America, and so it was, too, with the Social Contract. At
one point, Paraguay's Dr. Francia, one of the bloodiest dictators
in all world history, interpreted the Social Contract as meaning
that the Paraguayan people had delegated all their power to him.

But Latin America did progress—through the enlightenment,
through Romanticism, through Positivism, that philosophy
through which man was, step by step, progressing to a rational,
positivistic world. There was something in Latin America, as in
North America, something in the New World experience itself,
that nurtured the tender plants of republicanism and freedom.
As Arciniegas wrote, "The role of initiating the republican-
democratic system in the world was given to America." And he
meant both Americas, North and South.

CHAPTER 12

The New Women

"No man exactly looks upon the emancipation of women with pleasure." A young Cuban Communist married to a recently emancipated wife.

She is wearing a chic black dress and pearls. She is getting a little heavy in the soft, pink way that Latin women get heavy. She is sitting on a gold chair in the palace-home of Anita Fernandini de Naranjo, perhaps Peru's richest woman, and she is talking about "uplifting" the lower-class Peruvian mothers.

"The thing to do is to establish some sort of training for them," she is saying, with a good deal of intensity. "Not just to give them things—that's no good. We used to go to the *barriadas* and give them fancy clothes, and the man inside was drinking . . ."

"Alcohol is a vice," she says, and everybody nods. "The only choice this woman has is getting married and having children," another woman adds.

There are some hundred million women in Latin America, white-skinned Spanish beauties, olive-skinned *mestizos*, dark Negroes, exotic mulattoes, blond German and Polish types and primitive Indians who scamper naked through the primeval forests. They encompass every possible way of life. The Indian women practice trial marriage for one or two years before they are officially married; the upper-class and middle-class Spanish women look upon virginity with an almost medieval reverence. In Bahia and parts of Negro Brazil, Negro women are the priestesses of the cults and the spiritual intercessors to the gods; in the Spanish areas, women are almost ruled by the priests and the saints' days, and the church often takes the place of the "husband," who is never home. In the marginal towns of Peru, the *mestizo* women believe that if a baby sits in the lap of a pregnant woman and pushes down, the new baby will be born. In Chile they insist that an aspirin in the vagina is a contraceptive device. In some *mestizo* areas, a couple will not marry until they have enough money for a huge party, and this often does not happen until middle age; their children attend the ceremonies. To keep the whole system going, there are hordes of prostitutes, ten thousand of them in Montevideo alone.

That day in Anita Fernandini's sitting room, there sat an unusual and particularly interesting assortment of these women. Coming from all over Latin America, they were members of a club called the Soroptimists which originated in the United States to do public service of various kinds. They were remarkable because they were, first, professional women, which Latin women traditionally are not. They were, second, clubwomen, which Latin women traditionally are not. They had been meeting in Lima for a week, discussing how they could give civic service to their communities, which is still another thing that Latin women traditionally do not do. And they adopted some interesting declarations, such as, "Courses should be given in schools to teach boys respect toward girls." Mrs. Haydée de Benavanti, the Peruvian club's president, explained firmly the need for such a resolution: "Everything is taught to the girls to respect the men. To the boys they say, 'Well, you are a man. You can do what you want.'"

Most of the women were young and vigorous, particularly the more aggressive Brazilian women. Only Señora de Fernandini represented the "Old School." She was the prototype of the dowager Spanish aristocrat woman. Her house was all gold—it was her setting. In a certain sense of the old style, Anita de Fernandini possessed a civic conscience. She was the "Lady Bountiful" giving baskets to the poor. She had been mayoress of Lima once, during which time she became internationally noted for her unflagging attempts to clothe the naked statues in the capital.

As it happened I had the opportunity a few days later to be out in one of the *barriadas* to see the third type of woman that is common in Latin America—the *barriada* woman the clubwomen were talking about. Señora Fernandini's name was brought up. The speaker was a big, somewhat burly priest from Canada, Father Andrés Godín, who ran a large vocational school for boys from the Pampa de Comas *barriada*, as well as a clinic, and was affectionately called "Don Camilo with brains" by those few of his admirers who were literate.

Father Andrés' clinic, which was meant to serve the *barriada* and only the *barriada*, abutted the Fernandini hacienda, one of many they owned. Indeed, from Father Andrés' simple office in a plain square building, you could see the healthy rows of vegetables strung out across the valley. But despite her money and her palace, the Señora was sending her hacienda workers to the priests' free clinic, a fact which irritated the priest considerably.

"We have to educate the rich too," the stolid, nearly expressionless French Canadian said, standing outside his school with his arms folded in a "That is that" manner. "The upper classes have a false idea of the church. It is not to give alms. They have to understand the basis of charity is justice. We don't offer our programs to families from the haciendas. There we'll have to start labor unions."

Around Father Andrés' complex, the Latin women are quite different from the few Señora Fernandinis of the continent, and far more numerous. Poor, overworked, generally stricken with tuberculosis in some level of development, abandoned by one, two, or a number of "husbands," they kept coming to the American social worker in the clinic, a young woman named Jeanine Reiser, for help. "We're always working with the wives," she said. "It's hard to get the husbands to come in. I try to tell the women, 'You see the problems, you can help with your sons.'

"But the idea of teaching their daughters that their womanhood is something to treasure—it's too abstract to grasp. We try to show the women they have dignity by our manner; we try to stir something in them to responsibility, to develop confidence to build on, to impress them with the idea that in spite of being poor they have something to give. But they feel that everyone is picking on them. They feel everybody has abandoned them. They are fatalistic about men and they always say, 'Yes, that's the way men are.'" This interpretation seems closer to the truth than the public eulogies to "woman's place" and her happily passive condition.

All of these women, and many more, are women of Latin Ameri-ica, for there are, of course, thousands of types that come under the title "Latin American women." In contrast to the United States, where there is far more similarity, in Latin America the differences run broad and deep. There is a far greater difference be-tween, for instance, the turbaned Negress of Bahia with her African cults and the sleek Chilean intellectual than there is be-tween any two North American types. There is more distance psychologically, socially and educationally between the Ecuado-rean Indian woman from Otavalo and the girl from Ipanema than between the Negress from Alabama and the society girl from New-port. What this means is that the virtues of the "ideal Latin American woman" usually are simply the virtues of a tiny upper-class minority.

The virtues of the ideal traditional woman—the feminine, non-aggressive, recessive counterpart of the aggressive macho-style man—have revolved about the qualities of modesty, subservience and humility. In the Hispanic sense the good woman was a house-wife and mother who largely ignored her husband's peccadilloes outside the home or explained them away as proof of man's inferior carnal nature. But paradoxically, within the home the woman often wielded far more power than her North American counterpart. Latin women, too, tend to have stronger personalities than North American women because their place in society is so well defined, and the protection is so strong for the woman who accepts this place that she is not subject to the restless searching that typifies many American women.

Traditionally she has accepted the dictum of society that placed her among "good women" and "bad women." Very few rebelled against the fate that, whichever she chose to be, she would be considered not a mixture of complex human characteristics but the personification of either the Virgin Mary-like mother or the trullish woman of the streets.

Bearing and raising children has always been the life of the Latin American woman, and the family is a strong entity, protected by law in ways totally foreign to the United States. "Marriage, the family and maternity are under the protection of the state," according to the law of Bolivia. Non-Communist Cuba, Peru and the Central American countries express the same sentiments. El Salvador goes further by promising the enactment of laws and provisions for the "moral, physical, economic, intellectual and social improvement" of the family and for the "promotion of matrimony." A number of the other countries announce that they are friends of matrimony and facilitate the legal transformation of concubinage into common-law marriage. Under the Peruvian military regime of 1969 a law was passed assuring a child of mother's milk—military men think they can control everything.

Families are not so large as is imagined, tending to be more in the area of six members in all. A high number of families do consist merely of nuclear families; however, what are known as *familias grandes* or "big families" with cousins, spinster aunts, orphans and grandparents, all living with the nuclear family, are also typical.

Children are doted upon and spoiled, particularly the boys. The love she cannot give her husband the wife often showers upon the children. Little girls are disciplined, but little boys are often allowed to run free, leading to the early formation of the strong-willed *macho* who has never been bent to society's needs. Fathers take little hand in the raising of the children. Disciplining, teaching and training are supposed to be done by the time he gets home: he simply plays with them, briefly, before leaving the house again to go out with his male friends or his mistress. Men have little responsibility in the child-rearing task, and they are pampered in other ways, some of which approach the criminal. In poor *mestizo* and Indian countries, nutritionists discovered that one of the most severe causes of the terrible malnutrition among the children, many of whom die from it, is the fact that all the good food available to the families is given to the man.

The rigidity regarding women in Spain and their protection from everything outside the home is legendary. Even today Spanish males of a traditional stripe talk condescendingly of a woman's *tontería*—a quality of dim-wittedness that makes it improper for her to think of anything outside her own four walls. Even in the 1960s in Spain it was possible to put on a play in Madrid in which several "cunning" young women became lawyers and brought disgrace upon their families. "It's a fact that from all times, and not only in Spain, but especially in Spain," wrote the Spanish writer Consuelo de la Gandara, "the well-cultured woman, the woman who understands other things besides rearing children and putting good dishes on the table, has been ridiculed." Despite great changes since the Spanish Civil War, Spain still has the lowest percentage of women in its work force of any other country in Europe: only 16 percent of Spain's women work, while in France 35 percent work, in Italy 25 percent work, in England 31 percent work and in West Germany 36 percent work.

But in Latin America, from the time of the Conquest on, Spanish women exercised their abilities elsewhere than just at home. It is one of the apparent contradictions in Latin America that despite traditional female custom, Latin American history has been filled with strong-willed women who stepped out of the home and imposed their imprint on society. Often it was a case of class. Women in Latin America are often given the same power as their husbands. A woman of a higher class was privy to the power of her class and thus to more power than the male of a lower class. But there were also women of extremely low station, like Evita Perón, who have risen to rule nations.

The first woman to come to Latin America was probably from the Spanish province of Andalusia and probably she came with the supply fleet of Antonio de Flores in 1494, only two years after Columbus reached the New World. In this strange world she found Indian tribes that ran the gamut in male-female relationships. In Colombia there was said to be a tribe whose women spoke a language of their own which they kept secret from their men. The

Aztecs held women in low esteem, but around Lake Nicaragua there was a matriarchy so severe that the husbands were often beaten by their wives.

The first massive male-female experience in the New World—the seizing and raping of the Indian women by the conquistadores—is seen by historians as having molded the psyche of the Latin American for all time, as has been noted. Yet there were happy Spanish-Indian mixtures, too. In Peru, many of the conquistadores mixed with the *coyas* or women of the Incaic elite. When they were baptized, they became "ladies" and were referred to as *doña*. Many of them married Spaniards, and from one unmarried union came the famous half-breed, the Inca Garcilaso de la Vega, son of an Inca princess and a Spanish gentleman. He became the greatest chronicler of the Incas.

Gradually, however, Spanish wives and women desiring to marry in the New World began to cross the sea. The Spanish crown encouraged the trend, believing that the steadying influence of wives from home would stem the anarchic passions of the conquerors. Men who appeared in no hurry to send for their wives were admonished by the king, and high officials were required to carry their wives with them. Meanwhile the conquerors were notably fecund; Francisco de Aguirre, one of the conquerors of Chile, was reunited with his wife after twenty-three years and the siring of fifty *mestizo* children.

After 1510 the number of women and children crossing the Atlantic greatly increased. This included single women who, however, needed licenses from the king to make the trip. There were remarkable women like Doña Beatriz de la Cueva, who married Pedro de Alvarado, captain general of Guatemala, and ruled the country herself after his death. Single women came, but all were not enchanted with the gnarled and tired old conquistadores they found as prospective husbands. Story has it that the aging veterans of the Guatemala campaign were brought into a room in the capital of Guatemala as the young women watched. "Do you mean we are to marry these broken-down old men?" one exclaimed. "They must have escaped from hell, they look so crippled. Some have lost an ear and others an eye. Some of them have only half a face and the best of them have long scars across their faces."

Another girl answered: "We are not marrying them for their elegance, but for their Indians. Since they are old and worn out, they will soon be dead. Then we can have young husbands. It will be like changing a broken old bottle for a strong new one." It is told that one of the conquerers turned on his heel and went immediately to marry a noble Indian woman by whom he already had two children.

During the later colonial period, the place of women changed dramatically. The *limeñas* or women of Lima became notorious in the eighteenth century for their antics, as they strode around the sensuous city that was Lima. They dressed in a cape called the *manto*, which was draped over the head and one eye, leaving only one flirtatious eye free. These *tapadas* or veiled ones, as they were called, frolicked through Lima, flirting outrageously and challenging the pretense and pomp of the time. Often they would flirt with their own husbands and, at the moment when the flirtation was to go further, pull the *manto* back. The favorite saying of the time was that Lima was a paradise for women, a purgatory for men and a hell for burros.

With none of the traditional modesty of the Spanish woman, the *limeñas* would listen, as to a compliment, to scandalous proposals by men, then thank them for their kind reactions to their attractions and move on. Though they displayed their breasts, this was not considered provocative; what *was* provocative to the men at the time was small feet.

Many Latin American writers have noticed the difference between the attitude of the North American pioneer toward women and that of the Latin American. "For the colonizer of Brazil, a man of the Renaissance, woman is an object of prey," Vianna Moog wrote. "For the Puritan, a man of the Reformation, woman is his companion in work, welded like himself to the duty of earning her bread by the sweat of her brow."

There was another difference. The Portuguese had been under Moorish sway for centuries; the sulky dark-skinned woman was not a slave, as in the United States, but a member of the ruling class and, as such, she was eminently desirable. When he saw the Indians ("very good-looking and elegant, with very long black hair down their backs and their breasts so high, firm and pointed and unconcealed by their hair that we stared at them openly"), there was nothing to stop him from mating with her.

The Latin American women who have come down to us through history are, though largely unknown outside of Latin America, as extraordinary and romantic a lot as any in the world. All strong personalities of a type seldom seen, even in the Anglo-Saxon countries, they cut a dramatic swath through history, sometimes leaving the world in pieces around them. All the complex strains of Latin womanhood are symbolized by the women who walked down that stage.

One of the most remarkable was Sor Juana Inés de la Cruz, who carried beneath her nun's wimple one of the most original minds of her day. Sor Juana was born in Mexico in 1651. A Latin scholar at five, at fifteen she was a beautiful and brilliant woman who was already flailing her arms in a society that had no place for such a maverick. She offered to don men's clothes in order to be able to attend the university, but even that was not acceptable: women were banned from the halls of learning. At sixteen she became a nun, and in the convent she read, wrote plays and poems, and made scientific observations. Carlos de Sigüenza y Góngora, the first scholar of the viceroyalty, wrote of her, "There is no pen than can rise to the eminence which hers o'ertops." Her poems of love, to the man she never found in her lifetime, have been described as the "gentlest and the most delicate that have come from the pen of a woman."

Typically for her time, there was in many quarters little appreciation of her work. Her superiors ordered her to put away her books and to devote herself to religion. A feminist, she bitterly resented the fact she could change nothing for women, "those poor souls who are generally considered so inept." Having sold her substantial library of several hundred volumes, she gave the proceeds to charity. A thoroughly brilliant and thoroughly frustrated woman, she died in 1695 at the age of forty-four. She remains one of the greatest women in Latin American history.

Not all convent life, however, was so peaceful as that of Sor Juana's, despite its frustrations. In colonial days there was recurrent war between the convents and the monasteries. In Santiago the monks of Saint Francis of Assisi attacked the nuns of Saint Clare of Assisi, with whom they were supposed to share a "mystical love." The entire Franciscan cell attacked the nuns, pushed them about, and dragged them along the ground by their hair. But in Cartagena, Colombia, when the nuns tried to free themselves from their long obedience to the monks and to place themselves under ordinary ecclesiastical jurisdiction, the conflict was even worse.

At one point the Franciscans approached the nunnery, bringing with them locksmiths and carpenters to force the locks. The bishop ordered them publicly excommunicated, but the monks paid him no heed. Instead they marched to drumbeats on to the nunnery, declaring the bishop excommunicated. The city was split into two factions and put on a war footing, as urgent letters were dispatched to the pope and to the king. When the monks actually attacked, the nuns exchanged insults with them and bombarded them with stones.

The siege lasted six months. With townspeople forbidden to take food to the nuns, no one could understand how they could continue to hold out. Then it was discovered that food was entering by means of the underground sewers. Eventually the nunnery was broken into by the monks, and the nuns fled through the streets to take refuge in the bishop's palace.

On another level, no less turbulent, was the woman who will live in Latin American history as the "greatest lover": Manuela Saenz, the lifelong mistress and devoted companion of the Liberator, Simón Bolívar. Manuela, a gorgeous, white-skinned, dark-eyed, high-spirited, high-breasted Ecuadorean, was as outrageous in her clothes as in her manners. In her red hussar's uniform, she managed to infuriate almost the entire society of Quito and Lima. Already the wife of a British trader, she met Simón Bolívar at a ball in Quito in 1822 at which the victory of the creoles over the royalists at Pichincha was being celebrated. In addition to being the most celebrated man of his times, he was a lean, handsome man with dark, burning eyes.

The meeting of Manuela and Bolívar reverberated like an exploding powder keg. Unable to keep their eyes off each other, they danced together the entire night. From that night on, Manuela, a bold woman who would not be used and put aside as Bolívar's other loves had been, was his "lovable fool." She plotted with him in the independence underground and followed him all over the Andes, through the most difficult periods of the wars, carrying with her his valuable archives.

Over and over he left her and over and over, consumed with need and desire for her, he wrote to her the words that have become immortal in Latin American history: "Come. Come to me. Come now." Always she came. In the end when the independence had come, when it had already degenerated into egotistical squabbling among the leaders and when Bolívar had become a completely disillusioned man, she saved his life one night in Bogotá when she warned him of a plot to kill him. Because of her he was able to climb out the now famous window in his house in Bogotá and hide under a bridge until the plotters were gone.

Manuela was a totally free woman, tied only by her own desires to the man she adored above all else in the world, Simón Bolívar. She was a woman without compromises to society's will. In the letter of 1825, in which she broke with her husband, she wrote him: "Do you think for a moment that, after being beloved of this general for years and with the security that I possessed his heart, I would choose to be the wife even of the Father, Son or Holy Ghost, or of all three? I know very well that I cannot be united with him under the laws of honor, as you call them, but do you believe that I feel less or more honored because he is my lover and not my husband? I do not live for the prejudices of society, which were invented only that we might torture each other."

At the end she suggests that her British husband, who was always shocked by her escapades, will be quite happy in heaven, because "everything there will be quite British, for monotony is reserved for your nation—in love, that is, for they are much more avid in business. You love without pleasure. You converse without grace, you walk unhurried, you sit down with caution, you do not laugh even at your own jokes. These are divine attributes, but I, miserable mortal who can laugh at myself, laugh at you too, with all this English seriousness . . ."

Manuela Saenz was one of Latin America's most arresting women. But Bolívar, though he did love Manuela and could never quite bring himself to live without her, was also a typically *macho*-style man and he treated her in that fashion. In the end, when he was sick-unto-death and the whole independence movement was in the throes of gangrenous disarray, he left her in Bogotá, though he knew he was leaving her to the fangs of their enemies. When he died her name was on his lips, but while he lived, he never would marry her. She outlived him by years, to die a pathetic death of fever in a miserable Ecuadorean seaport. It was all typically Latin American. The great leader, the *jefe máximo*, does not have any one woman. He must be personified as "the man" and as "everyman" and as "all men." In much the same way that Fidel Castro, though he was married and divorced before he came to power, today has no "woman." He has many women, for he is many men, he is all men. And *no one* in Havana will speak of Fidel Castro's life with women. It is as if he is God. Does God have women? Does God have such desires?

Latin America today also has its women of singular passions and extraordinary abilities. Recent history has seen Evita Perón, the beautiful blond courtesan, rise through her marriage to Juan Perón to become the most powerful woman in modern Latin American history. Shrewd and knowing, Evita made herself into the saint of the poor, and indeed Perón's quarrel with the Vatican arose over his attempts to canonize her. She never dressed humbly; she dressed in elegant furs and jewels, for she was cunning enough to know that the poor did not want her to stay at their level. She was their symbol, their herald-bearer. She was to them the realization of what they could become.

But while Evita wielded fantastic power, particularly through her Foundation Evita Perón, which dispensed social welfare funds, she was clever enough always to defer to her husband. When she died of cancer in July 1952, hundreds of thousands crowded around the place where her body lay. Eight people were trampled to death and more than a thousand were injured. To the poor she was the "madonna of America." Her autobiography, *The Reason for My Life*, was made required reading in every school. Juan Perón's downfall can be traced from Evita Perón's death, and in a few years, he was leaving Buenos Aires on a gunboat. Evita's body, of course, has never been found. It has been hidden all this time. Perón's successors did not want to risk making of her the saint the poor people already thought she was. So first the body was hidden in the War Ministry; then one day it disappeared from there.

Another of the strong-willed women of Latin America is the famous mayoress of San Juan, Puerto Rico, Doña Felicia, who made a dramatic stand in 1964 when the conservative Catholic hierarchy instructed the Puerto Rican people not to vote for the governor, Luis Muñoz Marín. He had instituted a public birth-control program, and the fact that he was widely hailed as one of the finest leaders in Latin America made no difference. Doña Felicia publicly went out and voted. Since the hierarchy had threatened anyone who voted for the redoubtable Muñoz with excommunication, she went to New York City and took communion from Francis Cardinal Spellman.

It is indicative of the particular Latin American milieu that the struggle for greater rights for women did not take the obstreperous, often anti-male route it took in the United States. It has been a much softer route, and where women have been active —and they have been active—it has been in broad-based political movements rather than in specifically feminist causes. The traditional acceptance of the Latin American woman of her place has not been severely challenged, except in countries like Cuba. Indeed a survey taken in Costa Rica among women showed that young women placed faithfulness in a husband in fifth place among desirable traits and married women ranked it fourteenth.

There is a general trend toward women suffrage, but it is very slow, depending as it does upon the political party in power and not on any organized suffrage movement. Nine of the twenty republics provide for universal suffrage, but the way is fraught with barriers, for the men do not react to the idea with enthusiasm.

Although the Mexican constitution of 1917 included the vote for women, the necessary enabling legislation was only voted in 1953.

The mood is changing, however. One example of the trend occurred when the popular Peruvian magazine *Oiga*, or "Hear," took it upon itself recently to scold a Lima paper for the "most incredible article of which it could conceive"—an article it published on "how to get a man." "On the one hand," wrote *Oiga*, "when they decide to honor the woman they reduce her to the most nauseating and sentimental level. On the other hand, she is reduced to a category of inferiority, almost animal. If this were on a humorous note, we would be glad to laugh, but unfortunately it isn't. Literature—that is what they call this—of this class fills pages and pages of our press. They have decided that the Peruvian woman merits this type of spiritual treatment. In the future there is no other possibility than getting, seducing, retaining, fishing and hooking a man. And this in the era in which the woman has the right to vote, to fill the same hours of work as a man, and to continue the same technical education, besides having children, guiding them, being well groomed and adequately dressed."

This is typical of the modern press in Latin America, and it reflects the gradual internal changes. Many older Brazilians, for instance, recall watching their fathers padlock the door when they left for work in the morning. Until 1962 in Brazil women had the same legal status as the insane and even today some banks insist that a woman get her husband's permission to open an account. In the 1960s the Association of Women with Diploma, an organization of university women, began lobbying for a bill that prohibits job discrimination on the basis of sex. "Brazilian laws and values were determined by men for men," commented the sociologist Maria Alice Bessoa. "It will take a lot of re-education before they cease seeing a woman as a prisoner."

Foreigners have learned, often at their own cost, that the customs relating to love, sex and marriage are not changing as rapidly as they might wish. A Peace Corpsman in the Andes decided to meet all the local girls. But he didn't want any of them to take the encounter seriously, so he hit upon a plan. "I thought I had it all settled," he explained. "I decided to go out with one girl in the group one night, one the next." He wiped his brow. "Boy, that didn't work! They were all furious at me." This sort of thing simply is not done. Courtship is still rather traditionally celebrated, even though the girls are working with the poor or even serving as members of a militia.

With the continuing massive movements of people and their separation from the traditional extended families, individual and family life is changing rapidly. There are many disruptions of the old pattern, and they are often the cause of acute suffering. Neither are the wives simply accepting without question everything that comes their way. And it is indicative of the fact things have changed that they will now go to family counselors and psychiatrists when situations get too bad.

Three cases that came to one Latin American family counselor typify the problems. A Cuban woman married to a Peruvian had come, as she described it, to an "agonizing" time of her life. In her husband's opinion, their teenaged son was ready to be introduced to the facts of life through some "clean" older woman who would teach him things in a nice way. "You can't imagine my agony when I realized that my husband has all the same ideas as other men," she told the social worker.

Another woman, only eighteen years old, was taking part in highly respectable youth movements but her parents complained bitterly, because "a girl is supposed to be home nights" and the meetings didn't start until 8 P.M. Eventually she moved away from home to a supervised pension with ninety other girls, all more or less in the same boat, but this wasn't easy either. Cut off from their families in a culture which is traditionally family-centered, many of the girls became emotionally disturbed.

In a third family the father suffered a nervous breakdown when he lost his job because of political changes in the government. His wife, the epitome of the dependent, passive, "ideal" Latin wife, had no inner resources with which to aid him. Their pretty nineteen-year-old daughter meanwhile became a model on a television station and the main support of the family, a situation that only sent the father into deeper anguish.

Family life is opening up particularly in the more sophisticated cities like Buenos Aires and Rio de Janeiro. Foreigners begin to find themselves invited into homes, something that happened very seldom previously. Attitudes toward sex are changing, though most slowly of all since most Latin men traditionally would not have thought of marrying an unvirginal woman. Today many of the students experiment with premarital relations, leading the noted Peruvian poetess Cecilia Bustamante to comment: "They have a new concept of love. Now if the girl is not a virgin, the boy does not feel deceived and the girl does not feel violated. They say: 'If the girl is not a virgin, never mind. What is important is to understand her.' They can love her. I know young men who say they would marry a prostitute if they loved her."

Another change is in the attitudes toward birth control, interesting because it signifies a departure from the old female fatalism—"What God provides . . ." It was always popularly assumed that Latin American women, as well as men, wanted large families and that they would not accept artificial interference with the sex act. But now that a great deal of research has been done on attitudes toward contraception and toward the ideal family, it has turned out that none of the old attitudes are important. It is naturally a sensitive subject, given the position of the church, the *machismo* of the men, and the feelings of both extreme right and left that birth control is something imposed by the Protestants of the North to cut down the birth rate of the underdeveloped Catholic nations of the South.

Despite this, all the polls show the same result, in every country. J. Mayone Stycos, director of Cornell's International Population Program, found in surveys in Lima that while the upper classes considered four children ideal, the lower classes wanted three or less. "Studies of Catholics in Puerto Rico, Peru, Santiago de Chile and Mexico City show the lower classes to be overwhelmingly in favor of having small families and . . . generally favorable toward birth control when they know what it is." In Colombia, the country with the most conservative Catholic Church and the most conservative attitudes, surverys showed that the majority of poor women, even though they had large families, thought a family of two children ideal. And the men agreed.

Nor were Latin women the wanton sensual creatures legend has made them out to be. The Colombian reports showed that they were actually quite frigid. Seventy-four percent in the lower income group reported having sexual intercourse less than once a week. Sixty-eight percent reported never or very seldom having had an orgasm. The pollers interpreted these two facts as rejection of new pregnancies.

To a great degree the changing status of women in Latin America—and their changing style—has come about through the progressive political movements. In countries like Bolivia, with its total social revolution in 1952, women are far freer than elsewhere. Women, indeed, took a crucial role in the revolution, particularly the strong-willed *chola* marketwomen, who often run all the market commerce in Latin American cities. In one crucial "battle," the marketwomen's role was to seduce the government guards at precisely the right moment. They are given credit for winning the battle, so avid was their participation.

Love, too, becomes more malleable with the mobility of a revolution. Divorce was instituted with the Bolivian revolution, and Bolivian couples immediately began to divorce each other with enthusiasm, until the figure reached seven a day in a country of less than three million. Gaby Touchard, a charming woman sociologist in La Paz, notes that in the total social turnover that accompanied the revolution, every new *cholo* leader who was coughed up from the social depths to a position of importance divorced his original wife and married a woman of the new higher class which he had just entered.

Indeed, while the "stability" of marriage and the home is stressed in law and lore throughout Latin America, it is a stability that exists only for the upper classes, and then not always for them. Of unstable marriages, desertions and the keeping of concubines, Professor Frank Lorimer of the American University in Washington, D.C., has pointed out: "The situation in Latin America, which contains one-third of all adherents to the Catholic faith, is particularly acute. Among seventeen countries from which statistics are available, there are nine in which more than half of all births are illegitimate."

One of the more interesting attempts to deal with this problem came in 1968 in Colombia, when the government of President Carlos Lleras Restrepo introduced a "Responsible Parenthood Bill" which, for the first time, forced a man to take responsibility for recognition and support of his illegitimate children. As mentioned earlier, the situation had become so deformed that women of the poorer classes, knowing that men would abandon them and that the state had no provisions to care for them, were actually seeking illegitimate children; they were their only security in old age. The bill upset many men because it gave all the advantages to the women—even one "association" with a woman sometimes made it necessary for a man to prove his innocence. The bill also had contained provisions for forcing all young women with a high school education—thus all the upper-class daughters—to give a year of social service to their society after graduation.

Many men were horrified (for good reason). The Catholic Church approved the bill but not with too much publicity, because, as one priest noted, "It cannot acknowledge that standards are as low as they are here." Government officials applauded it. "It represents a healthy shift in the power relationship between men and women in this society," one high official said.

But perhaps nowhere has the transformation of women's lives been so complete as in postrevolutionary Cuba. Women were put on a totally equal plain with men and many women held high positions in the new Communist state. Castro's private secretary, Celia Sánchez, held the post of secretary to the presidency, and wielded tremendous power. Haydée Santamaría, a heroine of the revolution, was a member of the central committee and one of the most powerful people in Cuba. But the Communist government not only emancipated woman, it provided facilities that made it possible for women to take full part in the economic life of the country; indeed, the government insisted they do so. By the mid-1960s the revolutionary government had built several hundred child-care centers in order to free women for work and for building, in effect, an entire new family structure. The ideal was to be the little town of San Andrés, where there would be "total Communism" and children would be raised from birth by the state.

Women were totally incorporated into the work force, and often in very unusual programs. There was a tomato-growing project in the eastern end of the island, for instance, in which they worked fifteen days in the fields and then spent three days at home.

The surprising thing was how little the Cubans objected, despite the traditional ideas of family loyalty and family exclusivity. Again, though this is difficult to judge, it probably was due to the fact that the people involved were not of the upper or middle classes, which had set the values for the previous eras. These were the poor marginal people who were suddenly being incorporated into the society and whose needs were suddenly being served.

Castro himself has emphasized the role of women in the revolution, time and time again, and he is especially courtly toward them. He often expresses concern for their sufferings in life and his conviction that the future will be different. "In the capitalist world and the colonial world the only role of the woman was to iron, clean the house, wash clothes and have children," he said one day to a cheering mass of five thousand students at the teachers' training school at Topes de Collantes. "On the contrary, to really have children, we have to get rid of this ironing, washing and cleaning. To create conditions to permit women to take advantage of their new situation of equality, we have to create conditions that permit them to incorporate themselves in the work force." The future of Cuba, he made clear, was for children to be cared for by the state, going home in the evening or, when they're older, on weekends. Only in this way could they create the perfect socialist conscience.

In affairs of the heart, equally interesting things have happened. Many wives left for the United States, with their husbands scheduled to come later. Instead the men stayed behind with their *queridas* or mistresses. "They had their own revolution," one Cuban Communist commented dryly to me one day. With regard to love and sex, Cuba is still a state in transition. The *posadas* or rent-by-the-hour love nests are still operated by the state. Though prostitution was done away with in the early days of the revolution and the prostitutes were "re-educated," the Commu-

nist state is realistic. There is one house of prostitution still permitted to operate on the outskirts of Havana as a kind of safety
valve for men without women.

In Cuba too the idea that a girl must be a virgin to marry well is
fading, but gradually. One revolutionary said critically, "Some revolutionaries have an absolutely feudal mentality when it comes
to this." The changes have been met with some gnashing of teeth
even among the most devout Marxists. My guide, a young believer
named Manuel Roldán, told me in a confiding moment: "No
man exactly looks upon the emancipation of women with pleasure. I have to admit that I was one of the ones who was backward.
I didn't want my wife to go out of the house to take part in anything." Haydée Santamaría commented sagely: "Ideologically the
man is advanced. But when he arrives at home he wants his wife
there, preparing the dinner."

Under the new state all the forms of marriage have changed
as well. A typical revolutionary girl will marry in the notary's office,
and marry the man she and not her family chooses; she will have
her wedding reception in the Palace of Weddings, which is the
former Spanish Club; and she will honeymoon in one of the attractive state-run resorts. She will work after marriage, put her
children in the *círculo infantil,* send her laundry out, serve in the
militia and be a member of the Federation of Women.

The federation, headed by Raúl Castro's attractive wife, Vilma
Espín, is the final link in the armor-like formation of the new
Cuban Communist woman. Before the revolution there were private women's groups—religious, social, largely based on class. Now
there is this one big centralized women's group whose activities
reach all over the country. It is an indispensable tool of the government in its efforts to indoctrinate and control the country.

"The organization is one arm of the revolution," Vilma, a
mother of four, told me, "to teach woman the role she has to play
in the new society and to prepare her for her incorporation into
society." She explained there would soon be a million members
and that the federation was financed 50 percent by the women
themselves and 50 percent by interested men. The programs included things like hospital work, sewing for the *círculos,* helping

students in their studies, teaching poor women hygiene, and working in the *zafra* or sugar harvest. They also work in special programs such as bringing the *campesinas* or girls from the countryside, to study in Havana. In a program unique to Cuba and apparently one that has been successful, the girls live for six months in Havana, are taught sewing and grooming and are sent to school. It is a way to break the backwardness of the countryside, and I was surprised at the poise of the girls I met in this program.

The Cuban Communists are quite aware that they are still in the process of transforming their society, and that elements of the past and the future exist now in juxtaposition. I saw a symbol of that ambivalence in the Lenin Hospital in Holguín. The hospital is a marble palace that was built in the "romantic" stage of the revolution, when money was poured into public works and into housing instead of being invested in the economy. In the maternity room of the hospital a young mother was giving birth. And in a hospital named after the patron saint of Communism, she was calling out to the "most sanctified holy virgin" to help her through her labor.

But the organization and utilization of women for political and social purposes was proceeding across the hemisphere, not only in Cuba. In Chile, in the crucial election of 1964, the women's vote was assiduously courted by both candidates, Eduardo Frei the Christian Democrat and Salvador Allende the Marxist. Both formed women's organizations. It had been the women's vote, always more conservative than the men's in Latin America, that had taken the election away from Allende in 1958. Both parties were conscious that the women could swing the election again. When the final figures did come in, the women had far outvoted the men in favor of Frei, and it was the women's vote that gave Frei the absolute majority he received. He repaid them after the election by opening mothers' centers throughout the country which did some of what the 4-H Clubs do in the United States— teach citizenship, sewing, crafts. It was typical that the Christian Democrat approach to the organization of women was totally home-oriented (giving the centers sewing machines, for instance) and not really revolutionary in the sense of the Cuban effort. Still Chile had been first in a more traditional women's program.

The Chilean campaign for the emancipation of women and for the vote for women had proceeded gradually over a period of fifty years. The noted Chilean feminist and educator Amanda Labarca began agitating for women's suffrage in 1914, when almost everyone was against it. But the movement was not as it was in the United States. There were no street battles, no biting of policemen on the ankles as they carted the women off to jail. It was all done with lobbying and persuasion. The Chilean Federation of Feminine Organizations was the women's group that worked in those days for women's rights and after suffrage came it wilted away.

"Imagine," Amanda Labarca told me in 1964, when she was seventy-eight and still vital and attractive, "we started in 1914 and by 1934 we were able to get the vote for municipal elections. In 1949 we were able to vote in the national elections for the first time. It advanced with difficulty, very slowly. We worked with the students a lot and worked to get legislation for women. Afterward young women who had taken part in the feminist organizations took their place in the men's world. Now there is no organization with the force of that women's group. They prefer to take part in mixed groups." She thought that while Chilean women had not introduced any new ideas to Chilean politics, they had "brought to the political world a great amount of honesty."

In Brazil in 1964 still another species of mass women's organization was created with the CAMDE group that staged spectaculars such as the "March with God for Freedom" that brought one million people into the streets in a demonstration against the leftist regime of President João Goulart. The CAMDE women were beautifully manicured, alabaster-smooth, upper-class women who organized against "Communism," as they saw it and where they found it, and they organized in little cells which were quite similar to a Marxist organization. They were instrumental in the overthrow of Goulart on April 1, 1964, and then became a major backer of the conservative military government that came into power.

Eventually they disbanded, but another mass organization was formed, CACOCA or the Campaign Against High Prices, which was soon staging mass protests against sales taxes on staple foods and high prices in general. It all symbolized the growing emancipation of women in Latin America and particularly in paternalistic Brazil, where 6.4 million females (of some eighty million people) are now employed and a number of women have made notable successes as performers, scientists, engineers and even ambassadors.

Still another curious part of the female emancipation picture occurred in Santo Domingo, after the 1966 election of Joaquín Balaguer to the presidency. Balaguer did the unheard-of thing of appointing women to all of the twenty-three governors' posts in the country. It is the governor who represents the president in each area and while he does not have a great deal of power, he is a key figure in reporting back to the palace. The women were appointed, he said, to cut down political hatreds and because women could smooth over differences. A year after their appointments they had made little difference in the big scheme of things, and had initiated nothing unusual, but they were a curious development.

And so the yeast is rising. Urged on by the spectacle of women emancipating themselves and changing their lives all over the world, the Latin American woman is changing too. But she is changing slowly and in accordance with her more family-oriented and hierarchical role. Even professional women constantly stress that they do not want to upstage their men. "One thing we are afraid of," said Mrs. Haydée de Benavanti, head of the Peruvian Soroptomists, "is we never want to lose the condition of being women. We like men to give up their seats for us. I don't agree that women can do anything. I don't agree with seeing a woman clean the streets, or being a mechanic. In politics, I think they can definitely take part. In public office, you have to have a great human feeling and I think women have it. But I don't think a woman should ever make a man feel not a man. After all, the part a man has in life is much more difficult. As a man, nothing is forgiven him. As a woman, she is treated more gently."

But even this attitude had its contradiction in the young Cuban revolutionary women I met. One militia girl, standing martially in front of the building she was guarding in Havana, said she used her gun "like a pencil." A young journalist named Consuela from Santiago asked, "Who would want to devote her life to a man?"

Unquestionably there are new Sor Juanas, new Manuela Saenzes and new Evita Peróns being born today.

CHAPTER 13

The New Military—
The Man on the Gray Horse

"We are the selfless idealists. We are the authentic guardians of the nation against Communism, atheism, political chaos and public corruption." An Argentine captain.

It all used to be so clear to liberal-thinking Americans interested in democracy and reform in Latin America—and, in truth, it generally was. The democrats were the "good guys," the Latin military were the "bad guys." Reform would come through the democrats, if only the military could be kept still and amused and far enough away from the *palacios del presidente*.

Then, suddenly, as the Kennedyian lights of hope and assurance of the early 1960s dimmed to the pragmatic shadows of the '70s, the entire picture began to shake and twist and blue like some mad psychedelic projection. Suddenly the military no longer were representing the wealthy oligarchies, as they had through most of Latin American history. Suddenly it was they who were the "social reformers."

People began talking about a New Military, about Nasserites and revolutionary colonels and juntas on horseback as one Latin military after another took over the democratic regimes. And one of the most brilliant American officials in Latin America, a man who all his life had enthusiastically believed in the sole efficacy of democracy, was heard to confide in a sadder-but-wiser tone:

"We always thought that when the revolution came in Latin America, it would be led by a man on a white horse. But if we are to be fair, we have to admit that maybe these young military officers will do it. Perhaps, after all, it will turn out to be a man on a gray horse."

These men on gray horses—for their motivations were as gray and mixed as were outside judgments of them—began riding across the continent opening new political and ideological paths. Coming largely from the lower classes, these new-style younger officers were not the bold *caudillos* of the past who had allied themselves with the wealthy and harangued the masses in the dark squares. These new men were very quiet about the whole thing, so very impersonal.

Not one had a dramatic public personality, and in many of the military-run countries, the leaders were unknown even to their own people. They were professionals, and their armies were highly institutionalized. They were distressingly, dramatically intense and sober—in contrast to the swashbucklers of old. They disdained —they hated—politics. Some called them military technocrats.

Many of them were class-haters with a passion that approached the class hatreds of the Marxists, with whom they soon came in certain instances to offer common cause. And though largely trained and advised by the American military, many of them were anti-American.

In the beginning of the 1960s, when President Kennedy launched the idealistic Alliance for Progress, only a few small countries like Paraguay and Honduras were under military rule. By the end of the decade, Brazil, Argentina, Peru, and Panama were tight in the military grasp. In the twenty countries of Latin America, 123 million people lived under military dictatorships, 12 million were under civilian dictatorships and 104 million were under democratic control. The total armed forces of the area, including Cuba, numbered 840,000, with Brazil having the largest single contingent of 195,000.

There were common reasons for the takeovers and, once in power, the new military regimes evinced common motivations and desires—showing that the phenomenon was a generational one with common roots. And so it came to be that from one military *casino* to another across the continent, you began to hear the same ideas—often expressed almost in the same words. Nationalize the land and distribute it. Impose reform from above. Remove politics from the control of the traditional parties and power groups. Curb the oligarchs. In all, the same basic impulses could be found lying just below the surface.

In the summer of 1969, when all Peru was shaken by the new military regime which was setting out to "restructure" the country, whispers began going around Lima. There was a mysterious "think tank" . . . a "band of revolutionary colonels" . . . hidden deep in the palace.

From them, the whispering went, came the regime's revolutionary legislation, one outrageous bill following fast on the footsteps of another. Only the week before, after a dramatic nonstop twenty-hour meeting, the colonels had decreed a total nationalization of all land in the country; it would be divided among the peasants. The colonels, who obviously meant it, had intervenors in the offices of the major haciendas the next morning; in sixty days, the state would take them over.

Next, the whispering went, would come a reform of private enterprise, which would give more power and profit to the workers, a reform of the fishmeal industry and perhaps even an urban property reform that would be not too different from Fidel Castro's.

The whispers largely were true. One day, having gained access to this regime, I traveled deep into the elegant old presidential palace for my first meeting with the group popularly called "the earthquake generation." There, in one of the formal, brocaded old parlors, with Francisco Pizarro's historic fig tree curling and twisting symbolically in a small patio outside, I came upon a graying, distinguished-looking man, Colonel Leonidas Rodríguez.

"These rooms are a little out of place to make a revolution in," he said, a wry smile playing on his lips. "We have our meeting here . . . papers all over everything. I'm afraid we mistreat them."

Rodríguez was a poor farmer's son from Cuzco and he spoke

Quechua, the Indian language. Yet he looked distinguished enough to be a diplomat from any country in the world. Soon he was joined by Colonel Arturo Valdés Palacio, a short, dark-haired, earnest-looking man who was one of the other of the eight "earthquake colonels" who made up the powerful Advisory Committee to the Presidency.

"The army took over the country because it was not ruled by truly national groups but by special interest groups," Colonel Rodríguez began. "Large groups were not incorporated into the life of Peru. This was always the great evil of Peru—privileged groups working to profit from the small groups."

"To say that democracy has been destroyed is a myth," Colonel Valdés interjected passionately. "There never was democracy. If you analyze the Belaúnde era, you see two political groups dominating both Congress and Belaúnde. He never could do what he wanted to do, for within these groups in Congress the men who dominated were the men with the large landholdings."

Most democratic-leaning observers had been shocked when the Peruvian military had overthrown Fernando Belaúnde Terry, long considered one of the best leaders in the hemisphere. There was the tacit assumption that this would mean an end to reform. No, said the colonels insistently. On the contrary, they had backed Belaúnde when he was elected in 1963 because his reform program "coincided with our ideas"; he was "a fine man," and they all admired him; it was when not enough reforms were made that they saw their mission as taking over.

"There are moments today in all Latin America when you have to change structures," Colonel Valdés went on. "We have avoided doing this bloodily. We will have reforms without blood."

"With the agrarian reform, we will create an internal market," Colonel Rodríguez interjected. "Today the peasants do not buy anything. They live from the land. With their own products, they dress themselves. We want them to be consumers, to have a secure future for their children. If we don't do this in Peru—if we don't create an internal market—we can't have industrialization. The peasants should be owners of the land. From the director of the land cooperative to the peasant, all should be equal."

The colonels grew excited and their voices rose when they talked about land reforms. They would form cooperatives all over the country; the idea apparently was to cooperativize all Peru. In place of the old *hacendados*, the *campesinos* or peasants would be the "new owners and workers." In each valley there would be a tractor station and a pool of technicians. "When a man owned his own land," they insisted, "there would be no talk of Communism." (It sounded, frankly, not unlike the Ukraine.)

They had not struck like lightning, without thinking this over, they went on. Ever since 1965 they had been traveling around the world studying land reforms—1965 because that was the year Peru had been threatened by a small and ineffectual band of Castroite guerrillas in the sierra. The army had put them down quickly, but . . .

"During this time when the armed forces had to resolve this problem, we were studying its roots," explained Colonel Rodríguez. "We realized that the origin was not that small group of guerrillas. It was the socio-economic condition of the countryside. We knew we were not going to destroy it with guns; you can't destroy ideas with force. We needed the total transformation of the country, we needed the government to help the forgotten people."

They made it clear that from this moment on they saw a clear and apocalyptic mission for the armed forces. "Democracy" had failed. "Capitalism" had failed. A Castroite Armageddon was at hand. It followed that the armed forces had not only the right but the duty to restructure Peruvian society in order to save it. And they believed that they represented the will of the people because most of them had come from the people. "We don't think we are especially prepared," Colonel Valdés said in one unusual moment of humility. "But then neither was an architect like Belaúnde especially prepared." He chuckled. "We don't have a school for presidents."

They did not feel that their aggressive campaign of opening relations with the socialist bloc was at all curious or questionable. "When I go to the store to buy cigarettes, I don't ask, 'Are they Communist or Aprista?'" Colonel Rodríguez said. "I just say,

'Are they good? Are they cheap? Give them to me.' The only thing that interests us is to have markets and loans."

Nor did they think they were being anti-American, just because they had nationalized the American-owned International Petroleum Company and refused the compensation demanded. They were going to nationalize the holdings of Peruvians as well. They were nationalists, pure and simple. What they did not stress was that they were economic nationalists—they believed in the control of much of the economy by the state.

Every day these colonels sat around in their formal sitting rooms, dreaming up new reform laws, calling in agronomists, sociologists, professors, anyone who happened to interest them, to testify for them. Then they chewed up the information and spat it out at a stunned public in their new laws.

The oligarchs who had helped put General Juan Velasco Alvarado in office six months earlier now were calling him an "ungrateful *cholo*" as they sat morosely aboard the yacht *Moriah*, where only six months earlier they had plotted with him. There was no one, but no one, who thought that Peru would ever be the same again.

Before I left the palace that day, I made the mistake of referring to their *golpe* or coup. Colonel Rodríguez looked, for just a moment, pained. "But please," he cautioned gently, "not a coup. This is a revolution."

The headquarters of the American-trained National Guard in Panama City is seamy. Paint peels from the walls in the steamy Caribbean heat, and swarthy men cradle submachine guns the way their women hold their babies. Inside, in a small windowless room where he slept the nights he didn't go home, General Omar Torrijos sat down at a chair by the desk. He seldom smiled. His swarthy, expressionless face was like a Buddha's—a Panamanian Buddha's, if that can be imagined. Black eyes, brown face, handsome features . . . but no expression.

When he talked, this man in his early forties, his lips seemed almost not to move. But inside of him something was moving and churning—a deep and abiding hatred for the Panamanian oligarchy. It had driven him and such class-conscious officers as Colonel Boris Martínez, whom Torrijos had then driven into exile, to take over the government in October 1968. It would drive him to many other things.

"Eighteen years ago we had a National Guard which was poorly trained," he began. Again it seemed that even as he talked his lips were perfectly still. "When professionals began to come into the Guard, they began changing its physiognomy.

"The Guard had been used only as a political instrument . . . to correct the mistakes of the politicians. When we went out to correct their mistakes, we realized the kind of problems we really had.

Torrijos was also the son of a rural family, his father a respected but poor schoolteacher, which placed him socially against the oligarchy. "We were permanently on call against labor and demonstrators," he went on. "But the problems this showed would not have existed if we had had good government.

"In one province, for instance, the inhabitants put cars across the road and closed it. It was because the government engineer had taken $5 million and had not built the road. The Guard was called in—to support the engineer, not the people."

In Panama the local nickname for the oligarchy is the *rabi blanco* or white dove, a name which stems from a sociological study done by the Panamanian professor of history Manuel Gaztiazoro. After studying the country's social system Professor Gaztiazoro decided to systematize it according to birds. The white dove was the aristocratic bird; the *rabi prieto* or black dove was a lower-class Negro man; the *rabi colorado* or mulatto dove was the woman who married and rose from her class, as when she married an American soldier.

Torrijos insisted he did not really "hate" the *rabi blanco*. "I've talked to them," he said. "I've told them all we want is for the law to be complied with by all." He paused, and for the first time one could almost sense a small, wry—but at the same time dead serious—smile play on his lips. "It's more agreeable that way," he added.

"They didn't pay taxes. They had special contracts and diplomatic passports. They understand now, and they're accepting things. I ask them, 'What have we taken from you?'"

In many ways, it is true, Panama is an anachronism in Latin America. It is a small, devilishly, deadeningly hot half-moon of steaming jungles and savages with strange earlobes and solid gold jewelry. Never a "real" country, Panama was carved out of the continent by the big American knife when we needed its narrow waist of land for our canal.

And yet . . . even poor Panama shared in certain fundamental Latin Americanisms: an oligarchy which controlled everything, corruption and poor, disfranchised masses. If anything Panama was a heightened example of Latin problems, for here there was more corruption, more neurotic anti-Americanism, and more slums.

And there was the National Guard—created, trained and financed by the United States in the same manner as that of Nicaragua and the Dominican Republic. For years the Guard had had especially close relations with the massive military establishments in the Canal Zone. And it was with this American influence that, in the early '60s, the Guard began to get a new vision of itself . . .

"It started with Fidel Castro . . ." General Torrijos began. "Suddenly there was a new orientation. We had more contact with the people. In all the military schools the orientation changed immediately. After Cuba there was a preoccupation with social forces in the courses. We studied the case of Cuba . . . philosophy . . . social justice. We came to the conclusion that there was a direct relationship between social justice and explosive violence."

The true motivation of men like Torrijos remains, of course, open to question. Much of it, no question, was personal ambition and aggrandizement. When the Guard took over, it was worried that President Arnulfo Arias, a charismatic oligarch who was wildly popular with the poor, would abolish or *emasculate* the Guard—and later the Arias followers called Torrijos and his men "Marxists." But there was also the question of social change, of administrative disorganization, of political control being totally manipulated by a few.

As the Guard delineated its program, it became clear that it was putting community development, political reform, administrative reform (thousands of people were paid for jobs in the ministries without working), and agrarian reform, at the top of the list, if only because the times demanded they do this to justify their moves. "This is a bastard regime," Nicolás Barletta, the regime's bright young planning director, said frankly. "But if it makes reforms, it will go down in history."

"All over Latin America, there is a new military generation with things in common," General Torrijos said as I left. "Everyone is seeking an escape from the corruption in which we have lived. We now read Mao." He almost laughed. "If I had read while I was a cadet, they would have thrown me out."

As sleazy and grimy and scrofulous as is the headquarters of the Guard in Panama City, just as elegant is the Army's General Staff School in Rio de Janeiro. The old Portuguese building, looking like a palace, sits on the Praia Vermelha, a jewel-like arc of beach just below the sheer rain-ridged rocks of Sugar Loaf Mountain. Sitting in such a secluded spot, the military school looks straight out into the blazingly blue ocean, with its back to the teeming city.

In the fall of 1968, both here and at the Officers' Advanced School, the younger officers, mostly captains, had risen in anger, impatience and jealousy against their top officers. They wanted better salaries. And more bite to "the revolution" which the military began in 1964. They wanted better professional standing, an all-out attack on the oligarchy, and more sobriety in government.

First, four hundred captains issued a manifesto, deploring their economic and professional grievances and the slowdown of "the revolution." It began to look dangerous when other groups of younger officers across the country began preparing sympathy declarations. It was becoming a national movement, sidetracked at the last moment only by a sudden grant of pay raises and promises.

The incipient captains' revolt then passed over to the Praia Vermelha, the beautiful little bay. Here, the knowing General Reynaldo Mello de Almeida nipped the blossoming revolt in the bud by circulating a questionnaire to all the younger officers asking them—before they could start asking *him* things—what their complaints were.

What it all added up to was a little Brazilian expression of latent Nasserism—a revolt of the younger officers against the higher ones in the name of better pay and social reform. And when I spoke to the officers at the school nearly a year later, there were many expressions in the conversation of what had come popularly to be called Nasserism. The men—mostly majors and colonels, plus one lone general—spoke freely, but did not want their names used.

"In a country like ours, you can divide people between the poor and the very rich," one colonel said. "Inside Brazil you see the boss and the worker, as in the sugar plantations in the northeast. They work hard—they must work all day long. It is important to understand this to understand anything. The rich want to be as rich as possible. And they want to keep man as poor as possible."

A major interjected. "In Brazil, as everywhere, everyone wants profits. Here, this is aggravated by the fact we don't have laws to contain profiteers. And usually a man like this is the one who pays for the political campaign. What we're trying to do now is to have a special law or treatment for this man and to explain to the people the real laws they have inside their society. In Brazil today people do not have enough education to understand how the rich and the politicians are able to use them because of money . . ."

These younger officers had exercised their intense hatred of the rich by prompting, under a National Commission for the Investigation of Illicit Wealth, a series of investigations into just about everybody who had any money at all. They were calling in the rich, with a sober puritanical passion, to question them about their assets. And before they did so they went to the bother of opening mail and plucking out such things as Swiss bank statements.

In several cases the military's naïveté about capitalism and its daughter, the profit motive, became so intense that businessmen being investigated found themselves giving the investigating officers a sophomore course in economics.

One Brazilian businessman was called in and questioned about whether he had a bank account abroad. "Yes, I do," he said, "I often travel to the United States, and I keep about six thousand dollars in a bank in New York."

"That is all?" the investigator asked.

"Yes, that's all."

"Then you wouldn't mind signing a statement to that effect?"

As soon as the man signed the statement, the investigator, smiling slightly, brought a bank statement out of his desk drawer. It was a statement from the man's Swiss bank account, and it had been taken out of his mail. "You seem to have forgotten this," he said.

These Brazilian officers wanted to "change the structure." But unlike in Peru, where the military received the support of the church and of leftist groups, they were doing it in Brazil in such a brutal manner that it was receiving almost no public support at all. With clubs and machine guns and torture, they had, five years after "the revolution" of 1964, antagonized almost every sector of society with their brutality and their disrespect for the most basic human rights.

Even General Reynaldo feared the passions of the younger officers. "We know we have enormous corruption in Brazil," he said. "But you cannot strike at it like this . . ." He brought his right fist down suddenly into his left palm. "You cannot simply throw out all of the wealthy men in Brazil. If we do, we would have enormous social problems. We would be like the French revolution—a poor man without a head."

Still, every few months another list of *cassados*—men deprived of their political rights—was published. And these men were soon not only out of politics but also out of the country and out of work. Students, the church, all the civilian groups soon were aligned in complete opposition to the government.

To the military men, each *cassado* was either a Communist or a

corrupt man—they saw shadows and threats and political hob-
goblins everywhere. And they defined "democracy" in their own
terms—they were the "democrats," elections meant nothing because they were controlled by the rich, and true democracy would
come through their representing the desires of the masses.

But the fact was that in their passionate puritanism they were
destroying an entire generation of political leaders, including
some of the best men in the country. One, a handsome and genteel
Negro from Santos, Esmeraldo Tarquinio, had risen from the slums,
put himself through law school and, after years of struggle and
suffering, got himself elected mayor of Santos.

"I was so enthusiastic," he reminisced later. "I had something
to show for the years of my life. And the funny thing is I was
never an instrument of political schemes." When he was elected,
he told friends, "I plan on four years of a great deal of work. We're
very poor. My biggest job will be to show people we are humble
enough to change our mentality. We must enlarge the labor
market, create better patterns of civic life."

Then in the winter of 1969, along with whatever were the
dreams of ninety others who also were "cassated" the same day,
his dream died. Observers agreed that Tarquinio represented the
"Brazilian dream," much as poor Americans rising to the top represented the "American dream."

"Sections of high society began gossiping and intriguing against
him," a diplomat who knew the situation intimately said. "It
simply was not acceptable, even in Brazil, where race is not supposed to matter, to have a Negro as mayor of a city like Santos.
At one meeting an army colonel said to him, 'You are a subversive
Negro, you ought to go to Russia where you wouldn't be able to
talk.'"

Yet Tarquinio was not "subversive." He was incorruptible, and
his only crimes had been being a Negro and attending a student
meeting at which he did not even speak. Yet Tarquinio—a typical
case—was cassated for ten years. By that time he would be fifty-
two—too late, he thought, to start running for office again.
Esmeraldo Tarquinio was not a bitter man, but, like many other
Brazilians, he was a very sad one.

And these military officers, unperturbed, continued to talk of reforms and change as though they could simply be announced, as if the efforts and passions of the people did not need to be galvanized. "We hope to have this year new political reforms," a colonel told me that day. "We intend to replace the professional politicians and put inside the Congress better men, men who work for their country."

When I asked him how they intended to do this, one explained, "Before a man runs for election, he will have to be examined by an electoral judge. He will have to show his credentials." And these credentials? "He must be patriotic, intelligent and be a professional man." He added, with the supreme self-confidence of the politically naïve, "We hope to have this reform by next year and in the 1971 congress these men will be in office."

To some observers the New Military of the '60s was no more than a replay of tired old songs. It was Juan Perón all over again, his appeal to the poor against the rich, his cry to the younger officers to pry out the entrenched older ones.

But closer studies made clear that they were, indeed, something new. Perón was a *caudillo* par excellence, and now there were no *caudillos*, no charismatic leaders. The new men in charge—Arturo Costa e Silva, Juan Velasco Alvarado, Omar Torrijos, Juan Carlos Ongañía—were themselves such gray men, so uninteresting personally and so unattractive politically, that they might better be called anti-*caudillos*.

They eschewed public popularity. Rather, they institutionalized the junta to a point at which the new phenomena might be called "juntas on horseback." They abhorred public displays of wealth such as, for instance, Pérez Jiménez's in Venezuela, building his pleasure brothel for his Cuban prostitutes on the side of the mountain. These new men were economic sobriety and dull morality itself.

In each country there were of course differences. The sober Argentina regime which took over in 1966 concerned itself exclusively with economics; it abolished politics, and soon set the economic house in order only to be continually plagued by displays of political dissatisfaction. The brutal Brazilian regime which came to power in 1964 was equally overcome with economic problems, but at least talked of reforming the political life of the country.

Peru stood as the most social reformist of the regimes. And although it, too, was imposing everything from above, the colonels there were intensely interested in giving political power and purchasing power to the forgotten marginal people. Panama would rank with Peru in having more interest in redistributing wealth and political power.

And yet, there were certain common roots in all—a rurally influenced propensity toward economic statism, a class tension with the oligarchs, a violent and inclusive patriotism, and a deep distrust of politicians. These had always grown in Latin American soil. Even Bolívar had spoken contemptuously of politicians, calling them "those legislators, more ignorant than evil, more presumptuous than ambitious, who are leading us to anarchy."

The history of militarism in Latin America is not what it is popularly thought to be. Militarism does not, for instance, stem directly back to the Conquest, or even to the wars of independence, although the authoritarianism that goes with it does. Bolívar and San Martín pasted their ragtag armies together of everything and everyone they could find. Then after their blazing successes in battle with Spain, the armies fell into disrepair. The men straggled home to their families and, as the continent sunk into anarchy, local *caudillos* came to rule the continent in place of the republican forms Bolívar had hoped for. One historian wrote with cynical truth that the expulsion of the Spanish in 1825 marked "the last day of despotism and the first day of the same."

What Latin armies there were were at the service of individual *caudillos*—militaries striving to force the people into that mold of society perceived by the dictator, rather than liberating them as Bolívar's men had done.

The prevalent anarchy of this period of Latin history is shown by certain facts. During the nineteenth century Venezuela suffered fifty revolutions. Up to 1903 Colombia had experienced twenty-seven civil wars, one of which claimed eighty thousand lives and another a hundred thousand lives. By 1898 Bolivia had survived more than sixty revolutions. In the 125 years up to 1950 Honduras saw the executive office change 115 times. During the Mexican revolution of 1910 the Mexican general and later president Alvaro Obregón is supposed to have said of his military compatriots with rare insight: "We can get rid of clericalism, and we can get rid of capitalism, but who is going to get rid of us?"

Then almost simultaneously at the end of the nineteenth century the Latin American countries decided they had had enough of civil disorders. They began creating professional military services, and within two decades all had conscription laws and some form of military establishment, borrowed either from Germany or France. Not surprisingly it was all a little unbalanced for a time. In 1915 Brazil was devoting 50 percent of its gross national earnings to military service. Costa Rica had one officer for every two enlisted men (the dichotomy between form and the substance again). But Guatemala was unique—she had thirty-five hundred officers and no enlisted men at all.

Many Latins came to hate and despise their militaries, who seemed to exist not to fight wars but to oppress their own peoples in the name of the wealthy. Money flowed into the military machines, which had the power to demand what they wanted, whether in salaries or in fancy airplanes. By the late 1950s the military services were costing the nations nearly $1.5 billion annually, or approximately one of every six of their national tax dollars —compared to one in fifteen spent for education.

Between 1954 and 1959, John J. Johnson, the political scientist, points out, Brazil spent more on its armed forces than on all public works and development programs combined.

As the armies formed they naturally took on the contours and styles of their countries. Uruguay's military was always non-political. Brazil's was considered the most democratic. Venezuela's was the most corrupt and meddlesome, until 1958 when the Rómulo Betancourt revolution turned the military into a non-political body. Colombia's was the most professional. In the Caribbean the armed forces tended to be National Guards formed and trained by the United States—a leftover of American occupation. In almost every country there was one aspect of the Latin military's role that was totally different from that of the North American military. Their constitutions defined them as "guardians of the constitution" or some such similar thing, and gave them the right to step into political life when the security of the country was threatened.

In early times and in certain countries the officer class came in large part from the upper classes. But generally the armies drew from the lower classes and to join the army was the one way for a poor young man to make good. More important, that poor young man most often came also from rural origins and from small landholding families who had no experience with capitalism and distrusted it. This laid the basis for the anti-capitalist tinge to their statist mentality.

For the Latin militaries had a strong tendency toward statism or economic nationalism. The Argentine military long had controlled the steel industry, the airplane industry and a host of smaller but crucial industries; Argentine, as well as Brazilian, military men sat in influential spots on development and planning boards. When the Peruvian military took over in 1968 they clearly were statists—they embarked on a binge of nationalization comparable only with the Cuba of Fidel Castro, the man whose "way" they said they were trying to avoid. To many this represented "socialism without Marxism."

In effect, too, they came out of the marginal population. And here is another example—a crucially important one today—of the New Latins, who formerly took no part in the inner life of their societies, suddenly coming to run them and to impose their own imprint and values upon them.

As the twentieth century progressed the militaries suffered reverses. The Mexican military, which had supported the corrupt dictatorship of Porfirio Díaz, was destroyed in the revolution; a new military was formed which to this day remains totally and uncompromisingly nonpolitical. In Bolivia's great revolution of 1952 the army was similarly destroyed. First peasants and worker militias were instituted, and a new more democratic military was formed beginning in 1955.

It seemed to be a rule of Latin revolutions—the real social revolutions, not the palace revolutions—that the traditional army had to be destroyed. For the Cubans did the same thing in 1959. There, of course, the army of Fulgencio Batista simply deserted and on his march on Havana, Castro met them straggling home. It was one of the few cases in history where a people and an army were so demoralized that they simply disintegrated. It is telling that the one thing Castro feared most during the time he was in the Sierra Maestra was a revolutionary coup within the armed forces that would usurp his opportunities.

Other countries dealt with their militaries in other ways. In Costa Rica the army was abolished in the '50s and that pleasant little country has had only a police force ever since. In Venezuela, Betancourt in effect bought off the army's propensity to take over the country by giving them so many retirement and other financial benefits they couldn't afford to revolt.

But in the militaries that were left intact, different kinds of changes were coming—particularly after the coming to power of Fidel Castro. Father Vekemans early had warned that a "technocratic military" would be a greater threat to real democratic participation than the Marxists, but no one listened. Then, one after the other, democratic governments of differing worths fell to military coups—Brazil in 1964, Argentina in 1966, Peru and Panama in 1968 . . .

The continent began to see, as Dr. Johnson, who is the specialist on the Latin military, said, "the substitution of technically trained managers of violence for the heroic leaders of the past." He warned, too, that things had changed, that no one should expect a repetition of the past.

"There is absolutely nothing in the evolution of the Latin American armed forces to suggest that they can any longer be trusted to be the stronghold of tradition or that they will for much longer hold off the mob power of the left," he has written. "Those persons in and out of Latin America who fail to appreciate this face a rude awakening, as do those abroad who fail to understand that no group from which potential officers currently are being recruited has close ties with any foreign power." That is, the United States.

One of the most popular terms to describe the New Military was Nasserite, even though most often even the younger officers— the ones who were supposed to *be* Nasserites—either did not know or much care for the term. When I asked one of the Brazilian majors, for instance, if he considered himself a Nasserite, he looked at me with scarcely veiled hostility and said, "He is a man who has lost three wars."

Yet the Nasserite term did have some meaning. It was Gamal Abdel Nasser who had turned the younger officers against the superior officers in Egypt and thus started the United Arab Republic's social revolution. He had effected agrarian reform through destroying the power of the pashas and had given the land to the peasants. Nasserism also meant strongly nationalistic, anti-foreign sentiment.

"Nasserism is a combination of Puritanism, righteousness and sheer, naked jealousy of the rich," said one American military specialist. "They believe that foreign interests are exploitive. It represents a frustration on the part of the officers that their countries are being overtaken by world events. They are extreme patriots, and their motivation is not ideological but patriotic. They are idealists without ideas.

"Their elders have failed. They believe it is time to break hierarchy and rank. It is time for new blood. There is a distinct belief in statism, which then leads to socialism. This is all that Nasser did. It is unreal to say such pressures do not exist in the military, and there is no assurance things will stay the way they are."

Yet Nasserite was only one term to describe the New Military, in whom, actually, qualities were too mixed for any simple characterization. In some instances they could be called fascist; Peru and Argentina particularly had definite corporativist tendencies. Too, they were not at all unlike the Castroites they so despised—both were middle-class military regimes led by revolutionary officers. All believed in the imposition of change from above, stressing human "participation"—but a carefully orchestrated human participation. All to a greater or lesser degree believed in the control of the economy by the state. All were extreme nationalist, anti-foreign and aggressively, often irrationally, egotistical. If it were not for the labels they would have loved each other.

But more interesting even than the qualities of the New Military is the question of why the phenomenon happened. The answer is that it happened indirectly and largely through unexpected circumstances. It was the threat of Castroism, of Marxist military men in beards, which led the military to take over and try to change their own societies and to attempt to transform them—in ways that turned out to be strikingly similar to Castro's.

It is not that there was some military "conspiracy" across the continent—one military did not egg on the other. Certainly they influenced each other, and certainly they were under the same circumstantial influences, for they all attend each other's schools and they all talk to one another. But it was largely a reaction of similarly thinking men of similar class having similar training and similar fears and reacting in the same way. Another example, in effect, of the unity of Latin America.

All this time, through its various military schools, including the Spanish-speaking School of the Americas in Panama, the United States had thought it was training a "democratic military"— officers who would step back from political involvement and let the democrats do it. With this in mind the American officers instituted training in "civic action"—to teach the Latin military to help instead of using their people.

But instead this passion for "nation-building" only contributed to giving these officers a new and profound sense of themselves as the men with the sacred responsibility for transforming their societies. They looked upon their armies as democratic because many of the officers and all of the soldiers were from the lower classes and because most officers had spent some time in the rural marginal areas and therefore knew them. Thus they felt they represented the masses, without the bother of elections. In the army a man could rise from a poor soldier to president, as did President-General Juan Velasco Alvarado, leader of the 1968 revolutionary government in Peru. It was no matter to the officers that the masses of the soldiers were poor Indian recruits earning ten dollars a month with no choice in anything . . . they would train them.

Their new professionalism gave them the power. In addition the technical know-how they gained in the United States only caused them to become more politically involved, for professionalization of any armed forces always means a greater, not a lesser, political involvement.

General Edgardo Mercado, the Peruvian foreign minister under the original revolutionary government and one of the major players in the Peruvian drama, put it this way: "The professional military has suffered the impact of technological changes. It has made the army as modern a thing as industry. Today you can't tell where the military starts and where the politician ends. Today an officer knows the realities of his country. Today everybody who wants development realizes you need social structural changes, without revolution . . . as we are doing it."

A tremendous influence on all the officers came out of the changes in training in their own military schools, which in the '60s began to intensify training in the social sciences, in politics and economics. It is typical that the Peruvian military got much of their inspiration for their "economic nationalism" in their advanced military schools, where in recent years they have had civilian, Marxist and radical Catholic professors.

Many of the Marxist economists and lawyers stayed close to the regime and even acted as spokesmen in important negotiations, such as those with the United States over the International Petroleum Company. As for the priests . . . "They got some inspiration from *The Development of Peoples* (Pope Paul VI's encyclical that strongly criticizes traditional capitalism)," said Father Darrell Hunt, head of the Catholic Information Center in Lima. "They talked a lot at the military academies about land reform, taxes, anti-capitalism and anti-Communism.

"One Jesuit, Rómeo Luna Victoria, taught at the army intelligence school. There was definitely some influence of the Christian social principle, even the idea of using violence against the 'structures of violence.'" Asked if most priests could accept the military as a means of doing away with the old structures, he said: "I'm sure they could. The military have the power. We'll have to work with them."

What became clear was that there was a strange convergence of ideologies and forces going on—the Nasseristic military working with the radical clergy working with the Castroite New Marxists. What did it matter, after all, whether you called it the military's "national statism," the Marxist's "socialism" or the Catholic's "communitarianism." It all meant basically the same thing— control of production and land by the state or in the name of the workers.

These military men were, in truth, men on gray horses. Men socially drawn from the gray, marginal areas of their own societies. Men ideologically gray, for what they believed in they drew from a mixture of military experience, Marxist collectivism and Catholic radicalism. And across the continent the reaction to them was very curious.

Many ultra-leftists praised those of them, like the Peruvians, who nationalized foreign industry and cooperativized the big land-holdings. Many questioned whether it would not have to be "men with guns" who would be the only ones able to defeat the rich and make the necessary structural changes to build modern societies.

"People feel that if there is to be change, it will be by way of the army. The liberals . . . they are dead. It is a new epoch, embryonic," Carlos Quijano, the influential editor of the leftist review *Marcha* in Uruguay, told me. "We are back to the two historic Hispanic powers, the army and the church.

"What is happening today in Latin America is a renaissance of nationalism. There is a feeling against the political parties—a feeling that they have been too responsive to foreign interests." He squinted his eyes in the darkness of his study and pondered what many were pondering on the continent. "Is it possible," he asked, "that, after all, the representative government of the Anglo-Saxon world does not fit here?" Then a sad look came over his face and he added, "We are passing through things that we ourselves do not understand."

Many feel that the time is now so late that the only thing any longer of importance is that the changes be made . . . however

. . . by whomever. "We cannot wait any longer for reform," Gilberto Freyre said of Brazil. "We must have it at once. We cannot wait for the liberal way through parliamentary, legalistic means. People think historically that military rule means reactionary rule. On the contrary, it may mean very progressive rule."

Even the Castroites are carefully watching these regimes, although they are watching skeptically. "You cannot divide Latin America between the civilians and the militaries," Carlos Rafael Rodríguez, the major Cuban ideologue told me in a rare interview while he was visiting Lima in 1969. "Peru and Cuba are close on many things, but they have considerable differences. I can't say we are putting our hope in these military regimes. It could be that the dynamics of the situation could bring the military to a more dynamic position in terms of national sovereignty. We might be forced to re-evaluate."

Perhaps the best analysis of the special characteristics of the New Military has come from James Rowe, a political scientist at the Brookings Institute. To him, what characterizes the new regimes are these elements:

They are now determined to remain in control of the situation for years and years, instead of stepping in at moments of crisis and then stepping out as they have historically done. Their obsession with Castroism and Communism is a crucial element. They now have a "new and much more sophisticated interest in geopolitics." In the old days, defense was national frontiers; now it is international defense. They want to integrate rapid economic developments clothed in the national security concept. Some military "schools of thought" are imbued with the idea that there is "one best way to organized things, that politics is evil, and that managers and operations research specialists can apply to the operation of a country the same principles they would apply to the operation of a hospital."

There was a certain naïveté about it all, for despite their classes in their military schools most of them remained painfully uninformed about economics and social change. "These men have had only modest exposure to the outside world," one economist commented who had studied the situation. "They have been brought up to the sophomore level, where everything is perfectly clear. They see how manageable everything is, if only people as disciplined as they could put things in order."

Their economic nationalism was based both on a feverish nationalism and on the benefits they saw accruing to their class—the middle class. They believed, too, that they could simply organize human beings to march toward development as they organize soldiers to march to parades. The kind of long-term power they had grasped in the '60s was, in truth, a kind of toy to them—they were talking about concepts they did not fully grasp, about human experiences they had not really participated in with their whole beings.

It might be that these military regimes would simply come and go. It does not look like it.

CHAPTER 14

The New Church

"In Colombia we are Catholics until sixteen, then Communists until twenty-five and liberals after that. We used to go to mass every day. Now the country is on the road to development, and we don't have time for that. We go less often, but we believe. It is not so formal as before, but I think we are better Catholics." A Colombian university student.

"The relation to God—yes, it is changing. We are realizing that the way of arriving at God is man. It used to be an individual religiosity; now it has more collective aspects." Father Rafael García-Herreros, prominent Colombian priest.

I met the young Colombian priest Father Camilo Torres in July 1965 just six months before he became a guerrilla and was killed in the mountains. He was radiant with confidence then, the knight-errant of the students and the talk of Bogotá.

When I called him on a Saturday afternoon for an appointment, he said, as though it were a matter of great importance, "Ah, but I am leaving tomorrow at 9 A.M." There was a moment of silence and then he said typically: "Never mind. Can you come at 7 A.M.? We will talk before I leave."

When I arrived at his little apartment near the tudor-style

Catholic University where he taught sociology, he was bustling around, his servants watching his every move with adoring eyes. Camilo was like that—he was so handsome, so intelligent, he had so much charisma, he drew everyone to him. A medium-sized, well-built man with an arresting smile and curly brown hair, he was one of the most strikingly good-looking Latins I had ever met. He exuded a certain warmth that was at the same time both spiritual and very, very sensuous. The perfect leader, especially for Latin American women, I thought—handsome, sensuous and a priest.

It was precisely that week that rumors had started that the conservative Cardinal Luis Concha Córdoba, whose only action at the Vatican Council a year later was to vote against the *schema* on religious liberty, was going to defrock Camilo. For there was a restless, free spirit in the young priest that did not fit within the austere gray robes of the ultra-traditional Colombian Church.

Once, his friends said, Camilo had asked the cardinal to allow him to be a priest on Sundays and a revolutionary on weekdays. He sometimes accompanied friends to the Bogotá whorehouses, where he gave absolution to the girls. He was going too far with his talk about "mass movements" and political change, and had the cardinal not said, "It must be borne in mind that the Church cannot involve itself in socio-economic measures that may fail, for the truth of the Church is forever"?

But Camilo dismissed this. "I consider the work of a priest is to take a person to God," he explained to me that distant Sunday morning, "to work toward the love of one's brother. I consider there are circumstances that do not permit a man to offer himself to God. A priest must fight those circumstances, and for me they are political. The grave problem is political, because the fundamental decisions have to be political decisions, and these decisions are now produced by the minorities and not the majorities. Because of this, the majority must produce pressure groups; it must take political power."

This young priest then in his late thirties, trained at the University of Minnesota and the Belgian University of Louvain, talked about starting a newspaper and showed me letters from backers who had promised to help him. Still smiling that radiant smile, he said good-bye and left for the airport, where several hundred cheering students saw him off to a sociologists' meeting in Peru.

But within weeks Camilo *had* been defrocked. He tried for a while to work with his mass movement idea. Then, impatient and driven by whatever devils or saints inhabited him (his friends insist there were quite enough of both), he joined the Marxist guerrillas. On February 15, 1966, the government announced that Father Camilo Torres had been killed in an encounter with Colombian troops.

His death marked the beginning of the Camilo legend, and the birth of perhaps the single most important martyr of this Catholic generation. Colombian students marched with placards reading, "Camilo, we will not mourn you, we will avenge you." The Christian Democrat youth in Venezuela held a conference, with a moment of silence observed in Camilo's memory. In Uruguay young Catholic workers, students and priests held a large meeting to discuss *Camilismo*—Camilo's thought. His mother was told, "*Señora*, Camilo does not belong to you, or to Latin America; Camilo belongs to the world."

Father Germán Guzmán, the priest-sociologist, broke the clerical silence on the Camilo affair with the prophecy that "generations which fight for authentic democracy will realize his sacrifice" and that "every day he grows closer to the conscience of people who want to be free."

Camilo's friends insisted that it was the aged, aristocratic Cardinal Concha Córdoba who had driven Camilo to his final sacrificial act, but it was not nearly so simple as that. Actually the cardinal defended him until he turned to violence. But basically the clash was inevitable, for they were two totally different and unreconcilable men with two totally different and unreconcilable views of the world.

"The case of Camilo was not simple," the heavy-set cardinal, with his ponderous howls and his kindly smile, reminisced two years after the scandal that shook and threatened his Church. We were sitting in the elegant old rooms of his mansion—so different from the rough mountains where Camilo had died. The cardinal was retired—at rest, too, but in a different way from Camilo. His fingers, chubby and deeply jointed like a child's, rested on his large belly.

"I appreciated him greatly—I had a great affection for him," he went on, a touch of sadness to his voice. "But he finally became a guerrilla. In no case is violence licit to change social conditions. It is very sad for a priest to die like this."

The cardinal felt that "the Church should give social formation, but it should not enter into solutions for social problems. The Church's mandate is for spiritual things. In solutions, one day you can be correct, and the next day you're not correct."

It was precisely this type of view, though it might be right in terms of the long-term mission of the Church, that sent young priests into angry, frustrated spasms and that led to the "rebellion of the priests" against their superiors all across the continent. For, working close to the people, they did not see things getting "better" at all. They saw schizophrenic societies where reality bore no relation to the traditional forms the cardinal treasured.

They saw the famed Colombian religious piety on the surface —and chaos underneath. They saw the terrible Colombian *violencia*, like a dark religious orgasm beneath the surface piety of lace mantillas, antique colonial confessionals and Roman-gowned priests in round black hats.

Not unrelatedly, Camilo was one of the sociologists who had studied *la violencia*, that terrible pathological killing, earlier discussed, in which some three hundred thousand Colombians died in twelve years. "*La violencia* was a way to escape the isolation of the village," was the way he interpreted it to me that morning. "It was a way to rise above frustration. It instilled a means of social mobility. It was a way, but a pathological way."

Strangely enough Camilo himself then turned to violence— almost as a catharsis, it seemed, almost as a way to break through his own isolation and rise above his own frustrations. It was typical of the Latin need to theorize about everything that a "theology of violence" arose among Camilo and many of his generation of young Catholics. But—even more strange when you consider the Camilo saga—it turned out that he was always obsessed with violence.

"When Camilo returned from his visit to Peru that July, he asked me if I was in agreement with his ideas," his mother, Señora Isabel de Torres, reminisced in 1968, two years after his death, sitting in her small sitting room in the capital city. "I said yes. 'To the ultimate circumstances?' he asked. 'To the death?' 'To the death and beyond,' I answered.

"I was certain they would kill him," his mother, a white-haired woman with beautiful, aristocratic features, continued. "He was too, but he said it didn't matter." She paused. "But he didn't think it would happen so rapidly, nor did I.

"He always said he would go to the mountains. He never thought the political movement could be enough. But he thought it would come much later. One night in October he told me he wasn't going to sleep here that night, that he was going away to rest for a few days. I was perfectly tranquil. I didn't know it would be the last time I would see him . . ."

His death, like Che Guevara's, is surrounded by the kind of mystery and irresolution the Latins so adore. No one knows where his body is buried. His mother says the death-mask picture shows that the body identified as Camilo's is not his. He never could grow so heavy a beard, she said, and besides, friends of his told her they saw him in Bogotá without a beard four days before his alleged death.

To those around him who do accept his death, it was almost as if the young priest—symbolizing the drives of many young Latin Americans—sought to make a sacrificial offering of himself to atone for the selfishness, shallowness, and egotism of Latin American men of the past.

"He wanted to show people that he was not talking just to talk, that he could die for his ideas," Ruth Arcandona, the young sociologist who worked closely with Camilo, observed long after her colleague was dead. "Dying for one's ideas is very important—showing you can carry them through to the ultimate consequences. But Camilo was not a *caudillo*. He was a scientist who analyzed things very carefully. He didn't want love, honor, glory. He was totally a modern man."

In many respects, Camilo *was* a modern man. But there are many liberals—even rebels—within the Church who interpret modernism in other terms. The "Camilo syndrome" of symbolic sacrifice—demonstrating the inherent violence of constituted society through the example of counterviolence—is by no means the only current flowing in the pounding rapids of the Latin American Catholic Church today.

The Camilo group—the violent Christians—no doubt is the most dramatic. But the progressives or liberals are certainly the largest group, believing profoundly in change but in peaceful, programed change. Both stand against the old conservatives, now a dwindling minority.

For the Church is riven and tormented with change, with everything from revolts of the priests to Catholic political reform movements in power to brilliant young clerical sociologists mapping out the continent for change right under the noses of conservative bishops. The organized political arm of the reform movement is the Christian Democrat party; the social arm is a gaggle of institutes with stacks of money from West Germany, Belgium and the United States; and the intellectual arm is the number of eager young priests situated in influential positions and seeking to change the way of things.

You can also divide them between those who would put aside human will and choice for a generation or two in order radically to transform society . . . and those who believe there will be no real transformation of society unless you involve, in a most profound level, individual human will and talent. And all of these impulses, though only really coming to fruition now, have existed throughout church history in Latin America.

Traditionally there were three pillars to Hispanic society—three existences almost of themselves, with their own laws, rights and privileges. These were the Church, the military and the bureaucracy. The bureaucracy probably will curse Latin America forever, but both the military and the Church have changed so much today as to be almost unrecognizable in historic terms.

Historically the Spanish Church clearly formed and encouraged Hispanic man in his consummate, egotistical individualism. For the Spanish faith, heavily influenced by Judaic elements, was concerned with individual salvation and not with the *bien común*—the good of the community and the relation of man to his fellows. Punitive measures were strong, and the individual Catholic was obsessed with the idea of future punishment. "Morality" in a universal sense counted little, and worship concerned itself largely with the forms, the externals and the mechanics and not with the substance. The forms, for their part, were dramatic—the mass took on an almost pagan splendor in Spain and the glory of the cathedrals was designed both to dwarf and to inspire man. At the same time Spain was noted for its mysticism, and nowhere else in Europe were there so many *alumbrados* or *iluminados*—in effect, "lighted" or "illuminated ones."

The entire apparatus of the Spanish and Portuguese churches was transported to the New World, even the Inquisition, which came in 1570 with passion to such ecclesiastical centers as Cartagena, Lima, and Mexico City. Only the Indians, considered not to be *gente de razón* or "reasonable people," were exempted from the relentless doctrinal eye of the Holy Inquisition.

Much of the religious jurisdiction of the New World was entrusted to the religious orders—the Dominicans, Franciscans, Augustinians and Jesuits. To each was given a "province," a practice that greatly exacerbated inter-order rivalry until colonial cities like Antigua, Guatemala, became virtual museums of convents, great churches and monasteries.

The literature of Latin America has many stories of opportunistic, grasping, venal priests, and it was largely the Church, standing with the aristocracy and using the military, which kept the continent in religious and social bondage. Still, even in the early days there was the counter trend. In addition to the predatory impulses of the Catholic Church, there existed also the concomitant strain of idealism and utopianism.

In 1511 Antonio de Montesinos, a Dominican friar in Hispaniola, voiced the famous cry on behalf of the enslaved Indians: "I am a voice crying in the wilderness . . . You are in mortal sin

. . . for the cruelty and tyranny you use in dealing with these innocent people. Tell me by what right or justice do you keep these
Indians in such cruel and horrible servitude? Are these not men?
Have they not got rational souls, are you not bound to love them
as you love yourselves? Be certain that, in such a state as this, you
can no more be saved than the Moors or Turks."

The cries of Montesinos were listened to with anger by a soldier
of fortune and slaveowner, Bartolomé de las Casas. But three
years later, Las Casas himself, now a priest, suddenly awakened
to the truth of Montesinos' charges. Las Casas was to be named
"Protector of the Indians" by the Church and to spend a lifetime
fighting for the alleviation of the suffering of the Indians.

In 1537 Las Casas attempted to win to the Cross an area of
Guatemala where the Indians were so unfriendly to the Church
that it was called "The Land of War." In one of the first attempts
at a utopian society in Latin America, he gradually won over the
Indians by singing songs in the Mayan language about the peace-
fulness and love of the friars.

For a time he was successful, and he sanguinely named his experiment "The Land of True Peace." But it ended like most of
the utopian dreams of Latin America. More predatory settlers
came into the region, and the Land of True Peace resorted to its
true belligerency.

Always the Church was one—or two or three—steps behind
secular trends. It supported the Spanish crown during the independence wars, then formed the base for the conservative parties
which were to war with the more secular-minded and progressive
liberal parties during the nineteenth century. The Church had to
fight hard to preserve its privileged position in the many countries
where it was the "official faith" and enjoyed a concordat with the
governments.

It was during the Mexican revolution in 1910 that the Church
faced its greatest threat. Effete, arrogantly rich, allied with the
forces of the past, the Church enraged the revolutionaries—and
the latter struck back ruthlessly.

The Church was stripped of its properties, public celebration of
religious services was prohibited, and education was turned over

to the state. To this day, it is illegal for clergy to wear their traditional garments in public. The famous Constitution of 1917 refers to "religious associations called churches," and says that freedom of belief "shall be maintained by complete freedom from any religious doctrine, and, based on the results of scientific progress, shall struggle against ignorance and its effects, servitudes, fanaticism and prejudices."

All over the continent the old Latin Church had come to be a static, moribund structure, the stronghold of ritual and form. Usually allied with the state, its priests usually paid by the state, it was a church in which bishops rode around the poverty-stricken Guatemalan Indian country in baby-blue Mercedes Benzes and in which each church or orphanage in the Andes had its own haciendas with Indian peons tied to them. To gain access to God was still to observe most astringently the forms and motions of the Church; charity toward one's fellows was personal and hierarchical. Its schools were for the rich, its prayers for the poor.

Then suddenly in the mid-twentieth century observers began to realize that the Church no longer was the Church of tradition and history. In Chile, Christian Democratic party laymen, acting in the political sphere, influenced the Church hierarchy to liberalize. Both by taking definite action and by passively no longer taking part, the Catholics of Latin America forced the Church to change.

The Church was dying by attrition. There was one priest for every fifty-seven hundred Catholics—compared to one per eight hundred in the United States. In most Latin countries native seminarians had become so rare that the work of the Church was effectively being taken over by foreign priests (the numbers reached 80 percent in Bolivia, approximately 50 percent in other countries). Church reports showed Catholics falling away to the African cults, to the Evangelical and Pentecostal churches.

The divorce of Catholicism from the affairs of daily life, from true morality, had come to take its toll. The forms no longer were enough. The Latin Americans had come to a fork in their spiritual road—they wanted ethical teachings to be related to daily affairs, large numbers wanted a social gospel in place of the tired old rituals and forms.

And the New Church? What would it be? It became clear as the shadows began to take life that the New Church was stressing community in place of exclusivity and social responsibility instead of the traditional Latin's individual relationship to God. In place of an organization that had oppressed and frustrated the ability of man to develop himself as a free man, the Church had become, by the 1960s, the most important force for the development of man against both the dictators and the technocrats. In short, the formerly rigid and exclusive Roman Catholicism—influenced by Protestantism, influenced by the modern world, influenced by the changes in the Vatican—was becoming a broad, inclusive Catholicism.

Within even the short period of time of the years of the '60s, it could without exaggeration be said that the Latin American Church changed from a predominantly conservative Church to a predominantly liberal Church. In most countries it was placing itself on the side of social change through peaceful measures. Many of the younger priests were rebelling against even these measures as too tame. And in countries like Brazil, under the sway of an oppressive military regime, the Church soon came to take a strongly anti-government stand.

Before, the twin pillars of Church and military not only had held up society, they had braced up each other. Now in country after country, they were at war.

How and why the Latin Church, long the very essence of conformism, the protector of classical capitalism and the citadel of oligarchic reaction, should have changed so dramatically and on so many levels at once, is an amazing story to many students of the situation.

One acute observer, Thomas Sanders, a professor of religion who reported on the changes in the Church for the Institute of Current World Affairs, decided that "perhaps the major reason why thoughtful Latin American Catholics have succeeded in leaping from traditionalism to modernity, and even unconventionality, lies in the magnitude of the problems they have confronted."

And indeed the emptiness of the chalice did seem to lend to the experimentation proceeding on all levels. But there were other reasons, too: the old forms did not fit or were no longer relevant; statistics showed the situation of the Church degenerating in Latin America; the Latins had developed sociologically and psychologically beyond the "old spirituality."

Neither should the sheer influence of liberal foreign missioners and churches—the American, the Belgian, the French, the German —be underestimated. Around midcentury, foreign priests, many of them trained in that seedbed of revolutionary Catholicism, Belgium's University of Louvain, poured into Latin America and soon were in key influential positions. Many of the changes in the Latin Church, too, were clearly orchestrated from the Vatican, which began turning its attention to a forgotten Latin America in the early 1950s. Rome became aware that if Latin America, the only part of the underdeveloped world that was both Western and Christian, could not be saved for Western civilization, probably no part of the underdeveloped world could be.

In 1955 Pope Pius XII invited all five hundred and forty Latin American bishops to gather in Rio de Janeiro for the International Eucharistic Congress. From this meeting, at the request of the bishops (and with the opposition of certain highly placed Vatican politicians) came the Latin American Bishops' Conference of CELAM, which went on to sponsor some very leftist projects such as *concientização* in northeastern Brazil—a literacy project of "making people conscious of their state" that the military government then dubbed "Communist." In place of the ingrown national churches of the past, there was now a unity—with this new organizational structure, the Church became an entity to be dealt with.

The 1955 meeting was followed by a meeting in Washington in 1959 of bishops from Latin America, Canada and the United States. More and more as they got together and began to flex their ecclesiastical muscles in unison, the bishops liberalized their churches. When Pope Paul VI visited Colombia in 1968, thus becoming the first pope to step foot on Latin American soil, his visit was followed by the Medellín documents.

In them the bishops placed on record forever the fact that the Catholic Church no longer was the defender of the status quo; it was now on the side of social reform and—perhaps most important—on the side of the development of Latin America through the development of the individual. No longer, in effect, would the Church stand as it always had, behind imposing power from above; now it would stand for the consciously formed power of man rising from below.

One of the first and most important developments in the New Church—and perhaps the one most in conflict with Church history in Latin America—was the idea that the Church should not as a church involve itself in society's social or political problems. Instead it would be the individual Christian, working as an individual man and representing his own individual integrity, who would work within society. It happened very soon that this newly freed and thinking individual began reaching out with an astonishing ecumenicity beyond the Church to form alliances with others of other ideologies who shared his ideas on certain levels—and these included even Marxists.

One of the most interesting examples of this took place in the Bolivian tin mines, deep in the wildest and most remote part of the Andes. There, Father Gregorio Iriarte, a soft-spoken, kindly faced but indomitable Basque priest set out to achieve a dialogue with the Marxists and ended up by replacing the Marxist mine leaders with Christians.

The area around the Catavi and Siglo Veinte mines is one of the starkest places on earth. It resembles nothing so much as the face of the moon, with its barren mountains, its pock-marked earth surface and its eerie magnificence. But it is a hard life. The beaten-down descendants of the outskirts of the Inca empire now work the old Patiño tin mines for the state, ending more often than not at age thirty with a hopeless silicosis. Those who can't get work in the mines squat around the dismal town sifting the sand, scratching open the earth with their hands and scavenging for the tin dust that lies in the dirt.

Father Gregorio arrived in 1964 in Catavi, always the most suicidally explosive of the Bolivian mines. Soon enough he ran up against the Old Church. The Church radio station, Pius XII, according to him, "represented the Church, but in the name of anti-Communism. It was totally against the unions."

No fewer than nine times had it been dynamited by the miners, and the priest in charge had been burned in effigy. "I knew that if this happened, he was doing something wrong," Father Gregorio told me in his dry way.

In the politically and socially ecumenical spirit of the New Church, he set out to get to know the Marxist labor leaders. One of them, the notorious Chinese-line leader Federico Escobar, he particularly liked. "Men like Escobar believed that Communism was a fight for the poor," he observed. Escobar invited the new priest to his house, and they talked things over. "I fight for the poor too," the priest said. "Good, let's get together," said Escobar. "And we both developed a friendship without anything ideological," the priest related.

Their friendship grew stronger. One dark May night in 1965 the government decided to invade the mines once and for all and break the power of the mine leaders, who often had fought the government troops with machine guns. The order went out: take Escobar prisoner.

The Communist's first thought was that his friend Padre Gregorio would help him. So he walked across the cold, dark town to the parish and told the priest, "I have to flee and I need your help." Without answering, the priest studied the map. "It will have to be Chile," he concluded. Bolivian revolutionaries traditionally escape to Chile when things get too hot. Escobar wanted to go by the mountains, across the weird moonscape of southern Bolivia, but the priest said no, "If you go with me, we go by the road."

At the army barriers they were stopped by troops searching for Escobar. "Who is your friend?" the troops asked the cassocked priest.

"A businessman," Father Gregorio said.

"You understand we have to be very careful," the soldier said. "Escobar could escape."

Escobar did escape, but only through the help of the very postconciliar priest who today is leader of the hundred or so "mining priests." Since that time, they have changed the name of the once-despised Church radio station to John XXIII, which now offers secular programing. Since that time Father Gregorio has afforded a rapprochement between the Catholic priests and the Marxists and supported the Catholic hierarchy's negotiating with the government in behalf of benefits for the miners.

But that was not all. Once the Marxist leaders were driven out by the government Father Gregorio helped gradually to replace them with the Christian union leaders that he is training. It is a crucial element of the "new way" that these leaders will not work in the unions as Christian leaders per se. Gregorio is decidedly against this. Instead they work as individual men, with values forged in a general Christian outlook.

Father Gregorio also partakes of the common reaction among most priests in Latin America against traditional capitalism. "Before, Catholics always insisted upon the right of private property," he said. "Now they are insisting more on the *bien commún*. Private property, as an absolute right, is negated. Free competition is negated. We can open a dialogue with the Communists over this."

This kind of political and economic ecumenicism has led to a surprisingly activist Christian-Marxist dialogue and to a distinct ideological convergence among probably the majority of the younger priests and the new, Castro-style Marxists. Castro himself has said, for instance, that the United States should not worry about the Soviet Communists in Latin America for they were no longer revolutionaries. Instead the Americans should worry about the Catholic revolutionaries, because they were. On the occasion of his speech commemorating the tenth anniversary of the Cuban revolution, Castro went so far as to dedicate a school in honor of Camilo Torres and to end his talk with the exhortation, "Christians and Marxists, together!"

For a time in the mid-'60s, despite the fact that the Church within Cuba had been totally emasculated, there was a dramatic coming and going between Castro's Cuba and liberal Latin churchmen. The papal nuncio in Havana, Bishop César Zacchi, called Castro "ethically a Christian if not ideologically one" and urged Catholics to work for the revolution, pointing out that the obstructive middle-class Catholics largely had left the island.

But whereas in Europe the Christian-Marxist dialogue was proceeding largely on an intellectual plane, in Latin America it was taking place on an action level on a continent where all the social and political options still were open. For priests such as Colombia's Father Gustavo Pérez-Ramírez, the influential director of the Colombian Institute of Social Development, "the Christian-Marxist dialogue starts on a humanist level. It begins with the idea that you must change structures. They must disagree on many things, but they all are aiming at the same thing."

Contacts with Marxist violence led to the strange formulation of a theory of "Christian violence," with Christians such as Camilo going to the mountains with the guerrillas and Guatemalan students trying to form a Christian guerrilla front. This raised many and tormenting problems, and led to some fascinatingly labyrinthian theological ponderings.

The young "violent Christians" liked to quote Albert Camus to the effect that "violence is at the same time unavoidable and unjustifiable." And in March 1968, on the first anniversary of the pope's encyclical *The Development of Peoples*, which the rebels use to justify just about everything they want, the Jesuit scholar C. Jarlot of the Gregorian University in Rome said, "There is only one way to escape from an unjust situation: an unjust violence can only be defeated by a just violence."

Even this convergence on the role of violence in the revolutionary transformation of society has not led, however, to really close relations between the Christians and the Marxists. Once in Venezuela during a student federation election in Central University, Gerardo Escalona, president of the Catholic Movement, advanced an invitation to the Marxist students to debate the common points between Christianity and Marxism.

"Our surprise was that they responded by making a poster making fun of Christ," he related afterwards. "They had Johnson and Betancourt (Rómulo Betancourt, former president of Venezuela) in the crucifixion and the oil companies as the two thieves. We were offended." Then during the campaign the Marxist students attempted to capture the Catholic votes with murals making comparisons between "scientific Christians and Marxists." There were murals showing the "good Catholics" like Camilo. "Then after the election they didn't want to accept the dialogue any more," Gerardo said sadly. "It was only strategic. For the election."

Still, the basic ideas of the Marxists and the liberal Catholics are similar—collectivism on the one hand, "communitarianism" on the other, the formation of the "marginals" as a necessary component of development on both parts. Both were strikingly anticapitalist, and both were together against oppressive military regimes like the one in Brazil.

But the convergence of ideologies, albeit under different names, had reached such a point—frequently incongruous—that even the young military officers were anti-capitalist and economic statists. In the winter of 1969, for example, because of the bad relations between the Church and military in Brazil, there was a movement to hold several private, confessional meetings in which churchmen, military officers and businessmen got together to try to fathom one another's point of view.

The former economics czar of the 1964 "revolution," Roberto Campos, felt the anti-capitalism of both the military and the Church had grown so profound that he opened one meeting with these words: "There is a spurious and unconscious alliance between the Church and the military in the belief that capitalism has not worked in Brazil and so it is time to move to another system. I would estimate that sixty percent of you clergy and forty percent of you military are anti-capitalist. Because you are also anti-Communist, you accept capitalism. But you want capitalism without profits. You clergy want to subvert capitalism; you military want to purge it."

The very opposition of the Brazilian Church to the military government—its opposition to all dictatorship across the continent—was another symptom of change, for all through history the two had stood together—usually against the people. But by the winter of 1969 Pope Paul had sent a letter to Cardinal Agnelo Rossi of São Paulo offering his support in getting the Brazilian bishops to stand up against the oppression of the military government, which was then going so far as to torture and imprison priests. The letter was not necessary, however—the bishops made their own statement, an indicative one. Since the military regime existed and had taken unto itself extraordinary powers, they would recognize it although they did not approve of it. But they insisted that it then use this power to reform and restructure the country.

Not in all military-run countries, however, were the churchmen in opposition. In Peru, where the Nasseristic military regime was nationalizing land, the Church tended to support its social reform aspects. "It may be the only way to do it," said one influential priest.

Even in Brazil, such influential churchmen as Recife's liberal archbishop Dom Helder Cámara, based their hope for the future on the younger military officers who would or might be social reformers. Asked whether she could ever see a union of the Church and the younger reformist officers, the prominent Catholic laywoman Marina Bandeira, who is close to Dom Helder in thought, said: "Of course. They will come to see that if they are to have the support of the people they have to make reforms. And they may be the only ones with the power to do it. What difference does it make if you call it 'national statism' or 'socialism'?"

All of this leads to another schism in a church already dangerously schizmatized. This is the division between those, like the Christian Democrats, who believe that man must be developed from below to take an integral part in his own and his society's development, and those who would support the military reformers because they have come to think that only the imposition of reform through sheer power will work.

The first group, which is nonviolent, believes that the use of violence only leads to its continuation through history as a weapon of change—that what Latin America needs is an institutionalization of change, not change brought about by the passion and courage of the moment. As Dr. Ricardo Arias-Calderón, a prominent philosopher and Christian Democrat in Panama, says:

"I personally see no improvement in going from the pre-Castro to the post-Castro stage. I want to see Latin societies change from the types of society that try to avoid change to societies that install avenues for change; a revolution to institutionalize revolution, not to create the scene for another revolution. The problem is very complicated: how to find the means that really foster change and yet not condemn us to a new means of non-participation."

Of what the future will bring for the Roman Catholic Church no one can be sure. But there are many well-informed prophecies. It seems almost certain, as seminaries close all over the hemisphere for lack of seminarians, that before the end of the 1970s a married priesthood or deaconate will be established. Foreign priests, too, are questioning their role—whether they can make the necessary "reincarnation" to a new culture to be really effective. And more important, whether they can be effective "serving" unless archaic feudal societies are totally reformed.

Holding this latter thought, many priests have literally shed their cassocks and clerical collars and taken themselves to the socio-economic institutes. The Chicago-centered Franciscans in La Paz did this. They closed the seminary they had been sent to teach in (nobody much was coming anyway) and opened an institute that was to study Bolivian society and offer solutions to that charming if daffy country's multitudinous problems.

They became so involved in the economic life of the country that at one point two of the priests traveled on their own money to New York to tell Grace and Company, an American firm with the best reputation in Latin America, that they weren't paying their workers high enough salaries. This is typical of the new collarless priests of the economic catacombs.

There are those who think that this kind of obsession with the economic and the social at the expense of the spiritual and the mystical will, in the end, cost the Church as severely as the old overemphasis on the religious and the spiritual did. But the ecclesiastical clock is clearly ticking in favor of the social reformers.

Whatever the immediate future holds, it will in the end be a New Church. Some, like Panama's influential Father Leo Mahon, believe the 1970s will see a total confrontation of the Latin

Church—as a unity, as a "Latin American Church"—with the Vatican, even a schism. The unity under CELAM will lead to this, he thinks, as will the fact that the Latin Church is moving faster toward reform than an uneasy Rome will permit.

When he hesitantly broached the idea to a very influential liberal-moderate archbishop one day that this would happen within five years, the archbishop shook his head in disagreement. "No, no," he protested. "I don't agree. It will take at least ten years."

CHAPTER 15

The New Latins

"South America has the same Christian laws and usages as we have; she contains all the germs of civilization that have grown amid the nations of Europe or their offshoots . . . Why, then, should she always remain uncivilized? It is clear that the question is simply one of time; at some future period, which may be more or less remote, the inhabitants of South America will form flourishing and enlightened nations." Alexis de Tocqueville, *Democracy in America*, 1835.

I had been traveling all day, from five o'clock in the morning, around the barren beige perimeter of Lake Titicaca, which lies between Peru and Bolivia, with members of the Peruvian development bodies—the housing board, *Cooperación Popular* and the cooperative league. There was beauty all around us, for the lake is spectacular; the air at twelve thousand feet is icy and so thin it causes colors to stand out with a mysterious clarity.

The lake itself was strangely diaphanous and reflected the intense blue of the sky. To the Quechua and Aymara Indians who lived around it and for whom it had a mystical significance, not only was it in ancient cosmological myth the birthplace of the sun, it was also the place where the Incas threw fabulous stores of gold from the temple on the island of the sun, to keep it from the Spaniards.

But as dramatic as the scenes of the lake were, even more dramatic were the scenes involving the young Peruvians. At one spot we drove out across the land until we came to a very remote village where the pure-blooded Aymara Indian women were sitting in rows, their cheeks red from the wind off the lake and their bowler hats set at rakish angles. They were chattering like children. Their laughter sounded like the twittering of birds. Their hands worked quickly as they spun alpaca wool into yarn for blankets for the Peruvian army.

The cooperative spinning was a new project begun by *Cooperación Popular* and directed by Peruvian university students. At one point one of the young Indian women, pretty in their firm-cheeked, square-jawed way, came running out of the adjoining public building crying, "I earned ten *soles*." Forty cents. A large daily salary on the *altiplano*.

At another spot, Santiago Blair, the cooperatives man, gathered the Indians together in a little community house close to the lake and talked to them about the consumers' cooperative they were building. He stood under a picture of Tupac Amaru, the leader of the last great Indian rebellion in 1783, and showed them a picture of two donkeys hooked to the same cart but pulling away from each other. Naturally neither one was getting anywhere. "Of course, we're not animals," he explained, smiling. "It is just to make the point that the cooperative movement includes everyone . . . all races, religions and sexes. No one can be excluded. This means the women too. It means democracy: one person, one vote. The man with money has no more votes . . ."

Still farther down the road, closer to Bolivia, we stopped in a particularly forsaken spot to visit several Peruvian girls—all university students and obviously of the middle class—who had been assigned to a little town consisting mostly of Indian and *mestizo* women. The men were gone most of the time, smuggling things across the border.

The girls looked pale and discouraged—it was their first encounter with "doing good" and they hadn't quite been prepared for what it would be like. Inspired by President Belaúnde's ideas of development, they went there to do good and found they could not even speak the people's language, which was Quechua and not Spanish. But they were holding up. "We know it's very little," Haydée Patilla, a pretty dark-eyed law student from Lima said, as we left, "but it's something. We've started, at least." What she meant was *her* generation had started, at least. As we drove away, they waved and waved until we were out of sight. Three forsaken little figures which, however, loom large in the Latin America of the future.

That evening one of the student leaders of the program in Puno, a young man named Victor Montesinos Ramírez, came over to my hotel and took me out to supper. We ate in a little restaurant downtown, and he talked for a long time.

"We don't work in the cities," he explained, in his intense but efficient way, "we work in the country, in the forgotten places where nobody is. Where there is neither prefect, politician nor police, where no one has gone—we go. The last will be first is our principle. We come as ambassadors, and then the communities have a voice.

"In all of Peru there is this sentiment of community," he continued, "and in Bolivia and Ecuador too. There are borders, but it is really all one country."

Speaking of the Indians he estimated that "the worst developed are those in the service of the haciendas. They have lost their liberty, they live like animals. Why have they lost their liberty? Man is free when he has land. When he has land, he can have a community.

"We know these people," he insisted. "We go to their houses, we converse with them. The others—the bureaucrats—they're very serious. We're not like them. They call us extremists." He laughed —a nice young laugh.

"Many say we are not friends of the United States. That isn't true." And he plucked the now commonly heard string of unity and interdependence. "We are all from the same America."

"Revolution has always been shooting people. For us, this is not revolution. We want the revolution of development, the revolution of peace. We can't be Communists for one simple reason: the Communist approach lacks liberty and we love liberty."

Finally, talking about the former presidents, he said, "We had one president—all he wanted to do was build buildings. There were new buildings everywhere. He built a big education building when we didn't have any schools. Another president—all he wanted to do was buy arms—I don't know whom they were to be used against. Now," he summed up, "we've finally got a government that cares about development."

Camilo Sánchez, twenty-three, was the second-in-command of the Fuerzas Armadas Rebeldes, the guerrilla force I lived with for several days in the Sierra de las Minas in Guatemala. He was classically Indian-looking and poor, but with a rich, honest smile. He had a broad, flat face with high cheekbones and he struck me as having a simple faith. But he was impressive to watch—he had natural leadership qualities and the men seemed to like him a good deal.

When I first asked Camilo to tell me how he became a guerrilla, he stared at me with an unmistakably pleased smile and asked with unconcealed surprise, "You want to talk to *me?*"

When I assured him I did, he sat down on a rock in the forest where we were resting and smiled for a moment to himself. Then he embarked on the talk, as on a journey. "What drove me to it most was the situation I lived in before," he began, speaking slowly, as if it could barely be worth the effort to listen to him. "It was the poverty. I was the son of a worker, and we suffered a great deal. Finally I came to an understanding of the origins of the suffering with which we lived. I arrived at an understanding that the only way to get out of the poverty was to make the revolution that we are making."

How had he made the decision? "There were different grades of decision," he went on. "I took part in student demonstrations first. When I saw that this did not resolve everything, I decided on violent revolution. We have to stop the exploitation of man by man. I'm going to fight to the end, until they kill us or we win . . ."

And what kind of society was he fighting for? "I would like to see a society without class, where all were equals, where there is no exploitation, where there are schools and land for everybody. My position is a revolutionary one that aims at being a Marxist-Leninist one." He said it with almost hushed respect. "I have to study more, I have to know more."

He had been there three years—three years in that miserable forest eating that miserable food, fighting that miserable little war. "I have never left since I came," he said simply, but obviously with pride. "The life is difficult, but it is good if you have a consciousness of what you are doing. You feel tired, you feel exhausted, but you do not feel burdened."

I never felt that Camilo harbored the qualities of a killer, though doubtless some of the guerrillas did. Still their business was killing and often enough they did it indiscriminately. Just before I was there they had ambushed a police station in a suburb of Guatemala City and machine-gunned the building until it looked like a piece of Swiss cheese. Three policemen were killed —"men of the people," the same men the guerrillas said they wanted to help.

Talking to the chief of the station, Lieutenant Antonio Anselmo Pineda, a day after the ambush, I asked him how he felt about the guerrillas. Did he feel any hatred for them for doing this? "Hatred?" he repeated, and his face looked blank. "No," he said slowly, "we don't even *know* them. They don't know us. We wouldn't have attacked them, but they were attacking us. I don't know why they did it. I don't know what their motives were."

He thought for a moment and raised his eyes questioningly to me. "Perhaps they know," he finished up.

The tragedy of that man's puzzlement, the uselessness of the sergeants going to their graves, remained in my mind. Later, up in the mountains with the guerrillas, I asked Camilo why they had killed the policemen. "After all," I said to Camilo, who had much the same open, honest way about him as Lieutenant Pineda, "these policemen are the sons of poor families. They are the ones you say you want to help."

"Yes, they are poor, and they are the same ones we are fighting for," Camilo said. "In the case of the policemen, they are there just to get a salary. It is a way to maintain themselves, and we believe it is not of their own choice. They are the very people who are going to receive the benefits of the revolution. But unfortunately they are the ones ordered by the government to oppress the people. So they deserve to be punished. It is one of the contradictions of the fight," he summed up, as though it were a simple everyday problem.

I went out one night to the affluent Miraflores section of Lima to see Dr. Guillermo Roose, a well-to-do dentist who was then secretary general of the Christian Democrat party. This pleasant, good-looking professional man, who much resembled one of his North American counterparts, put it as clearly as anyone I ever talked to in Latin America.

"What interests us is the internal construction of man," he explained, sitting there at eight o'clock at night after a full day's work and still in his white dentist's jacket. "Principle has a large importance with us. Traditionally, what Latin American man has believed in his personal life was one thing and in his political life another, so you found a double personality. If man is not the same in both, you find a Lon Chaney.

"There have been men in politics who can be immoral and at home they can be very moral fathers. For us, man is the same in the home, in work and in politics." He paused. "This is a new idea for Latin America," he added.

About all any medium-sized town can bear is one prima donna, but Recife, Brazil, has two—the irreverent sociologist Gilberto Freyre and the irreverent archbishop Dom Helder Cámara. They happen to be the town's two most famous citizens and they happen to be probably the two best-known citizens of Brazil in the world. They also happen to look at each other with very little delight.

Freyre, a charming, white-haired man with a devilish twinkle in his eye, is the author of *The Mansions and the Shanties, New World in the Tropics* and a whole list of sociological-historical books that form the backbone of research on Brazil. From the beginning he was an avid supporter of the military regime that took over in 1964; he believed that liberal democracy has failed in Latin America, that reforms must be imposed from above.

Dom Helder, a little, wizened man with a knowing expression, had become the symbol of liberal Catholicism in Brazil. He stood as the antithesis of the militarists, believing as he did that man must be developed from below, from within himself.

I called upon Freyre one day in his beautiful old colonial house just outside Recife, a hot, steamy town that is the capital of the desert-like Northeast. The shudder was barely noticeable when Dom Helder's name was mentioned. Then he asked, his eyebrows arched: "Did you know that Dom Helder was a Fascist in the '30s? Actually, today he is a candidate for the presidency in Brazil.

"Communists of the Russian type in New York and Paris have him as their candidate—they want to use him as a sort of Kerensky. Since he is a man with great political ambitions and very vain, I think he'd accept them without seeing the dangers of coming under Communist rule. Some liberals want him, too. They have said he is the ideal solution for Brazil—to free it from the menaces of militarism and dictatorship."

Freyre shook his head, then added quickly with a confidential air: "Oh, we are not enemies, though when we meet"—he shook his head slowly—"I feel he is a little too . . . cordial. He's a politician. His model was Dr. Goebbels. You see the influence when he goes on TV.

"And another thing. He travels all the time—he is never here."

He sighed a deep sigh, a worldly sigh. "It all shows the mistake of having a mother choose a career for you," he added.

The next day, as things happened, I was chatting with Dom Helder in the archbishop's palace in Recife. I asked him if it was true he wanted to be president.

He pounded his little fist on the table. "Gilberto Freyre!" he exclaimed. "He persists in thinking that my secret wish is to be president of Brazil! He cannot understand that my social position is a consequence of the Gospel. He understands only a political explanation.

"Really, really, I don't have any intention . . . any such intention at all. My wish is to help my people, to aid my people."

Now *he* shook *his* head. "I once wrote an open letter about him," he continued. "I said there are two Gilberto Freyre's, the sociologist and the politician. I wrote that I preferred the first, not the second. And you know," he added in a confidential tone, "he accuses me of traveling all the time." His voice was for a moment triumphant. "It is *he* who travels all the time."

Not only have the two men hurled their barbs at each other from across the city of Recife, they have also delighted in writing to and of each other in their respective newspaper columns.

Freyre once queried himself in his column: "Is it true as Dom Helder alleges, that you were a Communist at the time that he was a Fascist?"

"No, it is inaccurate," Freyre answered himself. "This is a mistake of the Most Reverend Archbishop. I hope he will not persist in making this error in his announced book. I have never been a Communist. I have never been on the verge of becoming a Communist. I have never belonged to the Communist party and I have never renounced Communism to which I have never belonged."

Today the two men are further apart than ever. Freyre believes that traditional democracy has failed. He says that "reforms must be made by whomever." For his part, Dom Helder thinks that there can be no reforms without participation of the masses.

Between the two of them, the two stars of Recife represent the aforementioned major conflict in Latin America—whether change will come through the development of the individual man, who then will make his wants felt, or whether it will come imposed from above. What is telling is that both of them know that change must come.

And despite the conflicts between the two, one gets the feeling that they sustain a perverse affection for each other. Indeed, what else would they have to talk about in a place like Recife?

On the third day, the day after I had seen Dom Helder, I ran into Freyre again on a plane bound for Rio. I told him I had seen his pal, and his face lit up.

"What did he say about me?" he asked eagerly.

My taxi-driver in La Paz was a merry, hard-working *cholo* type who obviously took pride in his work. I caught him one day during carnival in February, and he chatted freely with me as he drove, relating the story of some other Americans he had picked up.

"I picked them up one day and took them around," he began, "and they took my phone number and told me they would call me to take them to the airport when they left.

"Well, it was carnival and I had already started drinking in the Boda del Diablo. Sure enough, they called me at home, and someone brought the message.

"I'd just gone to carnival, but I went and took them to the airport. I wanted to show them that a Bolivian is a man of his word."

From inside the bizarre and wonderful house on the cliff, you can see the sand-eating waves, foaming like a maddened mouth biting at the mute and helpless shores. All along the magical coastline of Chile, rocks stood like black and lifeless sentinels, guarding the land and sending the foam reeling back into the sea in crazed patterns.

Inside the windows that opened on this magnificent scene stood a tall, handsome man whose poetry has much in common with the coast of Chile, his native country. "I watch the sea," he said as his eyes caressed the view wisely and lovingly. "Sometimes it is so good I applaud."

This kind of communication with the elements is part of life to Pablo Neruda, thought by many to be the world's greatest living poet. His lyrical poems reel like the foam, crash like the sea, and end, often, in the unresolved desperation of the repelling walls of the rocks.

He is an American poet. Like Walt Whitman. Where Whitman said, "I see . . . I hear . . ." Neruda says, "I look . . . I am listening . . ." Both see their societies, and hear and sense them, the new societies of America.

Asked about a problematical cultural unity for Latin America, he shook his head vigorously—yes. "I feel very good with my cousins," he mused. "Even though we are always saying funny things about each other. But when we are away in Europe, we always seek each other out." Why? What is it? He shook his head slowly in puzzlement. "It is such a powerful thing . . . like blood, you see."

His poetry is surrealistic, and he has spoken about a peculiarly promising ground for surrealism in Latin America. "Poetry in South America is a different matter altogether," he has said. "You see, there are in our countries rivers which have no names, trees which nobody knows, and birds which nobody has described. It is easier for us to be surrealistic because everything we know is new.

"Everything has been painted in Europe, everything has been sung in Europe. But not in America.

"I would say to the young poets of my country and of Latin America—perhaps this is our tradition—to discover things, to be in the sea, to be in the mountains, and approach every living thing. And how can you not love such an approach to life, that has such extravagant surprises?"

Neruda was a long-time member of the Communist party of Chile and a member of the central committee—yet he showed, too, in himself, in his own life and attitudes, the great tolerance Latins have for one another, the Latin Americanism that rises above and beyond ideologies or beliefs. He admitted that, in Chile, Christian Democracy had usurped the revolution that the Communists had long fought for. He had, he said, many American friends. Somehow he was never quite able to overcome his basic humanity, to divide people into rights and wrongs, reds and blacks, befores and afters. Throughout his poetry is posited the positivistic Communist—for whom the world could be changed if only one organized human life correctly—and the poet for whom life basically holds no ultimate meaning, no regenerating hope.

Through his life is evinced something else—he is far more than a political man. He is the living proof that there is a Latin American culture—a creative impulse that is purely, indigenously, intrinsically new and unique in the world.

These are all new Latins. Part of a vast body of young and not-so-young Latin Americans who are fighting and striving for change today and who are determined that it must come now, within this generation. What they say over and over is that they want societies without the rigid social distinctions of the past, societies where the fruits of development and prosperity accrue to the majority of the people. They want to control their own environments; as Frei has said, they want to be the "subjects" of history.

The new man often has the apocalyptic view that Latin America —the real Latin America—is being formed today and that he must form it. It is not enough to let it happen. Some see a vacuum— the historic vacuum—and believe it must be filled with an ideology. For the first time in history this ideology is emerging from Latin America itself and even what ideologies are being imported are being redefined within the Latin American milieu, even redefined for the world, in universalist terms. Others see the answer as a nationalist, non-ideological pragmatism. But both approaches aim basically at the same ends.

There is also embedded deep in the New Man the idea of redeeming Latin American man, of saving him from himself: the idea of curbing excessive individualism by forcing a man to vow loyalty to an ideology and to religious, political and social compromises which will force a man to abide by his promises. Everywhere there is present the strong idea of injecting morality into societies that have been hopelessly corrupt.

This is one of the qualities the Chileans stress about Frei— that he always has been what he is, that he never changed or sold out. It is one of the points the radical Catholics mention about Camilo—that he gave up his life for what he believed. It is what the Cubans say about Castro—that he and his men are thoroughly honest, in contrast to the terrible corruption of previous years.

Most of the New Latins work in fields that have a scientific or social science orientation rather than in the traditional areas of law and the classics. They are often technicians—engineers, architects, social scientists, anthropologists, sociologists. Even the military are so trained. It is no accident that the most influential young priests are almost without exception sociologists. For the goal of this kind of Latin man is to analyze his society *as it is* and not as tradition has said it was. Latin men have begun to learn that their traditional passion for spiritualism has led only to misery; that, contradictory as it seems, a bit of pragmatism leads to something spiritually good. They see the false forms, and they see the real substance, and they want to bring the two off-focus pictures together in a kaleidoscope.

Many of these *técnicos* are involved in an almost fanatic quest for development—which in the non-Marxist sectors is the new war of liberation. In particular, they are out to develop the frontiers and the interiors. It is enough for some observers to say that it is simply because they want to develop their countries—to build roads and dams and "new places"—because they are ashamed of their countries in the drawing rooms and across the conference tables of the world. It is easy to suspect their interest as simply a lust for wealth and for a higher social position. But there is more to it than that.

What Freyre calls the "interior quest" is psychological as well as physical. The idea is to reclaim the land, to seize it from the "occult forces" of history that have robbed Latin America. There is a strong element of proving—finally—one's mastery over the land, of turning one's back on the fatalistic determinism of the dark Spanish past and reveling in positivism of a new and developmental sort. Unquestionably it is related to the quest for the Latin man's own internal self. One often has the feeling, in talking to them, that they feel they will find themselves, finally, by digging into the mud and mysteries of the formerly spurned interior.

Finally it comes down to the basic idea that in the mountains and in the countryside and in the frontier and in the soil there is purity and there is the real indigenous Latin America—not necessarily Indian but a creative mixture of everything that has been put into it. Brasília was an attempt to recapture it. Father Vekemans' ideas of the coasts being "colonized" by creoles who have no genuine stake in Latin America and do not feel they are Latins is an attempt to analyze it. The Peruvian students working in the wildernesses with the Indians are an attempt to redeem it. And Castro's idea of revolutionary purity being found in the mountains and the peasants is an attempt to develop a philosophy about it.

To a great extent the New Latins are an expression of the dramatic class changes that have come in many countries. In every country a new middle class has been rising since the beginning of this century and particularly since World War II, that concerns itself with rescuing the "marginals" from their state. In certain countries, as in Chile with the Christian Democrats, the new political movements are a direct expression of their will to power and their dissatisfaction with things as they are. In a country like Bolivia, which has undergone a total social revolution, the classes have been so reversed that today you can find a member of the old aristocracy running a hamburger stand and selling hamburgers to the new *cholo* class that rose to take over the government after 1952. The leaders—the men of power—are coming more and more from the marginal and middle-class portions of Latin America, and this means new values are coming to the fore.

Probably nowhere have the classes been so overturned as in post-revolutionary Cuba, where workers and peasants actually became the New Class of the new Communist state. One hot sticky night on the eastern coast of Cuba in the town of Manzanillo, I was staying in the Communist party guesthouse. It was a house which formerly belonged to the wealthy Álvarez and Galleanos families.

As we sipped daiquiris served by a white-shirted, bow-tied waiter, the local secretary of the party, Victoriano Quintano, said: "Yes, these four houses were once owned by the same family. They owned the airport, ranches and sugar mills. They left, and now we use them for guests of the government." Before we sat down in the elegant dining room, at a table that could easily seat twenty-five persons, I went around the group—all were in military uniforms—and asked about their pre-Communist backgrounds. One had been a cobbler. Without exception, all had been workers and peasants and now they were high party functionaries, drinking Bulgarian wine and eating in the mansions once owned by the wealthy.

In talking to most of the New Latins, one discovers that even if they do not seek class changes as sudden and as dramatic as Cuba's, most of them do seek changes. They believe that the

structures of the past are outdated and though they are not cultural egalitarians, like North Americans, they do usually favor a
greater social equality than now exists. They also stress interdependence, a quality that is a new value in Latin American terms and
they are putting it into practice everywhere.

By the 1960s several of the richer countries had begun giving
aid to the poorer ones. Mexico had announced a program of
preferential trade for the Central American countries. In the Organization of American States meeting in Rio de Janeiro in 1965,
all of the countries agreed to aid each other—a remarkable development in terms of the historic jealousies they had always nursed like
tender roots. There were also a series of multinational projects
along formerly disputed borders, and the efforts at a Latin American Common Market which stumbled along fitfully.

The idea of Latin American unity is, of course, far from new.
In colonial times the entire continent was united under the
Spanish and Portuguese crowns. In the independence wars troops
of every country fought to free every other country. San Martín
brought his Argentine troops to battle in Chile, to pacify Peru.
Bolívar took Venezuelans, Colombians and Ecuadoreans on his
march to liberate Peru and Bolivia. Men from all over the Caribbean fought with the Cubans against Spain, and eight hundred
Haitians even fought in the American Revolutionary War, many of
them losing their lives at the Battle of Savannah.

The first governors of Peru were an Argentine and a Venezuelan;
two Venezuelans became presidents of Bolivia and Ecuador. It
was only later, during the age of the *caudillos*, that the Latin states
retreated behind their nationalist barriers and xenophobically
closed themselves off from each other.

As Bolívar said one day, speculating on the future with that inherent sadness that always seemed to be part of him: "It is a
grandiose idea to think of consolidating the New World into a
single nation, united by parts into a single bond. It is reasoned
that, as these parts have a common origin, language, customs and
religion, they ought to have a single government to permit the
newly formed states to unite in a confederation. But this is not
possible." Nevertheless, he went on to dream: "How beautiful it

would be if the Isthmus of Panama could be for us what the Isthmus of Corinth was for the Greeks! Would to God that some day we may have the good fortune to convene there an august assembly of representatives of the republics, kingdoms and empires to deliberate upon the high interests of peace and war with the nations of the other three-quarters of the globe."

The idea of unity never quite died, but neither did it ever quite approach realization until, in mid-twentieth century, it awoke again with a new force and urgency.

At the same time, the Latin Americans were also suffering cultural unity pains, and the suffering and searching over what it is to be a Latin American continued. When asked what countries they were from, students had begun answering, "Latin America." Magazines were publishing articles like the one in a Chilean magazine which discussed what the name of the "new country," of all Latin America, should be; this particular article decided the "country" would be called Colombia and Lima would be the capital. A meeting of Latin American intellectuals was held in Arica, Chile, to discuss what Latin American culture really was (without coming to any conclusions). Venezuela held a Latin American music festival at which only Latin music was played. And Fidel Castro had a Latin American guerrilla conference where all the continent's guerrillas got together to plot unified subversion.

There were no answers, but there were plenty of insistent questions. As Arturo Uslar Pietri, the Venezuelan politician and poet has written: "The first question we should ask ourselves is: What is Latin America? . . . What are we? . . . Never before has a society had, to such a degree, this tragic obsession, which might be called the 'ontological anguish of the Latin America.' The Latin American has always, somewhat like Hamlet, pondered his real nature, asking himself, 'What am I: white, Negro, Indian, *mestizo*, European, something that partakes of all this, or something distinct?' The deep concern for knowing what we are, what I have called the 'anguish of being,' has existed since the Conquest."

Today there are no answers, but there *are* affirmations. Latin thinkers almost without exception know that there *is* a Latin Americanism. When I asked about this of Gilberto Freyre, this

man who has studied Latin America's biggest country more profoundly than anyone, living or dead, he said: "We are in a moment
of transition. We are really going through in Latin America the
most serious revolution we've ever gone through. It is known as a
continent of revolutions, but there has never been anything compared to what we have now. It is a much more social type."

As to psychological unity, he said that it is present and increasing. "I remember a long time ago when I was young how little of
unity there was," he reminisced, "how little we knew of each other.
I had an interesting experience recently in Salamanca, when I lec-
tured at the university. There were many Latin American students
and through their questions I could see that the unity has become
a reality. They were greatly sensitive to their similarities. They
discussed this as a Latin American culture, they said that political
differences were insignificant.

"I presented a series of questions. Is there an Iberian culture,
an Iberian-American culture? We agreed there was. One thing we
had in common was our sense of time. It's not a joke, it's very
serious. A Latin American comes to a hotel and says to wake him
between ten and eleven, not at a precise time.

"There's the way of feeling about being democratic. It is not the
same way as an Anglo-Saxon or a Frenchman thinks. It is something more social than political. We have class differences, but
there is a great interpenetration between classes. Take an Englishman. British of certain classes don't associate at all with other
classes, despite their 'democracy.' That would be impossible in
Spain or Portugal or Latin America. It is perfectly possible for members of one class to associate with other classes through their sense
of social democracy.

"There is also an 'Americanism.' At Salamanca we spoke of the
influence Latin Americans were having on Spain and Portugal—
in customs and language. Today they're using expressions that
fifty years ago the academies would consider disgraceful. Indian
words. African words. I think there is a certain American attitude
toward life that is common to both North and South. It is more
free, more open."

The Argentine cartoonist Landru agrees on this "Americanism."

"My family came in the sixteenth century," this handsome, wry man told me one day; "we were one hundred and fifty percent Spanish. But really I feel Spain very little. I am American."

There was not only the cultural convergence, there was a strange convergence going on politically and socially. Whether Marxist or military or liberal Catholic or liberal democrat—all basically wanted the same thing, the total transformation of Latin American society.

Che Guevara told Augusto Olivares, a Chilean journalist, an interesting story once with regard to this. It happened at Punta del Este in 1961 during the ministerial conference that gave birth to the Alliance for Progress. Che was visited late one night by two young Peruvian military officers and the three men talked long into the night. Afterwards an astonished Che told Olivares: "I was amazed, they were more revolutionary than I. I said to them when they left, 'But you are wearing uniforms . . .' One looked at me and said, 'So are you.'"

To some observers none of these changes is very new. They point out that throughout Latin American history there were always numbers of good, unselfish, talented leaders—and that they always were eclipsed, in time, by the old-style *caudillos*. Latin life goes on as usual, they insist, with the same patterns repeating themselves—only under different names.

I recall Juan Lechín, the vice president of Bolivia and the leftist leader of the tin miners, talking about himself one day. Many considered Lechín, who was one of the major leaders of the 1952 revolution, to be a Communist or, at the very least, a man of vague Marxist ideology. But when we spoke that day about Latin America needing an ideology, Lechín said in his laconic way, "What Bolivia needs is not an ideology, Bolivia needs a *caudillo* like me."

And, indeed, it is tempting to think that this is, after all, all that Latin America will amount to. For even in midcentury, the continent wavered back and forth—between independence from the United States and a sick dependence upon it, between unity and atomization, between striding forward and sinking back comatosely into the womb. But it is too easy.

For even if you take these overlappings and confusions into

account, even if the Marxists turn out to be *caudillos*, and even if you approach the entire spectrum of Latin American change with humility and caution, it is still possible—necessary—to say that a new Latin American man is emerging in the new generation. He wants to redress the power imbalance, to help his fellow countrymen to enter the modern age, to develop classless societies, to achieve political and cultural unity, to step from authoritarianism to individual responsibility and to evolve a new, modern Latin American personality. All this is new. The man of the past did not strive for this, nor did he dream it was possible.

Certainly the strain of Spanish authoritarianism remains. But alongside that there has always been, in Latin America as in North America, the propensity for a freer, more democratic life, a unique New World liberty. "The answer is simple," Arciniegas says; "it is the force of political circumstance. The more deeply a European country was rooted in history, the greater difficulty it had in arriving at democratic formulas. The Americas never had to struggle to overthrow monarchies, never had a powerful nobility. The people of the Americas were commoners—plain Perézes in the Hispano-Indian colonies, plain Smiths in the English. Europeans who had been docile vassals in Europe emigrated to America as bold adventurers . . .

"All in all, substantial changes occurred in everyone. The white man in America became profoundly American. Almost without knowing it, he had brought 'his democracy' from Europe. 'His democracy' was a repudiation of the society he left behind him in Europe. The Spaniards had a name for their wanderers, their displaced persons. They called them *indianos*, a word meaning that they were born in Spain but had moved to the Indies and identified with their new home. The son of the *indiano* was the creole, whom centuries of colonialism transformed into a revolutionary . . .

"The idea of the free man emerged with the American, . . . the word 'liberty' rang with magic in America . . . In Spanish America, which lacked an aristocracy or a nobility, where a population alien to the traditional hierarchies of Europe had matured, everything was conducive to a search for a democratic system within which to order political life."

The Latin American, therefore, like the North American, was a New Man. He had other problems—and it took him longer to develop because of complicating Latin characteristics—but today he is developing, today he is changing, today he is in truth becoming a modern human being.

Even that most recalcitrant and mystifying area, the Amazon jungle, which has symbolized so dramatically the lack of hope for developing or changing Latin America, is yielding. Even the "Amazon syndrome" is finally proving beatable. Ford could not do it, nor Farquhar, whose dreams were left to rot in the rain forest. But the marginal people who have begun to move and the road-builders and the new technicians are doing it. They're parachuting air force men into the jungle to construct roads across the continent. The rubber-gatherers and gold-miners and colonists and individuals are invading the interior. In the next twenty or thirty years, it will all be tied together, and there will be new cities which face not Europe, but the interior of Latin America.

For many the new settlements and the changes have created only a deep sense of unease and a deep sadness. As the newcomers invade the land, river by river and ridge by ridge, and as the new houses are strung out along the streams where only the Indians were before, the Indians are dying off. The Brazilians call it the "great dying," and some are predicting that within fifty years there will be no more savage Indians in the Amazon. The white men bring in the common cold, and an entire tribe dies. Hunters and settlers savagely kill many of the aborigines. But it is more than all of this.

The anthropologists find that many Indians are dying of despondency. As they see the world they know changing in ways they cannot comprehend, they cease planting and stop hunting. They sit outside their houses and eventually they die. The old days of fighting against change—of attacking the Madeira-Mamoré workers in the night—are largely gone. The movements are too vast to fight now and most of them seem instinctively to know this. "These tribes believe the world came to life when a coconut fell from the moon," one anthropologist observed. "They can't understand what is happening."

So the picture of Latin America which persists no longer is that of an imperious Henry Ford trying to impose northern values on an intransigent Latin America. Nor is it the Madeira-Mamoré effort, to develop an area before it is ripe for such change.

The final frame on the roll of film might well be the sad, displaced Brazilian savage, sitting on the crooked old tracks of the Madeira-Mamoré, feeling himself dying, while Latin America claims itself.

BIBLIOGRAPHY

Adams, Richard N., and others. *Social Change in Latin America Today*. New York: Harper & Row, for the Council on Foreign Relations, 1960.

Alegría, Ciro. *The Golden Serpent*. Translated by Harriet de Onís. New York: Farrar, Straus & Co., 1943.

Arciniegas, Germán. *Latin America*. Translated by Joan MacLean. New York: Alfred A. Knopf, 1967.

Arévalo Bermejo, Juan José. *The Shark and the Sardines*. Translated by June Cobb and Raul Osegueda. New York: Lyle Stuart, 1961.

Beals, Carleton. *Eagles of the Andes*. Philadelphia: Chilton Company, 1963.

————. *Nomads and Empire Builders*. Philadelphia: Chilton Company, 1961.

Belaúnde Terry, Fernando. *Peru's Own Conquest*. Detroit: Blaine Ethridge, 1967.

Bishop, Elizabeth. *Brazil*. New York: Time-Life, 1967.

Bosch, Juan. *The Unfinished Experiment: Democracy in the Dominican Republic*. New York: Frederick A. Praeger, 1965.

Caldera, Rafael. *El bloque latinoamericano*. Santiago: Editorial del Pacífico, 1961.

Campos, Jorge. *Bolívar*. Barcelona: Ediciones Destino, 1963.

Castro, Fidel. Selected speeches.

Clark, Gerald. *The Coming Explosion in Latin America*. New York: David McKay Company, 1963.

Considine, John J., ed. *The Church in the New Latin America*. Notre Dame, Ind.: Fides, 1964.

————, ed. *The Religious Dimension in the New Latin America*. Notre Dame, Ind.: Fides, 1966.

————, ed. *Social Revolution in the New Latin America*. Notre Dame, Ind.: Fides, 1965.

Cowell, Adrian. *The Heart of the Forest*. New York: Alfred A. Knopf, 1961.

Crassweller, Robert D. *Trujillo*. New York: The Macmillan Company, 1966.

D'Antonio, William V. and Pike, F. B., eds. *Religion, Revolution, and Reform*. New York: Frederick A. Praeger, 1964.

Debray, Régis. *Revolution in the Revolution?* Translated by Bobbye Ortis. New York: Monthly Review Press, 1967.

Debuyst, Federico. *Las clases sociales en América Latina*. Madrid: Oficina Internacional de Investigaciones Sociales, Documentos Latino Americanos, 1962.

de Castro, Josué. *Death in the Northeast*. New York: Random House, 1966.

de Cervantes Saavedra, Miguel. *Don Quixote*. Translated by J. M. Cohen. Baltimore: Penguin Books, 1966.

de Cieza de León, Pedro. *The Incas*. Translated by Harriet de Onís; edited by Victor W. Von Hagen. Norman, Oklahoma: University of Oklahoma Press, 1959.

de la Vega, Garcilaso. *The Incas*. Translated by María Jolas; edited by Alain Gheerbrant. New York: Orion Press, 1961.

de Oliveira, Franklin. *Revolução e contra-revolução no Brasil*. Rio de Janeiro: Editora Civilização Brasileira, 1962.

Department of the Army, Headquarters. *Latin America: Hemispheric Partner*. Washington, 1964.

de Unamuno, Miguel. *Tragic Sense of Life*. Translated by J. E. Crawford Flitch. New York: Dover Publications, 1954.

Dorselaer, Jaime and Gregory, Alfonso. *La urbanización en América Latina*. Madrid: Centro Internacional de Investigaciones Sociales, 1962.

Draper, Theodore. *Castroism, Theory and Practice*. New York: Frederick A. Praeger, 1965.

————. *Castro's Revolution*. New York: Frederick A. Praeger, 1962.

Dubois, Jules. *Fidel Castro*. Indianapolis: The Bobbs-Merrill Company, 1959.

Elliott, J. H. *Imperial Spain 1469–1716*. New York: A Mentor Book, New American Library, 1966.

Espaillat, Arturo. *Trujillo: The Last Caesar.* Chicago: The Henry Regnery Co., 1963.

Evans, Joseph W. and Ward, Leo R., eds. *The Social and Political Philosophy of Jacques Maritain.* Garden City, N.Y.: Image Books, Doubleday & Company, 1965.

Foreign Areas Studies Division, Special Operations Research Office, The American University. *U. S. Army Handbook for Brazil.* Washington: Department of the Army, 1964.

————. *U. S. Army Handbook for Colombia.* Washington: Department of the Army, 1961.

————. *U. S. Army Handbook for Venezuela.* Washington: Department of the Army, 1964.

Freemantle, Anne, ed. *The Social Teachings of the Church.* New York: A Mentor-Omega Book, New American Library, 1963.

Freyre, Gilberto. *The Mansions and the Shanties.* Translated and edited by Harriet de Onís. New York: Alfred A. Knopf, 1963.

————. *The Masters and the Slaves.* Translated by Samuel Putnam. New York: Alfred A. Knopf, 1956.

————. *Portuguese Integration in the Tropics.* Lisbon: Tipografia Silvas, 1961.

Guevara, Ernesto (Che). *Guerrilla Warfare.* Translated by J. P. Morray. New York: Monthly Review Press, 1961.

————. *Reminiscences of the Cuban Revolutionary War.* Translated by Victoria Ortiz. New York: Monthly Review Press, 1968.

Guilisasti Tagle, Sergio. *Partidos políticos chilenos.* Santiago: Editorial Nacimiento, 1964.

Gunther, John. *Inside South America.* New York: Harper & Row, 1967.

Gutiérrez de Pineda, Virginia. *La familia en Colombia.* Madrid: Estudios Sociológicos Latinoamericanos, 1962.

Guzmán Campos, Germán, with Fals Borda, Orlando and Umaña Luna, Eduardo. *La violencia en Colombia.* Bogotá: Ediciones Tercer Mundo, 1964.

Hanson, Earl Parker, ed. *South from the Spanish Main.* New York: The Dial Press, 1967.

Harss, Luis and Dohmann, Barbara. *Into the Mainstream; Conversations with Latin-American Writers.* New York: Harper & Row, 1967.

Henríquez Ureña, Pedro. *A Concise History of Latin American Culture.*

Translated and with supplementary chapter by Gilbert Chase. New York: Frederick A. Praeger, 1966.

Herring, Hubert C. *A History of Latin America*. New York: Alfred A. Knopf, 1961.

Hoffman, Rodolfo and Debuyst, Federico. *Chile, una industrialización desordenada*. Santiago: Centro para el Desarrollo Económico y Social de América Latina, 1966.

Hyams, Edward S. and Ordish, George. *The Last of the Incas*. New York: Simon and Schuster, 1963.

Johnson, John J. *The Military and Society in Latin America*. Stanford, Calif.: Stanford University Press, 1964.

―――. *Political Change in Latin America*. Stanford, Calif.: Stanford University Press, 1958.

Lieuwen, Edwin. *Arms and Politics in Latin America*. New York: Frederick A. Praeger, 1962.

―――. *Generals Vs. Presidents*. New York: Frederick A. Praeger, 1964.

Lockwood, Lee. *Castro's Cuba, Cuba's Fidel*. New York: The Macmillan Company, 1967.

López-Fresquet, Rufo. *My Fourteen Months with Castro*. Cleveland: The World Publishing Company, 1966.

MacGaffey, Wyatt and others. *Twentieth-Century Cuba*. Garden City, N.Y.: Anchor Books, Doubleday & Company, 1965.

Mason, J. Alden. *The Ancient Civilizations of Peru*. Baltimore: Penguin Books, 1968.

Mayobre, José Antonio with Herrara, Felipe and Sanz de Santamaría, Carlos and Prebisch, Raúl. *Hacia la integración acelerada de América Latina*. Mexico City: Fondo de Cultura Económica, 1965.

Mindlin, Henrique E. *Modern Architecture in Brazil*. Translated by John Knox. New York: Reinhold Publishing Corp., 1956.

Moog, Vianna. *Bandeirantes and Pioneers*. Translated by L. L. Barrett. New York: George Braziller, 1964.

Morley, Sylvanus G. *The Ancient Maya*. Revised by George W. Brainerd. Stanford, Calif.: Stanford University Press, 1956.

Neira, Hugo. *Cuzco: tierra y muerte*. Lima, Peru: Problemas de Hoy, 1964.

Osborne, Harold. *Bolivia, A Land Divided*. New York: Oxford University Press, 1964.

Owens, Ronald J. *Peru*. New York: Oxford University Press, 1963.

Paret, Peter and Shy, John W. *Guerrillas in the 1960's*. New York: Frederick A. Praeger, 1962.

Paz, Octavio. *The Labyrinth of Solitude*. Translated by Lysander Kemp. New York: Grove Press, 1962.

Picón-Salas, Mariano. *A Cultural History of Spanish America*. Translated by Irving A. Leonard. Berkeley, Calif.: University of California Press, 1962.

Política, Ideas para una América nueva. No. 62. Caracas: Revista Mensual, 1967.

Poppino, Rollie. *International Communism in Latin America: A History of the Movement, 1917–1963*. New York: The Macmillan Company, 1964.

Porter, Charles O. and Alexander, Robert J. *The Struggle for Democracy in Latin America*. New York: The Macmillan Company, 1961.

Prescott, William H. *History of the Conquest of Mexico and History of the Conquest of Peru*. New York: Modern Library, 1936.

Pritchett, V. S. *The Spanish Temper*. New York: Alfred A. Knopf, 1954.

Rodó, José Enrique. *Ariel*. Edited by Gordon Brotherston. London, England: Cambridge University Press, 1967.

Rodríguez, Mario. *Central America*. Englewood Cliffs, N.J.: Prentice-Hall, 1965.

Rosarios, Ottocar. *América Latina, veinte repúblicas, una nación*. Buenos Aires: Emecé, 1966.

Rotundo, Humberto with Caravedo, Baltázar and Mariátegui, Javier. *Estudios de psiquiatría social en el Perú*. Lima, Peru: Ediciones del Sol, 1963.

Schmitt, Karl M. and Burks, David D. *Evolution or Chaos*. New York: Frederick A. Praeger, 1963.

Schulthess, Emil. *The Amazon*. Translated by H. A. Frey and C. Wayland. New York: Simon and Schuster, 1962.

Shapiro, Samuel, ed. *Integration of Man and Society in Latin America*. South Bend, Ind.: University of Notre Dame Press, 1967.

Sigmund, Paul E., ed. *The Ideologies of the Developing Nations.* New York: Frederick A. Praeger, 1963.

Smith, Rhea Marsh. *Spain.* Ann Arbor, Mich.: University of Michigan Press, 1965.

Smith, T. Lynn. *Brazil.* Baton Rouge, La.: Louisiana State University Press, 1963.

Szulc, Tad. *Twilight of the Tyrants.* New York: Holt, Rinehart & Winston, 1959.

————. *The Winds of Revolution.* New York: Frederick A. Praeger, 1965.

Tannenbaum, Frank. *Slave and Citizen.* New York: Alfred A. Knopf, 1947.

Tomlinson, H. M. *The Sea and the Jungle.* New York: A Signet Book, New American Library, 1961.

Torres, Camilo. Documents. Cuernavaca: Centro Intercultural de Documentación, 1966.

Vásquez, Mario C. Monograph: *Hacienda, peonaje y servidumbre en los Andes peruanos.* Lima, Peru: Editorial Estudios Andinos, 1961.

Vekemans, Roger. Selected writings.

Volman, Sacha. *La educación para el cambio social.* Mexico City: Centro de Estudios y Documentación Sociales, A. C., 1964.

Von Hagen, Victor W. *Realm of the Incas.* New York: A Mentor Book, New American Library, 1961.

————. *South America Called Them.* New York: Alfred A. Knopf, 1945.

Whitaker, Arthur P. *Argentina.* Englewood Cliffs, N.J.: Prentice-Hall, 1964.

————, ed. *Latin America and the Enlightenment.* Ithaca, N.Y.: Cornell University Press, 1961.

————. *The United States and the Independence of Latin America, 1800–1830.* New York: W. W. Norton & Company, 1964.

Ydígoras Fuentes, Miguel. *My War with Communism.* Englewood Cliffs, N.J.: Prentice-Hall, 1963.

Zea, Leopoldo. *The Latin-American Mind.* Translated by James H. Abbott and Lowell Dunham. Norman, Okla.: University of Oklahoma Press, 1963.

INDEX

Aguero, José de la Riva, 13

Aguirre, Francisco de, 241

Alape, Jacobo Prías (Charro Negro), 198

Alba, Victor, 33

Alberdi, Juan Bautista, 114

Allende, Salvador, 68, 154–55, 157–58, 159, 165, 166, 255

Alliance for Progress, 260, 317

Alvarado, Pedro de, 241

Amaru, Tupac, 302

Amazon river system, 3–5; natural wonders of, 3–4; "Amazon syndrome" as Latin American syndrome of failure, 4, 37; forests and timber of, 5; soil of, 5; "Amazon syndrome" proving to be beatable, 319

Ambassadors from U.S. of Latin descent, attitude of Latin Americans toward, 43

"American," pre-empting of term by U.S., 106

Americanism, 19, 316–17

Americanized Latins, attitude of Latin Americans toward, 43

Anchieta, José de, 229

Antonio de Montesinos, 288–89

Antônio o Conselheiro ("the Prophet"), 230–31

APRA party of Democratic Left in Peru, 25, 70–72, 118

Aprismo. See APRA party

Arbenz, Jacobo, 147

Arcandona, Ruth, 286

Arciniegas, Germán, 16, 23, 34, 113, 231, 234, 318

Ardino, Pedro Antonio, 197

Arévalo, Juan José, 116

Argentina: Latin Americanism of Argentines, 42; military take-over in, 271–72, 275

Arguedes, José María, 180, 187

Arias, Arnulfo, 266

Arias-Calderón, Ricardo, 298–99

Ariel (Rodó), 116–17

Artigas, José Gervasio, 43, 233

Attwood, William, 132

Authoritarianism in Latin America, 7, 17, 18, 24, 62–75, 191; in era of the great *caudillos*, 36; as heritage from Spanish, 68; and seesaw motion with progressive democratic ideal-ism, 72–73; and unquestion-ing acceptance of testimony of leader, 74, 163; as deter-rent to development into a modern society, 75; concern of Chilean Christian Demo-crats over abolishing of, 162–